Jihadi Terror in Pakistan
Sunni Jihadi Groups in Pakistan

Jihadi Terror in Pakistan
Sunni Jihadi Groups in Pakistan

Brig. S.N.Sinha (Retd.), PVSM

NEHA PUBLISHERS & DISTRIBUTORS
DELHI

Publisher
NEHA PUBLISHERS & DISTRIBUTORS
4832/24,Prahlad Lane,S-207 Ansari
Road, Daryaganj, Delhi-110002
Ph.: 43570976, 23278261
Email: nehapubdistributors@gmail.com

Edition: 2015

ISBN: 978-93-80318-75-2

Laser Typesetting
JEE-VEE Graphics, Delhi

Price: 1195/-

Printed
Vikas Computers, Delhi

Preface

Jihad, an Islamic term, is a religious duty of Muslims. In Arabic, the word *jihâd* translates as a noun meaning "struggle". The word jihad appears in 23 Quranic verses. Within the context of the classical Islam, particularly the Shiahs beliefs, it refers to struggle against those who do not believe in the Abrahamic God (Allah). However, the word has even wider implications.

Pakistan's intelligence agency, the Inter-Services Intelligence (ISI), has long faced accusations of meddling in the affairs of its neighbors. A range of officials inside and outside Pakistan have stepped up suggestions of links between the ISI and terrorist groups in recent years. In autumn 2006, a leaked report by a British Defense Ministry think tank charged, "Indirectly Pakistan (through the ISI) has been supporting terrorism and extremism—whether in London on 7/7, or in Afghanistan, or Iraq."

In India, Mumbai's police chief has claimed to have proof that the ISI planned the July 2006 bombing of the Indian city's commuter rail system, which was carried out by the Kashmir-based militant group Lashkar-e-Taiba.

Today's frightening instability in Pakistan comes in a world in which global terrorists are actively seeking nuclear weapons and the materials and expertise needed to make them, a quest that has been underway for more than a decade. Rapid action is needed to keep the Taliban's advances in Pakistan from creating new opportunities for these deadly adversaries.

This book is a modest attempt to discuss all these issues.

—*Editor*

Contents

1

The Meaning of the Concept of "Jihad"

Another concept that deserves clarification due in the context of our discussion is that of "jihad". The exact meaning of "Jihad" is "effort". Thus, in Islam, "to carry out jihad" is "to show effort, to struggle". The Prophet Muhammad explained that "the greatest jihad is the one a person carries out against his lower soul". What is meant by "lower soul" here is selfish desires and ambitions.

Assessed from the Qur'anic point of view, the word "jihad" can also mean a struggle carried out on intellectual grounds against those who oppress people, treat them unjustly, subject them to torture and cruelty and violate legitimate human rights. The purpose of this struggle is to bring about justice, peace and equality. Apart from these ideological and spiritual meanings, struggle in the physical sense is also considered as "jihad". However, as explained above, this has to be a struggle carried out solely for defensive purposes. The use of the concept of "jihad" for acts of aggression against innocent people, that is for terror, would be unjust and a great distortion of the true meaning of the term.

Killing Oneself, In Other Words Committing Suicide, is Forbidden in the Qur'an

Another important matter that arose in the wake of the latest terrorist assaults against the United States is that of suicide attacks. Some people who are ill-informed on Islam have made utterly erroneous statements to the effect that this religion of peace allows suicide attacks, whereas in Islam killing oneself and killing other people are both prohibited. In the words, "Do not kill yourselves." (Qur'an, 4:29) God has declared suicide to be a sin. In Islam it is forbidden for anyone to kill himself or herself, for no matter what reason. The Prophet reveals suicide to be a sin in a parable, when he says that those who commit suicide will be punished:

> *Indeed, whoever (intentionally) kills himself, then certainly he will be punished in the Fire of Hell, wherein he shall dwell forever.*

As this makes clear, committing suicide, and thus carrying out suicide attacks, and causing the deaths of thousands of innocent people while doing so, is a total violation of Islamic morality. God says in the Qur'an that it is a sin to put an end to one's own life. For that reason, it is quite impossible for someone who believes in God and says he abides by the Qur'an to do such a thing. The only people who can do such things are those who have a very mistaken perception of religion, have no idea of true Qur'anic morality, fail to use their reason and conscience, are under the influence of atheist ideologies, and who have been brainwashed with feelings of hatred and revenge. Everybody must oppose such actions.

Compassion, Tolerance and Humanity in the History of Islam

To sum up the facts we have seen so far, we can say that the political doctrine of Islam (in other words, Islamic rules and principles regarding political matters) is exceedingly moderate and peace-loving. This truth is accepted by many non-Muslim historians and theologians. One of these is the British historian Karen Armstrong, a former nun and an expert on Middle East history. In her book Holy War, which examines the history of the three divine religions, she makes the following comments:

> *... The word 'Islam' comes from the same Arabic root as the word 'peace' and the Koran condemns war as an abnormal state of affairs opposed to God's will... Islam does not justify a total aggressive war of extermination... Islam recognises that war is inevitable and sometimes a positive duty in order to end oppression and suffering. The Koran teaches that war must be*

> *limited and be conducted in as humane a way as possible. Mohammad had to fight not only the Meccans but also the Jewish tribes in the area and Christian tribes in Syria who planned on offensive against him in alliance with the Jews. Yet this did not make Mohammed denounce the People of the Book. His Muslims were forced to defend themselves but they were not fighting a 'holy war' against the religion of their enemies. When Mohammad sent his freedman Zaid against the Christians at the head of a Muslim army, he told them to fight in the cause of God bravely but humanely. They must not molest priests, monks and nuns nor the weak and helpless people who were unable to fight. There must be no massacre of civilians nor should they cut down a single tree nor pull down any building.*

After the death of the Prophet, the Caliphs who succeeded him were also very sensitive in exercising justice. In conquered countries, both the indigenous people and the newcomers led their lives in peace and security. Abu Bakr, the first Caliph, demanded his people adopt just and tolerant attitudes in these lands. All these attitudes were in compliance with the values of the Qur'an. Abu Bakr gave the following command to his army before the first Syrian expedition:

> *Stop, O people that I may give you ten rules to keep by heart: Do not commit treachery, nor depart from the right path. You must not mutilate, neither kill a child or aged man or woman. Do not destroy a palm tree, nor burn it with fire and do not cut any fruitful tree. You msut not slay any of the flock or herds or the camels, save for your subsistence. You are likely to pass by people who have devoted their lives to monastic services; leave them to that to which they have devoted their lives. You are likely, likewise, to find people who will present to you meals of many kinds. You may eat; but do no forget to mention the name of Allah.*

Umar ibn al-Khattab, who succeeded Abu Bakr, was famous for the way he exercised justice and made contracts with the indigenous people of the conquered countries. Each one of these contracts proved to be an example of tolerance and justice. For instance, in his declaration granting protection to Christians in Jerusalem and Lod, he ensured that churches would not be demolished and guaranteed that Muslims would not worship in churches in groups. Umar granted the same conditions to the Christians of Bethlehem. During the conquest of Medain, the declaration of protection given to the Nestorian Patriarch Yeshuyab III (650 - 660 AD) again guaranteed that churches would not be demolished and that no building would be converted into a house or a mosque. The letter written by the patriarch to the bishop of Fars (Persia) after the conquest is most striking, in the sense that it depicts the tolerance and compassion shown by Muslim rulers to the Book of People in the words of a Christian:

> *They [Abbasids] have not attacked the Christian religion, but rather they have commended our faith, honored our priests... and conferred benefits on churches and monasteries.*

All these are very important examples revealing the understanding of justice and tolerance of true believers. In a verse God commands the following:

> *God commands you to return to their owners the things you hold on trust and, when you judge between people, to judge with justice. How excellent is what God exhorts you to do! God is All-Hearing, All-Seeing. (Qur'an, 4:58)*

Canon Taylor, one of the mission leaders of the Anglican Church, expresses the beauty revealed by the Islamic morality in one of his speeches as follows:

> *It [Islam] brought out the fundamental dogmas of religion – the unity and greatness of God, that He is merciful and righteous, that He claims obedience to His will, resignation and faith. It proclaimed the responsibility of man, a future life, a Day of Judgment, and stern retribution to fall upon the wicked; and enforced the duties of prayer, almsgiving, fasting and benevolence. It thrust aside the artificial virtues, the religious frauds and follies, the perverted moral sentiments, and the verbal subtleties of theological disputants... It gave hope to the slave, brotherhood to mankind, and recognition to the fundamental facts of human nature.*

The false assertion that people in conquered countries converted to Islam under threat has also been disproved by Western researchers, and the justice and tolerant attitude of Muslims has been confirmed. L.Browne, a Western researcher, expresses this situation in the following words:

> *Incidentally these well-established facts dispose of the idea so widely fostered in Christian writings that the Muslims, wherever they went, forced people to accept Islam at the point of the sword.*

In his book The Prospects of Islam, Browne goes on to say that the real motive behind the Muslims' conquests was the brotherhood of Islam. The vast majority of Muslim administrators who have reigned over the Muslim lands throughout history continued to treat the members of other religions with the utmost tolerance and respect. Within the borders of all Islamic states, both Jews and Christians lived in safety and enjoyed freedom.

Georgetown University's Professor of Religion and International Relations John L. Esposito describes how Jews and Christians who came under the administration of Muslim states met with enormous tolerance:

> *Muslim armies proved to be formidable conquerors and effective rulers, builders rather than destroyers. They replaced the indigenous rulers and armies of the conquered countries, but preserved much of their government, bureaucracy, and culture. For many in the conquered territories, it was no more than an exchange of masters, one that brought peace to peoples demoralized and disaffected by the casualties and heavy taxation that resulted from the years of Byzantine-Persian warfare. Local communities were free to continue to follow their own way of life in internal, domestic affairs. In many ways, local populations found Muslim rule more flexible and tolerant than that of Byzantium and Persia. Religious communities were free to practise their faith-to worship and be governed by their religious leaders and laws in such areas marriage, divorce, and inheritance. In exchange, they were required to pay tribute, a poll tax (jizya) that entitled them to from Muslim protection from outside aggression and exempted them from military service. They were therefore called the "protected ones" (dhimmmi). In effect, this often meant lower taxes, grater local autonomy, rule by fellow Semites with closer linguistic and cultural ties than the hellenized, Greco-Roman elites of Byzantium, and greater*

> *religious freedom for Jews and indigenous Christians. Most of the Christian churches, such as the Nestorians, Monophysites, Jacobites, and Copts, had been persecuted as heretics and schismatics by Christian orthodoxy. For these reasons, some Jewish and Christian communities aided the invading armies, regarding them as less oppressive than their imperial masters. In many ways, the conquests brought a Pax Islamica to an embattled area.*

Another "Pax Islamica" brought by Islam was to women, a segment of society that was tremendously abused in the pre-Islamic times. Professor Bernard Lewis, known to be one of the greatest Western experts on the Middle East, makes the following comment:

> *In general, the advent of Islam brought an enormous improvement in the position of women in ancient Arabia, endowing them with property and some other rights, and giving them a measure of protection against ill treatment by their husbands or owners. The killing of female infants, sanctioned by custom in Pagan Arabia, was outlawed by Islam. But the position of women remained poor, and worsened when, in this as in so many other respects, the original message of Islam lost its impetus and was modified under the influence of pre-existing attitudes and customs.*

The reign of the Seljuk Turks and that of the Ottoman Empire were also marked by the just and tolerant outlook of Islam. In his book, *The Spread of Islam in the World,* Sir Thomas Arnold, the British researcher, explains the Christians' willingness to come under Seljuk rule because of this attitude:

> *This same sense of security of religious life under Muslim rule led many of the Christians of Asia Minor, also, about the same time, to welcome the advent of the Saljuq Turks as their deliverers... In the reign of Michael VIII (1261-1282), the Turks were often invited to take possession of the smaller towns in the interior of Asia Minor by the inhabitants, that they might escape from the tyranny of the empire; and both rich and poor often emigrated into Turkish dominions.*

Malik Shah, the ruler of the Islamic Seljuk Empire during its brightest age, approached the people in the conquered lands with great tolerance and compassion and thus was remembered with respect and love by them. All objective historians refer to the justice and tolerance of Malik Shah in their works. His tolerance also kindled feelings of love towards him in the hearts of the People of the Book. For this reason, unprecedented in history, many cities came under Malik Shah's rule of their own free will. Sir Thomas Arnold also mentions Odo de Diogilo, a monk of St. Denis, who participated in the Second Crusade as the private chaplain of Louis VII, refers in his memoirs to the justice administered by Muslims regardless of the subjects' religious affiliation. Based on the graphic account of Odo de Diogilo, Sir Thomas Arnold writes:

> *The situation of the survivors would have been utterly hopeless, had not the sight of their misery melted the hearts of the Muhammadans to pity. They tended the sick and relieved the poor and starving with open-handed liberality. Some even bought up the French money which the Greeks had got out of the pilgrims by force or cunning, and lavishly distributed it among the needy. So great was the contrast between the kind treatment the pilgrims received from the unbelievers and the cruelty of their fellow-Christians, the Greeks, who imposed forced labour upon them, beat them, and robbed them of what little they had left, that many of them voluntarily embraced the faith of their deliverers. As the old chronicler [Odo de Diogilo] says: "Avoiding their co-religionists who had been so cruel to them, they went in safety among the infidels who had compassion upon them, and, as we heard, more than three thousand joined themselves to the Turks when they retired."*

These statements by historians reveal that Muslim administrators who truly adopted the morality of the Islam always ruled with tolerance, compassion and justice. Likewise, the history of the Ottoman Empire which ruled lands on three continents for centuries abounds with examples of tolerance.

The way the Jews settled in Ottoman lands during the time of Sultan Beyazid II, after being subjected to massacre and exile in the Catholic kingdoms of Spain and Portugal, is a fine example of the tolerance that Islamic morality brings with it.

The Catholic monarchs who ruled much of Spain at the time brought grave pressure to bear on the Jews who had formerly lived in peace under Muslim rule in Andalusia. While Muslims, Christians and Jews were able to live side by side in peace in Andalusia, the Catholic monarchs tried to force the whole country to become Christian, and declared war on the Muslims while oppressing the Jews. As a result, the last Muslim ruler in the Granada region of southern Spain was overthrown in 1492. Muslims were subjected to terrible slaughter, and those Jews who refused to change their religion were sent into exile.

One group of these Jews without a homeland sought shelter in the Ottoman Empire, and the state allowed them to do so. The Ottoman fleet, under the command of Kemal Reis, brought the exiled Jews, and those Muslims who had survived the slaughter, to the land of the Ottomans.

Sultan Beyazid II has gone down in history as a most pious believer, and in the spring of 1492 he settled these wronged Jews who had been expelled from Spain in certain parts of his empire, around Edirne, and Thessalonica in present-day Greece. Most of the 25,000 Turkish Jews living in Turkey today are the ancestors of those Spanish Jews. They have adapted their religion and customs, which they brought from Spain some 500 years ago, to the conditions in Turkey, and continue to live most comfortably with their own schools, hospitals, old people's homes, cultural associations and newspapers. In the same way that they have traders and businessmen, they also have representatives in numerous professions, from technical subjects to advertising, with increasingly developing intellectual circles. While Jewish communities in many countries in Europe have for centuries been exposed to the fear of anti-Semitic racist attacks, those in Turkey have lived in peace and security. This example alone is enough to demonstrate the tolerance that Islam brings with it and its understanding of justice.

The compassion and tolerance exhibited by Sultan Beyazid II applied to all the Ottoman sultans. When Sultan Mehmet the Conqueror captured Constantinople, he allowed the Christians and the Jews to live freely there. André Miquel, who is known for the valuable works he has written about the just and tolerant practices of Muslims and the world of Islam, says:

> *Christians lived under a very well-administered government which they were unable to find in the time of the Byzantine and Latin states. They at no time saw any systematic oppression. On the contrary, the empire, and Constantinople in particular, became a shelter for those Spanish Jews who had been tortured. There was no forced imposition of Islam anywhere.*

As is clear from these facts, Muslims have at no time in history been oppressive. On the contrary, they have brought peace and security to all nations and beliefs wherever they have gone. They have abided by God's verse which says: "Worship God and do not associate anything with Him. Be good to your parents and relatives and to orphans and the very poor, and to neighbours who are related to you and neighbours who are not related to you, and to companions and travellers and your slaves. God does not love anyone vain or boastful." (Qur'an, 4:36) and have behaved well to all people. In short, friendship, brotherhood, peace and love are the bases of Qur'anic morality, and it is to these superior virtues that Muslims try to adhere.

ORIGINS

The beginnings of Jihad are traced back to the words and actions of Muhammad and the Quran. This encourages the use of Jihad against non-Muslims. The Quran, however, never uses the term Jihad for fighting and combat in the name of Allah; qital is used to mean "fighting." Jihad in the Quran was originally intended for the nearby neighbors of the Muslims, but as time passed and more enemies arose, the Quranic statements supporting Jihad were updated for the new adversaries. The first documentation of the law of Jihad was written by 'Abd al-Rahman al-Awza'i and Muhammad ibn al-Hasan al-Shaybani. The document grew out of debates that had surfaced ever since Muhammad's death.

Usage of the Term

In Modern Standard Arabic, *jihad* is one of the correct terms for a struggle for any cause, violent or not, religious or secular. The terminology is also applied to the fight for women's liberation.

The term 'jihad' has accrued both violent and non-violent meanings. It can simply mean striving to live a moral and virtuous life, spreading and defending Islam as well as fighting injustice and oppression, among other things. The relative importance of these two forms of jihad is a matter of controversy. A poll by Gallup showed that a "significant majority" of Muslim Indonesians define the term to mean "sacrificing one's life for the sake of Islam/ God/a just cause" or "fighting against the opponents of Islam".

In Lebanon, Kuwait, Jordan, and Morocco, the majority used the term to mean "duty toward God", a "divine duty", or a "worship of God", with no militaristic connotations. Other responses referenced, in descending order of prevalence:

- "A commitment to hard work" and "achieving one's goals in life"
- "Struggling to achieve a noble cause"
- "Promoting peace, harmony or cooperation, and assisting others"
- "Living the principles of Islam"

Distinction of "Greater" and "Lesser" Jihad

In his work, *The History of Baghdad*, Al-Khatib al-Baghdadi, an 11th-century Islamic scholar, referenced a statement by the companion of Muhammad Jabir ibn Abd-Allah.

The reference stated that Jabir said, "The Prophet... returned from one of his battles, and thereupon told us, 'You have arrived with an excellent arrival, you have come from the Lesser Jihad to the Greater Jihad—the striving of a servant (of Allah) against his desires (holy war)."

This reference gave rise to the distinguishing of two forms of jihad: "greater" and "lesser". Some Islamic scholars dispute the authenticity of this reference and consider the meaning of jihad as a holy war to be more important.

According to the Muslim Jurist Ibn Hajar al-Asqalani, the quote in which Muhammad is reported to have said that greater Jihad is the inner struggle, is from an unreliable source:

"This saying is widespread and it is a saying by Ibrahim ibn Ablah according to Nisa'i in al-Kuna. Ghazali mentions it in the Ihya' and al-`Iraqi said that Bayhaqi related it on the authority of Jabir and said: There is weakness in its chain of transmission." Hajar al Asqalani, Tasdid al-qaws, see also Kashf al-Khafaa'.

The best of Jihad

During the Arab Spring, many peaceful demonstrations in the Arab world faced violence and gunfire by their government's regime. The gunfire encouraged the protesters and led them to revolutions, based on their strong faith in what is called "the best of jihad". The best of jihad was encouraged by their prophet, Muhammad, saying:

"The best Jihad is the word of Justice in front of the oppressive Sultan [ruler]." In a battlefield context, when *jihad* is used to denote warfare, Ibn Nuhaas cited the following hadith to explain the meaning of the "best Jihad":

Ibn Habbaan narrates: The Messenger of Allah was asked about the best jihad.

He said: "The best jihad is the one in which your horse is slain and your blood is spilled." In a similarly worded Hadith to the one above, Ibn Nuhaas cited a hadith from Musnad Ahmad ibn Hanbal, where it states that the highest kind of Jihad, is "The person who is killed whilst spilling the last of his blood."(Ahmed 4/144)

It has also been reported that Muhammad considered performing hajj to be the best jihad for Muslim women.

Spiritual Struggle

Muslim scholar Mahmoud Ayoub states that "The goal of true *jihad* is to attain a harmony between *islam* (submission), *iman* (faith), and *ihsan* (righteous living)." In modern times, Pakistani scholar and professor Fazlur Rahman Malik has used the term to describe the struggle to establish "just moral-social order", while President Habib Bourguiba of Tunisia has used it to describe the struggle for economic development in that country.

Warfare (Jihad bil Saif)

Within classical Islamic jurisprudence—the development of which is to be dated into the first few centuries after the prophet's death —jihad is the only form of warfare permissible under Islamic law, and may consist in wars against unbelievers, apostates, rebels, highway robbers and dissenters renouncing the authority of Islam. The primary aim of jihad as warfare is not the conversion of non-Muslims to Islam by force, but rather the expansion and defense of the Islamic state. In later centuries, especially in the course of the colonization of large parts of the Muslim world, emphasis has been put on non-militant aspects of the jihad. Today, some Muslim authors only recognize wars with the aim of territorial defense as well as the defense of religious freedom as legitimate.

Whether the Quran sanctions defensive warfare only or commands an all out war against non-Muslims depends on the interpretation of the relevant passages. This is because it does not explicitly state the aims of the war Muslims are obliged to wage; the passages concerning *jihad* rather aim at promoting fighters for the Islamic cause and do not discuss military ethics.

In the classical manuals of Islamic jurisprudence, the rules associated with armed warfare are covered at great length. Such rules include not killing women, children and non-combatants, as well as not damaging cultivated or residential areas.

More recently, modern Muslims have tried to re-interpret the Islamic sources, stressing that Jihad is essentially defensive warfare aimed at protecting Muslims and Islam.

Although some Islamic scholars have differed on the implementation of Jihad, there is consensus amongst them that the concept of jihad will always include armed struggle against persecution and oppression.

Debate

Controversy has arisen over whether the usage of the term *jihad* without further explanation refers to military combat, and whether some have used confusion over the definition of the term to their advantage.

Middle East historian Bernard Lewis argues that "the overwhelming majority of classical theologians, jurists, and traditionalists (specialists in the hadith) understood the obligation of jihad in a military sense." Furthermore, Lewis maintains that for most of the recorded history of Islam, from the lifetime of the Prophet Muhammadonward, the word jihad was used in a primarily military sense.

Resistance against Globalization

Benjamin R. Barber used the term Jihad to point out the resistant movement against globalization (which he refers to as 'McWorld') as well as the modern-institutionalization of nation states. The forces of 'Jihad' come from fundamentalist ethnic groups who want to protect their traditions, heritage and identity from modernization and universalized markets. The resistance has led to fragmented, small-scale violent conflicts between cultures, peoples and tribes. Although 'Jihad' strengthens the solidarity within the resisting group, it obeys to hierarchy and cannot tolerate foreign influence, which discourages democracy.

HISTORICAL EXAMPLES OF JIHAD

With the exception of the battle of Uhud in 625 and the battle of the ditch in 627, all the battles of the prophet of Islam were offensive. All jihad wars undertaken after his death were offensive expansive wars. The Persian and Byzantine empires bordering Arabia were not a threat to the Muslim Arabs. In the West, Islamic armies conquered the Levant, North Africa, and finished the conquest of most of Spain by 715. Christians completed the liberation of Spain in 1492. In the East, the Muslim invaders conquered the Persian Empire. By 1206, they had invaded the Punjab, Sindh, Delhi, and beyond. Muslims stopped waging large scale jihad wars after 1683 because the Islamic world had grown too weak. Examples of jihad wars and the atrocities associated with it abound in Islamic history. We cite a few of them herein.

Wherever the Islamic armies invaded, they caused massive destructions, countless systematic massacres of extermination, enslavement and exile of a great portion of the population, and great human suffering. Looting and pillaging the wealth of conquered lands, periodic ransoms, and the jizya tax impoverished and ruined the conquered populations. Economic decline and general impoverishment followed in the conquered territories. More blood has been shed for Islam than for any other cause in history.

Some historians estimate that in India alone, more than 80 million people were massacred by the sword of Islam. In addition, 10 million Buddhists, 120 million Christians and African Animists, and many Zoroastrians in Persia were killed by marauding Islamic armies, both during their conquests and in the centuries that followed. The sword of Islam spread death, devastation and dark terror over many lands.

Examples of violent Islamic jihad in modern times are the civil wars in South Sudan, Afghanistan, Lebanon, the Russian war in the Caucasus, and the attacks in the West. To the Muslim fundamentalist, a Muslim terrorist who kills unarmed innocent non-Muslim men, women, and children in the predominantly non-Muslim West is a war hero. What the Islamists could not accomplish by military conquest in the world of today, they are attempting to accomplish peacefully by proclaiming the religion of Islam. The problem is that they do not tell the truth about Islam in their proclamations. Instead, they sugarcoat it in their attempts to sell it dishonestly to unwary Westerners.

The Early Islamic Era

Banu Qurayza, the last Jewish tribe in Medina, rejected Islam. They remained neutral in the battle of the trench (627). Muhammad, the prophet of Islam, questioned their loyalty, and besieged them. They surrendered. Muhammad appointed Sa'd ibn Muadh, one of his most fanatic followers, to decide their fate. Sa'd was wounded in the battle of the trench and lusted after revenge. He died soon after issuing his verdict. His verdict was that all the men of the tribe were to be killed, and the possessions of the tribe were to be divided among the Muslims. Muhammad ratified this unjust horrific judgment, and in order to justify the bloodbath, he claimed that his god sanctioned it (al-Ahzab 33: 26-27).

Muhammad ordered that a trench be dug in the night across the market place in Medina, and commanded that the male captives be brought forth to the trench in companies of five or six at a time, where they were beheaded and buried in the trench. This continued all day long into the evening till all the men of the tribe, numbering 800-900, were killed. Muhammad observed in person the horrific killings. If is important to stress that these tribesmen were not armed, and were not a threat to Muhammad and his followers. They were murdered in cold blood. Muhammad was responsible for the first Islamic massacre of 627 in the long bloody history of Islam.

The women and children of the tribe were sold into slavery, and its possessions were looted. Muhammad took for himself Rihana whose husband and all her male relatives had just perished in the massacre. Muhammad wanted to remove non-Muslims from Medina and Arabia by the sword, if necessary (Bukhari 4.52.288; 5.59.716; 4.53.392, 380). He started the process, and his followers completed it (Muslim 19.4366). In fact, till this day, it is illegal to build a church in Saudi Arabia. In addition, the religious police will raid a house where Christians are gathered to worship, will arrest the leader of the worship service and torture him in prison.

Muhammad warned the people who harassed him in the market place of Mecca saying that he would come back as slaughterer. The army that Muhammad led in his invasion of Mecca years later had a black flag signifying death with the word "punishment" written on it. Upon conquering Mecca, Muhammad ordered the killing of several persons for making satirical songs against him. In conquering Mecca, Muhammad brought to it death, not salvation. This contrasts with the peaceful triumphant entry of Jesus into Jerusalem riding a donkey, not bearing a sword and without an army.

After the death of Muhammad, the caliph Abu Bakr invaded Syria. During the campaign of 634, the entire region between Gaza and Caesarea was devastated. Four thousand Christian, Jewish and Samaritan peasants were massacred. During the military campaigns of caliph Umar ibn al-Khattab, the second guided caliph, in Mesopotamia between 635 and 642, monasteries were sacked, the monks were killed, and Christian Arabs executed or forced to convert.

In Elam, the population was put to the sword. The Arab invasion of the Middle East was not by any means a joyous liberating experience. It brought a great deal of death and destruction. The inhabitants of towns taken by storm were either killed or led into captivity, and their property was looted. Umar ibn al-Khattab was so brutal and despotic in his retaliation against the Persians for opposing Islam's spread that to this day the Iranians celebrate the anniversary of his assassination with great festivities.

Amr ibn al-As conquered Egypt in 639-642. As he advanced in it, he captured the town of Bahnesa near Fayum and put to the sword its inhabitants, including old men, women and children. He committed the same atrocities in other towns in Egypt. Similar atrocities occurred in North Africa. Tripoli was pillaged in 643. Carthage was razed to the ground and most of its inhabitants killed. The same pattern was followed in Anatolia, Syria, Iraq, and Iran.

Al-Hajjaj, the governor of Iraq (694-714), instructed his commander Muhammad ibn Qasim in 712 to invade India and destroy the unbelievers. After the capture of the port of Debal, the Muslim army took three days to slaughter many of its inhabitants. In the town of Brahminabad, the Muslim army killed more than 6000 men. In subsequent invasions, Islamic armies targeted the Hindu temples and monasteries in an orgy of pillage and arson. Those not killed were captured and sold as slaves. Mahmud of Ghazni (971-1030), the head of a Turco-Afghan dynasty, invaded India destroying, pillaging and massacring. He justified his actions by constantly referring to Qur'anic injunctions to kill the idolaters. At the battle of Somnah, the site of a celebrated Hindu temple, he killed about 50,000 inhabitants.

The Middle Ages

The Jews of North Africa and Spain suffered several massacres under the Islamic Arab rule, such as the massacre of more than 6000 Jews in the town of Fez (Morocco) in 1033, the massacres of

Cordoba and other places in Spain in 1010-1013, the massacre of the entire Jewish community of about 4000 in Granada, Spain in 1066, etc.

The Muslim Berbers Almoravids (1056-1147) arrived in Spain in 1086, followed by the more fanatic and violent Almohad Muslim Berbers who arrived in Spain in 1146-47. Almoravids deported from Spain a large number of Christians to Morocco in 1106, 1126 and 1138. The Almohads (1130-1269) wreaked enormous persecution on both the Jewish and Christian populations in Spain and North Africa, including massacres, slavery and forced conversions.

The Muslim Seljuk Turks invaded Asia Minor over a period of four centuries from the middle of the eleventh century. These invasions were accompanied with extermination of local populations or their precipitate flight. Entire cities, and whole provinces fell into decay. Some fertile districts were laid waste. Impenetrable thickets sprang up in vast areas replacing fertile fields and pasture. This was followed by Ottoman jihad campaigns in the European Balkans. The Turks practiced wide-spread forced conversions which persisted throughout the sixteenth century.

In the fourteenth and early fifteenth centuries, Timur the Lame (known as Tamerlane) launched jihad wars against both non-Muslims and Muslims accusing the latter of lukewarmness towards Islam. He combined Mongol barbarity with Islamic fanaticism. He massacred in the thousands out of Qur'anic piety, as a duty and sacred mission.

The following is a sampling of his massacres: his cold-blooded slaughter of 100,000 captive Indians near Delhi in December, 1398, his burying alive of 4000 Armenians in 1400-1, his erecting 20 towers of human skulls at Aleppo and Damascus in the same year, his massacre of 70,000 of the inhabitants of Isfahan in November 1387, etc.

The Wahhabis of Arabia condemned most non-Wahhabi Muslims as infidels, and waged jihad against them. In 1801 and 1802, the Saudi Wahhabis under the leadership of Abdul Aziz ibn Muhammad ibn Saud attacked and captured the holy Shia cities of Karbala and Najaf in Iraq, massacred parts of the Muslim population and destroyed the tombs of Husayn ibn Ali, the grandson of Muhammad, and Ali ibn abi-Talib.

The Armenian Genocide

In the nineteenth century, the Armenians demanded their equal rights and attempted to break out of their Ottoman Islamic dhimmitude peacefully.

They sought reforms in the Turkish/Ottoman system of government. As a result, the Armenian genocide began. The Muslim Ottoman Turks massacred more than 200,000 unarmed Armenian civilians in 1894-96 during the reign of sultan Abdul Hamid II (the Sassoun massacre).

That was followed, under the young Turks regime, by the Adana massacres of 25,000 Armenians in 1909. This climaxed in the 1915 genocide when additional 600,000-800,000 unarmed Armenian civilians were massacred. The Muslim perpetrators who committed these bloody atrocities were guided by Islamic Sharia prescriptions providing that if the dhimmi requested his equal rights, and freedom from his bondage, he forfeited the protection of the caliph.

The genocide of the Armenian Christians in World War I was an ethnic cleansing of central Turkey by an Islamic jihad wherein Muslim Turks systematically murdered unarmed civilian Christian Armenian males over the age of twelve en masse in 1915. Women and children were deported from their centuries-old Armenian villages. Many of them died or were killed in their arduous journey. Others were given out as slaves, or forced to convert to Islam. The Armenian properties were looted. At the end, about one and a half million Armenian civilians died and were killed in those atrocities. Turkish Armenia ceased to exist. The four elements of the Armenian liquidation in central Turkey—deportation, enslavement, forced conversion, and massacre—reproduced the historic conditions of Islamic jihad carried out from the seventh century on. Successive Turkish governments have consistently refused to acknowledge the historic fact of the Armenian genocide, and to pay compensations to the Armenians.

The Sudanese Genocide

During the brutal civil war between the Muslim Arab North of the Sudan, and the Christian and animist black South (1955-72, 1983-2005), Sudan was the site of the most vicious anti-Christian persecution raging in the world. The Islamist government of the Sudan committed genocide in the South and the Nubba mountains, including massacres, rape, looting, and slavery. Hundreds of Christian villages were razed to the ground. The end result was a devastated economy, a divided country, the death of approximately two million people, and the displacement of over five million people. South Sudan seceded from the Sudan, and became an independent state on July 9, 2011.

Despite the relentless cruel Islamic persecution, the Sudanese Church grew very fast in that period. Many Muslims and animists came to Christ in the Sudan than anywhere else in the world. In twenty years, Christians grew from 5% to over 20% of the Sudanese population (and 80% of South Sudan). South Sudan is the Christian bulwark against the southward advance of radical Islam into central Africa.

In the late nineteenth century, the British General Charles Gordon succeeded in breaking the back of the slave trade in the Sudan. However, the Muslim Sudanese Mahdi, Muhammad ibn Abdullah, that succeeded him in 1885 declared jihad warfare, and restored the slave trade in the Sudan. During the civil war, the soldiers of the Islamic government of the Sudan and the Arab militias armed by the government attacked African villages, kidnapped and sold as slaves tens of thousands of Sudanese Christian and animist men, women and children. There is no doubt that slavery is still widespread in the Sudan, including exporting slaves to Muslim countries in the Persian Gulf.

Jihad Atrocity in the U.S.A.

On Sept. 11, 2001, the Islamist organization of al-Qaeda attacked the U.S.A. this resulted in the death of about 3000 innocent civilians. None of the leading Islamic clerics in the Muslim world condemned the 9/11 atrocities. In fact, some praised it?! Misguided Muslim crowds celebrated it in the streets of the Middle East.

Muslim governments, who call for tolerance of Muslims in the West, have never apologized for 9/11 atrocities. The U.S. military was able to locate the leadership of al-Qaeda and destroy it.

AN IN-DEPTH ANALYSIS OF JIHADISM

Jihad is an Arabic word that literally means "combat" or "striving" and jihad is sometimes regarded along with allegiance to the Iman as the violent Sixth Pillar of Islam, although orthodox Islam only recognizes Five Pillars. The idea of jihad being the violent Sixth Pillar comes from the Khawarij sect, which was part of the fundamentalist Islamism movement that started in the early 20th Century. The Khawarij sect is named after Dhul-Khuwaysarah, a man that Muhammad prophesied would have an overprotective love of religion. The Khawariji interpretation of the role of excommunication is completely the opposite of the Salafist interpretation of excommunication (*takfir*). Salafism is rather restricted about who should be declared an infidel and therefore excommunicated. Followers of the Khawariji interpretation, or Jihadists, see few if any restrictions on who can be declared an infidel, and therefore justify unrestricted warfare or terrorism against infidels. Even traditional Qur'anic interpretations hold that those who reject Islam reject God, and one of the principal characteristics of rejecting God (*kufr*) is the inclination toward violence and oppression, encapsulated by the broad concept *zulm*, which means transgression against one's own soul or human nature. Now, many if not most Muslims reject the duty to propagate Islam by force and limit jihad to self-defense (Hashmi 2006), but then again, there is no such thing as a pacifist movement in Islam, and most Muslims respect the necessity of a continuous tension between incessant warfare and peace.

There is some controversy in Islamic thought as to whether jihad can be declared before or after an enemy attacks, or in other words, in a pre-emptive strike or in self-defense. A strict and literal reading of the Qur'an says self-defense only, but Islamic law has always justified a first-strike position. Just saying that women ought to have a right to vote is a crime of violence against all of Islam, and this can trigger a Jihadist reaction against not only the person who said that, but against whomever they got that idea from — a kind of scorched earth policy or nipping things in the bud. The basis for most anti-Americanism among Muslim extremists is part of the notion that any country that would give women the right to vote, or all minorities equal rights, is probably a country populated by infidels who are attacking Islam with crimes of violence. It may be important to note the quite popular opinion in the Muslim world that it was under attack by America first.

Jihad is also part of the name in at least two terrorist groups that make up the shadowy umbrella group called Islamic Jihad, which has millions of supporters throughout the Islamic world because these supporters agree with militaristic interpretations of jihad. The two main groups are the Egyptian Islamic Jihad and the Palestinian Islamic Jihad, both formed in the mid-1970s with origins going back to the 1928 Muslim Brotherhood.

Egyptian Islamic Jihad: This is the Cairo-based group that assassinated Egyptian President Anwar Sadat in 1981, and is responsible for a number of other assassination attempts inside of Egypt up to 1993. Since then, it has targeted American and Israeli interests around the world, and has a well-funded network operating out of Egypt, Yemen, Afghanistan, Pakistan, Sudan, Lebanon, and the United Kingdom. They succeeded in bombing one embassy in Pakistan during 1995, and the CIA thwarted another embassy bombing attempt in Albania during 1998. They are involved in a number of criminal activities, besides terrorism, around the world.

Palestinian Islamic Jihad: This is a relatively small group that operates out of Syria and is fanatically dedicated to the killing of Jews and total destruction of the state of Israel. By comparison, Hamas is a more moderate group. Formed in the Gaza Strip during the mid-1970s, it has been the consistent target of Israeli counterterrorism raids. They regularly conduct suicide bombing infiltrations into Israel, but are also known to target other Arabs seen as too moderate or too Western, having carried out attacks as far away as Malta and in Jordan and Lebanon. In February, 2003, the FBI arrested their alleged North American leader, a Univ. of

South Florida professor, but in December, 2005, the trial resulted in acquittal.

Suicide bombings (a tactic that came into popularity around 1983) are a trademark of jihadists. The religious element involved is that believers think they will attain a heavenly reward for their sacrifice. The political element involved is that it sends a message of how desperate and passionate the believers are. Expert opinion is mixed on the effectiveness of suicide bombing as a strategy of asymmetric warfare. Experts also agree that it is difficult if not impossible to profile a suicide bomber. Some say it ultimately backfires by turning public opinion against the bombers and those who support them. Support often comes in the form of charitable donations to the family of suicide bombers. Many poor parents in the Arab world may be inclined to encourage their children to become suicide bombers. For its photogenic value in a globalized world of mass communication, suicide bombing is a weapon of genius.

The Guarantee of Heaven for Islamic Martyrs

Suicide, under orthodox Islam, is a sin. However, Jihadists consider the circumstances to cleanse the sin, making it the act of a holy martyr, not a suicide. The actual percentage of Muslims who agree with this interpretation is hotly disputed, as is the concept of martyrdom. A martyr is technically someone who dies for their religious faith, but the outcome also matters, in terms of who gets to write history. Martyrdom, therefore, is intimately tied up with Islamic arrogance that their goal of religious domination will be victorious in the end. The study of all things in the end is known by the religious term *eschatology*, and Islam contains strong elements of Zoroastrianism, the world's first religion to have a full-blown eschatology. Many experts believe that Zoroastrianism, a religion that existed from 1500 BC to 700 AD in Persia and still popular in parts of Iran and India, had a significant impact on Islam. In a nutshell, the basic idea that Zoraster had is that earth is a battlefield between good and evil, and that good is destined to win out over evil, and anyone who allies themselves with good is guaranteed to be part of this destiny. What Mohammed took from this is the idea that whoever martyrs themselves for the sake of good goes directly to a special place in heaven, or in a worst case scenario, goes to hell for a short time and then goes to heaven. Satan, as the embodiment of evil, also plays a big role, as a real entity who tempts people to renounce their faith, and the martyr with the most guarantee of a special place in heaven is the one who fights Satan.

Demonizing America as the "Great Satan" makes it a fitting opponent in the predestined war between good and evil. Heaven is more than a transcendental place to Muslims. Orthodox Islamic eschatology holds that the afterlife is physical; people are said to have bodies, and they will experience material pleasures, including unlimited food, drink and sex. Heaven is known to some Muslims as the Gardens of Paradise where unimaginable spiritual and sensual pleasures await. To other Muslims, the rewards are quite imaginable, such as the 72 virgins waiting to have sex with each martyr every day (their hymens miraculously regrow the next day). This account was popularized by the media in 2001 when a CBS reporter interviewed a Hamas recruiter who talked about it. According to one translation, the Koran 78:31 reads "*As for the righteous, they shall surely triumph. Theirs shall be gardens and vineyards, and high-bosomed virgins for companions.*" Some Islamic scholars argue this is a false translation, and that passages like that are referring to angels or heavenly beings. Other Islamic scholars argue it's only 70 virgins instead of 72, and that your wife is always one of them. Yet other Islamic scholars say the whole thing is intended to be taken in a transcendental way, the pleasures of heaven being so great it's like having an eternal erection or first-time sex all the time.

JIHAD: ISLAMIC HOLY WAR

Two variant forms of jihad are distinguished in Islam: a spiritual mode (inner struggle), and a violent mode of striving in holy war to spread Islam and expand the Islamic state domain by force. Only 2% of the Bukhari hadiths that relate to jihad refer to the spiritual mode. The other 98% of the hadiths devoted to jihad claim that the violent mode of jihad is the supreme Islamic religious act. The small marginalized heretical Sufi sect adheres to the first mode of jihad. However, the paramount mainstream understanding and usage of Islamic jihad throughout fourteen centuries of Islamic history has been striving in offensive military conflict to expand the territory of Islam, conquer new populations for Islam, and establish Islamic law (Sharia). This is the classic primary meaning of jihad codified in Islamic law (Sharia) and attested in Islamic history. Contemporary Islamists are striving to impose Sharia globally and restore the totalitarian Islamic caliphate which Kemal Ataturk, the father of modern Turkey, abolished in 1924 in order to modernize Turkey.

There is no doubt from the historical record of Muhammad, the prophet of Islam, and his followers that he meant the jihad verses in the Qur'an to be understood literally, not spiritually (an-Nisa' 4: 95; al-Anfal 8: 65; etc). In fact, the Islamic scholarly consensus on the definition of jihad as aggressive warfare against non-Muslims was achieved over a thousand years ago. Muhammad was born into a culture of tribal conflict and bloodshed. Instead of improving it, he incorporated it into Islam through the concept of violent jihad. He retained the tribal warring culture as the basis for Islamic survival. Jihad warfare is a central doctrine of Islam. It helped define Islam from its very dawn. Islam was born as an ideology of totalitarian terror.

While wars are the exception to the norm in the history of any civilization, it is the norm in the Islamic civilization in dar-al-harb (the house of war), which is the territory of the non-Muslim populations. Jihad warfare is an Islamic institution, not a mere isolated event in Islamic history. The long bloody history of Islam reflects these teachings. It is rife with continuous harassment, persecution, subjugation and killing of non-Muslim infidels. All the battles of Muhammad were offensive except for the battles of Uhud (625 AD) and the ditch (627 AD) which were defensive.

Although Muhammad proclaimed in the Qur'an, al-Baqarah 2: 256 and al-Kafirun 109: 6 that there is no compulsion in religion, he abrogated that concept in al-Baqarah 2: 193; Al-'Imran 3: 83, 85; an-Nisa' 4: 89, 101-102; al-Anfal 8: 9, 12-13; al-Tawbah 9: 5, 29; Muhammad 47: 4; al-Hashr 59: 7; etc. In fact, the verse of the sword (al-Tawbah 9: 5) commanding Muslims to fight all who choose not to convert to Islam, whether they are inside or outside Arabia, abrogated at least 124 verses in the Qur'an that speak about love, peace, and forgiveness. Muhammad taught and practiced persecution, military conquest, subjugation, coercion and killing of non-Muslims. While Islam prohibits Muslims from paying or charging interest, it permits them to extort money from infidels and suppress them with usury to gain the upper hand.

At the end of his life, Muhammad, the prophet of Islam, said: "... I have been made victorious with terror, and while I was sleeping, the keys of the treasures of the world were brought to me and put in my hand ..." (Bukhari 4.52.220). On his deathbed, he commanded his followers to purge Arabia of non-Muslims (Bukhari 4.52.288; 5.59.716; 4.53.392, 380). He started the process (Muslim 19.4366), and his followers completed it (Bukhari 3.39.531; Muslim 10.3763). In fact, till this day, it is illegal to build a church in Saudi Arabia. In addition, the religious police will raid a house where Christians are gathered to worship, will arrest the leader of the worship service and torture him in prison.

THE ISLAMIC DOCTRINE OF JIHAD

Islam is not a religion of peace. It provides a recipe for perpetual war. It is the only major religion in the world of today that institutionalizes violence against non-Muslims, which it calls jihad (normally translated "holy war," as it is usually used in that context. The literal translation is "struggle" or "strive"). Many verses in the Qur'an exhort Muslims to wage jihad against those who reject Islam, and against Muslims who do not practice Islam to its fullest. An entire sura 8 is called al-Anfal which means "spoils of war." There is no sura called "peace." Only 56 verses in the entire Qur'an mention peace, and most of them occur in the context of the Islamic greeting of "peace be upon you." Others deal with the peace that occurs after a military battle. The most vivid and repeated themes in the Qur'an are on jihad and the punishment of hell.

The Arabic word "jihad" appears in its various forms about thirty-five times in the Qur'an: nine times in the Meccan chapters (suras), and twenty-six times in the Medinan ones. The Arabic word "qatal," means "kill" (it does not mean inner struggle against vices). It appears in its various forms, meaning "kill" or "fight," about one hundred and twenty-three times in the Qur'an: thirty-four times in the Meccan chapters (suras), and eighty-nine times in the Medinan suras.

The increase of these words in the Medinan Qur'an reflects the rise of the military power of the prophet of Islam after he immigrated to Medina, though a few uses of these words are not in a military context. In sura 9, al-Tawbah of the Qur'an, thought to be one of last suras given, each of these two words appear ten times in the context of war. In fact, verses al-Tawbah 9: 111 and an-Nisa' 4: 74 each contains three words rooted in the Arabic word "qatal" (meaning to kill): "God has bought of the believers their lives and their possessions, promising them paradise in return, so they fight (from "qatal") in God's cause, and kill (from "qatal"), and are killed (from "qatal")..." (al-Tawbah 9: 111).

In contrast with that, the Holy Bible (KJV) provides 420 verses on the subject of peace. Man strove for peace since ancient times (Isaiah 52: 7). Deep inner peace is the gift of the living God. Man cannot create his own peace. "The peace of God, which surpasses all understanding, will guard your hearts and minds through Christ Jesus" (Philippians 4: 7); "Now may the Lord of peace Himself give you peace always in every way" (2 Thessalonians 3: 16; James 3: 17-18); "There is no peace," says the LORD, "for the wicked" (Isaiah 48: 22; 57: 20-21; 59: 1-4, 7-11; etc).

In fact, the whole of the Qur'an and Islam support jihad in its various forms: jihad with money, with the written and spoken word and with the sword.

The verses that do not refer to jihad directly or indirectly marshal the Muslims into a militant fraternity (ummah) on the basis of a common belief system, a common set of rituals, and a common code of conduct. Jihad in any form can be practiced only when there is an organized and disciplined community to practice it. The Qur'an marshals and motivates the ummah to impose Islam on the rest of mankind by every possible means, including the sword.

The purpose of jihad is the islamization of the conquered populations either by pressuring them to convert to Islam, or by forcing them to submit to Islamic rule. The main purpose of jihad is political, not religious. It is an instrument for both the universalization of the Islamic religion, and the establishment of an imperial world state. Islamic jihad must continue until the whole world is under the rule of Islamic law. All the Sunni and Shia Islamic schools of jurisprudence command waging war against unbelievers in order to establish the rule of Islamic law over them. War is the main vehicle of Islamic religious expansion. Without the sword of Muhammad and his followers after him, Islam will not exist today. Over a thousand years of unprecedented military expansion, the Islamic armies invaded vast territories in the Middle East, North Africa and even Europe. Muslim Arabs and Moors had controlled Spanish territory for eight hundred years, Portugal for six hundred years, Greece and Bulgaria for five hundred years, Romania and Serbia for four hundred years, Sicily for three hundred years, and Hungary for one hundred fifty years.

Authoritative Muslim historians, such as Ahmad ibn Yahya al-Baladhuri (d. 892) and al-Tabari (838-923), attest the fact that Islam was spread by the sword.

Jihad in the Qur'an, Hadith and Sharia

Violent jihad is a central Islamic doctrine. The prophet of Islam repeatedly stressed that there is nothing better and nobler for a Muslim to do than to engage in jihad warfare (Bukhari 1.2.26; Muslim 20.4642). He claimed that engaging in jihad warfare is more meritorious than prayers, fasting, pilgrimage, etc. He warned Muslims who did not participate in jihad warfare of punishment (Abu Dawud 14.2497). He taught that Muslims who fight in jihad would be rewarded with a higher level in the Islamic paradise (an-Nisa' 4: 95; Muslim 20.4645).

Muslims are called upon to proclaim Islam by subduing and conquering non-Muslims, murdering them, destroying their temples, and looting their possessions.

In general, the obligation to participate in violent jihad is a collective one. It becomes a personal imperative one for every

Muslim when Muslim lands are invaded by uninvited non-Muslim forces (Reliance of the Traveler, o9.3).

The violent activities of the Muslim zealots are fully supported and encouraged by the Islamic teachings. Muhammad said: "I have been ordered to fight with the people till they say, 'None has the right to be worshipped but Allah ..." (Bukhari 4.52.196; 1.2.25; etc). Jihad is a Muslim religious duty and obligation, like pilgrimage (al-Baqarah 2: 216). Rejecting jihad amounts to rejecting a fundamental Qur'anic dogma. The Qur'an condemns Muslims who refuse to fight in jihad (al-Anfal 8: 20, 47, 49; al-Tawbah 9: 24, 39, 81-82). Some Islamist groups consider Muslims that do not participate in jihad infidels. Those who wage jihad rank highest in Islam.

References to jihad, and killing of infidels who reject Islam and of apostates who leave Islam abound in the Qur'an. It contains about 164 verses that refer to jihad warfare against non-Muslims and distributing the spoils of war. 24% of Medinan Qur'an is devoted to jihad.

"Fight against such of those to whom the Scriptures were given (Christians and Jews) as believe in neither god (the god of Islam) nor the last day, who do not forbid what god and his apostle (Muhammad) have forbidden, and do not embrace the true faith (Islam), until they pay tribute out of hand and are utterly subdued" (al-Tawbah 9: 29)

"When the forbidden months are past, then fight and slay the Pagans wherever you find them, and seize them, beleaguer them, and lie in wait for them in every stratagem; but if they repent, and establish regular prayers and practice regular charity, then open the way for them: for Allah is Oft-Forgiving, Most Merciful" (al-Tawbah 9: 5, 12, 14, 19, 20, 29, 36, 38, 39, 41, 73, 81, 86, 88, 111, 123; al-Baqarah 2: 190, 193, 216, 244; Al-Imran 3: 169; an-Nisa' 4: 47, 74, 76, 77, 84, 89, 95; al-Ma'idah 5: 33, 51; al-Anfal 8: 12-17, 39, 59-60, 65, 67, 74; al-Anbiya' 21: 44; Muhammad 47: 4-6, 35; al-Fath 48: 16; al-Hujurat 49: 15; al-Mumtahanah 60: 1, 11; as-Saff 61: 4; at-Tahrim 66: 9; etc).

The Qur'an urges Muslims to kill, even those willing to surrender (al-Anfal 8: 67). The Qur'an claims that Islam is superior to all other religions (Al-Imran 3: 85; al-Tawbah 9: 33; al-Fath 48: 28; as-Saff 61: 9; etc). The jihad warfare commands for waging offensive, aggressive and unjust wars to Islamize all the non-Muslim populations are open-ended, perpetual, global, and generic in nature. That is what motivates Islamists to terrorize and kill non-Muslims following the example of Muhammad, the architect of Islam.

To read such blood thirsty injunctions in the Qur'an, the holiest book of Islam, is shocking. It grants Muslim jihadis a license to kill in the name of the Islamic god in the Islamic jihad. Extreme hatred and bloody violence against the non-believers are built into the religion of Islam. It is a historical fact that, with the exception of some Indonesian islands, no nation has ever willingly converted to Islam. On the other hand, no nation has ever unwillingly been converted to Christianity in the first three centuries of the Christian era. In addition, the Hadith collections of Sahih al-Bukhari and Sahih Muslim include hundreds of references to jihad warfare. A sampling of the Islamic teaching on violence is provided herein from the Hadith of Sahih al-Bukhari which is second in authority only to the Qur'an in Sunni Islam. It contains about 199 references to jihad in the sense of armed warfare against non-Muslims. Muhammad, the prophet of Islam, said:

"The example of a Mujahid in Allah's Cause— and Allah knows better who really strives in His Cause— —is like a person who fasts and prays continuously. Allah guarantees that He will admit the Mujahid in His Cause into Paradise if he is killed, otherwise He will return him to his home safely with rewards and war booty" (Bukhari 4.52.46; 1.2.35);

"Nobody who dies and finds good from Allah (in the Hereafter) would wish to come back to this world even if he were given the whole world and whatever is in it, except the martyr who, on seeing the superiority of martyrdom, would like to come back to the world and get killed again (in Allah's Cause)" (Bukhari 4.52.53);

"There is no migration (after the Conquest of Mecca), but Jihad and good intentions, and when you are called for Jihad, you should immediately respond to the call" (Bukhari 4.52.42; etc).

All the four principal Sunni schools of jurisprudence, the Maliki, Hanbali, Hanafi, and Shafi'i, agree on the importance of jihad. Prominent Islamic scholars of antiquity from each of the four major schools of jurisprudence in historical Islam clearly understood the Qur'anic injunctions of jihad to command holy war. This includes al-Tabari (838-923), al-Biadawi (d. 1286), Ibn Khaldun (1332-1406), Ibn Kathir (1301-1373), Ibn Taymiyya (1263-1328), al-Ghazzali (1058-1111) who was a peaceful Sufi, etc.

Reliance of the Traveler (Undat al-Salik), the Shafi'i manual of Islamic law, devotes three sections o9, o10, o11 (eleven pages) to jihad. Making war on unbelievers is one of the responsibilities of the Muslim nation. The Islamic umma (nation) must exist in a state of perpetual war, interrupted only by temporary truces, with the non-Muslim world in order to compel either conversion to Islam, or subjugation to its rulers. When the Islamist regime is militarily weak, it reaches out for truce and peace simply in order to buy time to build up its strength (Muhammad 47: 35). Those that reject the invitation to convert to Islam are required to pay the poll tax (jizya) in humiliation and subjugation in their homelands. Should they refuse, war is to be declared against them (Muslim 19.4294; etc). In addition, Shia Islam calls for the necessity of jihad. Islam lacks any doctrine of equal coexistence. Islam lacks any doctrine of coexistence with non-Muslims in equality. In fact, peaceful coexistence as equals in a pluralistic society is not an option in Islam.

Islam divides humanity into two classes: a superior class of Muslims (Al-'Imran 3: 110; at-Tawbah 9: 33), and an inferior class of non-Muslims (infidels). There are more than four hundred verses in the Qur'an that describe the torment of hell that the god of Islam has prepared for the infidel. There are approximately seven hundred verses in more than fifty Qur'anic suras that have explicit negative references to the Jews (an-Nisa' 4: 47; al-Ma'idah 5: 13; etc.). The Qur'an dehumanizes and demonizes the non-Muslim infidels and calls them "... the vilest of animals ..." (al-Anfal 8: 55; al-A'raf 7: 179), and the vilest of all creatures (al-Bayyinah 98: 6; al-Mujadilah 58: 20). It claims that Jews were transformed into apes (al-Baqarah 2: 65 and al-A'raf 7: 166), and

Jews and Christians into swine (al-Ma'idah 5: 59-60)? It likens Jews to asses (al-Jum'ah 62: 5). It tells Muslims that Jews are cursed because of their unbelief (al-Ma'idah 5: 78). Muhammad claimed that Muslims will eventually exterminate the Jews in a global holocaust. "Allah's Apostle said, The Hour will not be established until you fight with the Jews, and the stone behind which a Jew will be hiding will say, O Muslim! There is a Jew hiding behind me, so kill him" (Bukhari 4.52.177; Muslim 41.6981-5).

The Qur'an goes as far as commanding Muslims to eschew friendships with infidels, including Christians and Jews (Al-'Imran 3: 28, 118; an-Nisa' 4: 89, 101, 144; al-Ma'idah 5: 51, 82), even if they be their fathers, sons, brothers, or kin (al-Tawbah 9: 23; al-Mujadalah 58: 22). Abu Obaida, son of Garah, who was praised by the prophet of Islam, killed his own father who refused Islam. Musaab, son of Omair, never listened for his mother's cries for help and left her to die because she rejected Islam. Abu Bakr, the first guided caliph, told his father he would kill him if he refused Islam.

Traditional orthodox Islam promises the jihadist that if he dies fighting for the god of Muhammad in Islamic jihad, he is guaranteed to be rewarded with the sinful Islamic paradise of sexual promiscuity and gluttony (as-Saff 61: 10-13; ad-Dukhan 44: 51-56; at-Tur 52: 17-29; ar-Rahman 55: 46-78; al-Tawbah 9: 111; Al-Imran 3: 157-8, 169; an-Nisa' 4: 74; al-Fatir 35: 50; Muhammad 47: 6; etc). Muhammad said: "Know that Paradise is under the shades of swords" (Bukhari 4.52.73, 72, 46, 48, 53; 4.53.386). Muhammad promised these fictitious rewards, which are merely a desert mirage, in order to motivate his fighters. Unable to give them a reason to live, he gave them a reason to die.

On the other hand, should the jihadist survive and live, he gets a share from the spoils of war, which enriches him (al-Anfal 8: 41, 60). In addition, he obtains forgiveness of his sins (as-Saff 61: 11-12), and the love of the Islamic god (an-Nisa' 4: 95; al-Anfal 8: 16). According to orthodox Islamic belief, martyrdom in Islamic jihad is the only sure way a Muslim could take to avoid the horrifying torments of the grave and hell, and to get into the Islamic paradise. In fact, when a Muslim dies in jihad, his corpse is not washed or dressed in clean clothes. It goes in his coffin just as he died. The stains of blood on it are a witness for him before the Islamic god. It is a sign of honor that would prompt the angels to treat him in a special distinguished way.

The Example of the Prophet of Islam

The history of Islam to-date has been one long jihad (holy war) against non-Muslims. Muslims are exhorted to emulate Muhammad's pattern of behavior (al-Ahzab 33: 21). In the ten years that he lived in Medina (622-632 AD), Muhammad, the prophet of Islam, was the aggressor in seventy-three of seventy-five raids and conflicts he got involved in. He initiated seventy-three raids, military expeditions, full-scale military campaigns, and small assassination hit bands to kill his opponents. This adds up to more than seven slayings, raids or battles for each of the ten years he ruled in Medina in the beginning of the Islamic era. There is a lot of blood on his hands. He did not personally participate in forty-eight of those raids. He personally accompanied his Muslim fighters in twenty-seven raids. In eight of them, he was in the battlefield fighting alongside with them. Muhammad used to order his followers and commanders to kill those who disbelieved in his god, not making any distinction between combatants, and civilians.

The prophet of Islam financed his military expeditions through a variety of avenues. His economic lifeblood was the plunder usurped from defeated enemies, and the jizya tax levied on unbelievers. The majority of the Arabs who adopted Islam and fought in the military battles of jihad did so in order to acquire booty usurped from the conquered tribes and peoples who did not submit to Islam. The Muslim fighters have been motivated mainly by their greed for the booty of wealth and women (al-Fath 48: 19-20). Four-fifths of the booty went to them, and one-fifth to Muhammad, or to the caliph after him (al-Anfal 8: 41). That was how the god of Islam made Muhammad and his followers wealthy (ad-Duha 93: 8; al-Tawbah 9: 74; Bukhari 3.37.495). Muhammad distributed his share of the booty as he wished to close relatives, orphans, the needy, travelers, and new converts to Islam to coax them to stay in Islam (al-Tawbah 9: 60; Bukhari 4.53.373; 4.55.558; Muslim 5.2313).

Sura 8 is titled "al-Anfal," which means "the spoils of war." The entire book no. 53 of Bukhari is called "One-fifth of Booty to the Cause of Allah (Khumus)."

The battle plunder included captive women and children who were sold as slaves for profit. Slave trading flourished in Arabia in the early Islamic era. The Qur'an describes the loot as "...lawful and good...," and supports pillaging and plundering infidels, enslaving their children, and placing their women in concubinage (al-Anfal 8: 69; an-Nisa' 4: 24; etc). In fact, the first Islamic raid on the peaceful Meccan merchant caravan at Nakhlah was to loot and rob the caravan. This is what motivates bandits and pirates.

THE RULES OF JIHAD

Based on Islamic jurisprudence derived from the Qur'an, the Hadith, and classical Islamic legal opinions, the principal rules of Jihad are summarized herein. These rules are immoral and exploitative:

1. Muslims may enslave women and children of the conquered non-Muslim populations (Reliance of the Traveler, #o9.13). Islam codifies slavery in its religious law (Sharia). Selling humans into slavery produced a lot of wealth for Muhammad and his followers. Slaying women and children is prohibited, not for mercy, but for profit. However, if a Muslim slays them, he is not censured.
2. The marriages of those women are annulled upon their capture. They may be forced to marry their Muslim masters and added to their harim (an-Nisa' 4: 24).
3. Worse off, Muslim jihadists are allowed to rape the captured female prisoners of war. Ali, Muhammad's cousin and son-in-law, did this abomination, and Muhammad defended him (Bukhari 5.59.637). Islam codifies and legalizes rape for conquering jihadist Muslim men (Muslim 8.3371, 3373-7, 3432). Islam is the only religion in the world that condones and encourages the crime of raping female captives of war as a reward to victorious Muslim soldiers for conquering the infidels.

4. Muslim jihadists are allowed to kill old men and Christian monks (Reliance of the Traveler, #o9.10), and women and children in night raids (Bukhari 4.52.256; Muslim 19.4321-4323).
5. The non-Muslim prisoners of war may be killed, enslaved, ransomed (exchanged for money or a Muslim captive), or released (al-Ahzab 33: 26; Muhammad 47: 4; Reliance of the Traveler, #o9.14).
6. Pagan Arabs were pressured to convert to Islam on pain of death. Enemy men who converted to Islam were allowed to keep their property and children (al-Tawbah 9: 5, 11, 14, 33; Bukhari 4.52.263).
7. The Muslim jihadist invaders may confiscate or destroy non-Muslim civilian property, including homes and groves (al-Ahzab 33: 27; al-Hashr 59: 5, 2; Bukhari 4.52.262, 263; Muslim 19.4324).
8. A Muslim jihadist who kills a non-Muslim in jihad gets his belongings. This is called personal booty. In addition, he gets his share from the four-fifths of the collective spoils of the battle.
9. The Muslim jihadist invaders give the people of the Book (Jews and Christians) three options (al-Tawbah 9: 29) either to convert to Islam, to keep their faith and pay the submission tax of jizya (poll tax) while living under Islamic rule, or to get killed fighting if they refused the first two options. However, Muslims can mount surprise attacks on the infidels, slay them and usurp their property. This is not censured because the victims are not Muslims, and they are not protected in the Islamic state.

Although Islam permits Jews and Christians to remain in their faiths as dhimmis under Islamic rule (second class citizens in their homelands), from the dawn of Islamic history till the present, forced conversions are widely practiced in the Islamic world. This is because Islamic teachings scorn non-Muslim infidels who are, according to Islamic culture, bound to the Islamic hell. Battle, animosity and hatred directed towards the non-Muslim infidels are part of Islamic mindset.

The Dhimma

The concept of the dhimma was first introduced by the prophet of Islam. After conquering the Jews of the oasis of Khaybar in 628, he agreed to let them continue to cultivate their oasis only if they gave him half their produce. He reserved the right to cancel out this treaty and expel the Jews whenever he liked (Bukhari 4.53.380). This type of treaty is called a "dhimma."

Peoples that came under Islamic rule and agreed to pay tribute (jizya) in return for Muslim protection are referred to as "dhimmis." They were ultimately reduced to the status of a tiny culturally derivative marginalized minority in their homelands. The only peoples that escaped Islamic dhimmitude were those who were successful in resisting and eventually, after centuries of armed struggle, defeating Islamic imperialistic jihad: the Christians of Europe and the Hindus of India.

The dhimmis (Jews, Christians, etc. under Islamic rule) were not equal to Muslims in dignity and rights. They lived in subjugation to Islamic rule. The terms of the dhimma were first articulated by the second guided caliph, Umar ibn al-Khattab (634-644). The dhimma was an agreement imposed on conquered populations. It required them not to build churches, monasteries, and synagogues, nor restore them. It also required them to wear clothes different from those worn by Muslims, not to acquire weapons, not to ride horses, to refrain from using church bells and from erecting crosses on top of the churches, not to proselytize Muslims, to pay the poll tax (jizya), etc. The jizya indicated the dhimmis submission and inferiority to Islamic rule (at-Tawbah 9: 29). It led to the overall humiliation and abasement of non-Muslims. Payment of the jizya often took place in a demeaning ceremony to ensure the belittlement and humiliation of the dhimmi. The Muslim tax-collector slapped the Christian man on the back of his neck or on his head telling him: 'O unbeliever, pay al-jizya.' This was followed by the Christian man handing him the tax money with his head bowed down and his back bent while the tax-collector held him by the beard. The dhimmi was not allowed to marry a Muslim woman. The penalty for such marriage was death. The dhimmi was barred from public office. The history of Muslim dealings with the dhimmis is one of oppression, random massacres, avaricious greed and plunder, extortion under the threat of persecution, rape, systematic degradation and slavery.

According the Shafi'i school of Islamic Sharia, the dhimma pact is broken if the dhimmi fights the Muslims, refuses to pay the jizya, or disobeys Muslim laws. It is also broken if the dhimmi violates the dhimma's additional stipulations, if any, by having relation with a Muslim woman, leading a Muslim away from Islam, killing a Muslim, or slandering Muhammad and his god. When the dhimma is broken, the rules of the prisoners of war will apply on the dhimmi subjecting him to either death, slavery, ransoming, or release. By denying basic human rights to non-Muslims in Islamic controlled lands, Islam has sanctioned slavery on an unprecedented scale. Jihad slavery in its various forms (slave soldiers, harem slavery, child slavery, etc.) became a powerful tool to both expansive islamization and the support of Muslim society.

The dhimma terms and requirements are codified in Islamic Sharia (Reliance of the Traveler, #o11). Under Western pressure on the weakened Ottoman Empire, the dhimmis were emancipated in the mid-nineteenth century. Although Islamic Sharia is enforced at this time only in a few countries, such as Saudi Arabia, Iran, and the Sudan, many of its elements are practiced in Islamic countries. It is surprising indeed that the dhimmi communities have survived at all despite the Islamic pressures on them throughout centuries of Islamic rule.

2

The Rise of Islamist Terrorist Groups

Despite Islamic teachings against suicide and killing innocent people in battle, terrorist groups like Al Qaeda have used a fundamentalist form of Islam to justify an unholy war of terrorism.

In recent years, the terrorist group Al Qaeda has committed terrorist acts killing many innocent men, women, and children. It was responsible for the September 11, 2001, suicide terrorist attacks on New York's World Trade Center and the Pentagon, which murdered close to 3,000 people. On August 7, 1998, Al Qaeda terrorists almost simultaneously set off bombs 150 miles apart at U.S. Embassies in the East African countries of Kenya and Tanzania. The blasts killed 12 Americans and about 250 Africans, most of them Muslims. On May 12, 2003, Al Qaeda suicide terrorists set off bombs in three housing compounds in the capital of Saudi Arabia. The bombs killed 35 people, including 12 Americans. Al Qaeda has been linked to many other attacks and continues to be a threat.

In a 1998 interview, Al Qaeda's leader, Osama bin Laden, called Americans "the worst thieves in the world today and the worst terrorists . . . ." He went on to say that, "We do not have to differentiate between military or civilian. As far as we are concerned, they are all targets." He justified targeting Americans in the name of Islam. He said: "The terrorism we practice is of the commendable kind for it is directed at the tyrants and the aggressors and the enemies of God . . . ."

Other groups also commit terrorism in the name of Islam. The U.S. Department of State lists, to name a few, Lebanon's Hizbollah, Algeria's Armed Islamic Group, Egypt's Islamic Jihad, Palestine's Islamic Jihad and Hamas, Uzbekistan's Islamic Movement, the Philippines' Abu Sayyaf, and Pakistan's Jaish-e-Muhammad (Army of Muhammad) as foreign terrorist groups. Unlike Al Qaeda, most of these groups do not commit terrorism internationally. Instead, they use terrorism to help overthrow the regimes in control of their countries. Although their goals differ, they all want to set up Islamist states, based on Islamic fundamentalism. (The political form of Islamic fundamentalism is sometimes called Islamism.) The vast majority of Islamic fundamentalists are not terrorists, but their teachings have been adopted by terrorist groups to justify their actions.

Islamic fundamentalism calls for a society ruled by Islamic law. It rejects most things Western (except technology). Islamists believe their culture has been infected by Western ideas and practices, which must be rooted out. They want a more equal society with less division between the rich and poor. They want women to return to their traditional role and dress. This can mean women taking care of the family, staying out of the political and business worlds, wearing a veil, and even dressing in garments that cover them completely. Fundamentalists call for a return to a strict, "pure" Islam as practiced in the seventh century by the Prophet Muhammad and his immediate successors, the first four caliphs.

But the Encyclopaedia of the Orient states that:

. . . there are no Muslim sources indicating that the Islam of the Golden Age was as strict and conservative as the Islamists believe. All indications show that it was the liberal Islam that paved the ground for cultural, social and military achievements of those days--values foreign to all major Islamist groups. Hence, there is reason to say that the Islamist idea of the Golden Age is a dramatic falsification of history.

Islamist terrorists, like Al Qaeda, view themselves as following Muhammad's example. Muhammad in A.D. 622 had to flee from Mecca with a small band of followers. Yet in 630, he returned with an army of followers to conquer Mecca and then spread Islam throughout the Arabian Peninsula. The terrorist groups see themselves as small bands that will lead Islam to victory.

But terrorist tactics run against the basic teachings of Islam. The Koran, the holy scripture of Islam, set strict rules against suicide and killing women, children, and old people in battle.

The overwhelming majority of Muslims deplore terrorist attacks and view them as violating the Koran. Even many fundamentalist Muslims believe terrorism violates Islamic law. Nonetheless, Al Qaeda and other Islamist terrorist groups draw their supporters from the ranks of Islamic fundamentalists.

Secular States After World War II

Islam is the religion of more than 80 percent of the people in North Africa, the Middle East, and Central Asia. Islamic empires controlled these areas for more than a thousand years. The last great Islamic empire--the Ottoman Empire --finally collapsed after World War I. During the 200 years it was crumbling, European nations were busy adding most of the predominantly Islamic areas of North Africa, the Middle East, and Central Asia to their empires. Following World War I, they carved up most of the remaining parts of the old Ottoman Empire.

European control ended state by state. Most countries in this heavily Islamic area gained their independence shortly after World War II. Almost all the new leaders who emerged in countries like Iraq, Syria, and Egypt chose to follow a secular model of government pioneered by Turkey after World War I. Many adopted European or American legal systems and other Western ways, forcing Islamic law and culture into the background.

The most significant leader of the era was Egypt's Gamal Abdel Nasser . In 1952, he led a group of Egyptian military officers in overthrowing Egypt's weak monarchy, which was supported by the British. Nasser set Egypt on a secular path and tried to unify his people by promoting loyalty to the nation. Islam would remain important, but no longer dominate government, the law, and education.

Egypt under Nasser adopted a socialist economic system and an authoritarian government with close links to the military. For a while, Nasser was an inspiration and hero to many Egyptians and others in the region. But poor management and corruption in the Egyptian government resulted in massive unemployment, increased poverty, and political repression. The same was true most of the other newly independent states.

The Jewish State and the PLO

In 1948, the United Nations, with the strong support of the United States, partitioned the land then called Palestine into Jewish and Arab states. The surrounding Arab countries, however, rejected this partition and attacked Israel. They viewed the partition as another case of European colonialism, with Jews displacing Arabs and taking land that they had occupied for more than a thousand years. But Israel defended its new borders and even gained territory.

In 1967, Nasser asked the U.N. to remove its troops along the Egypt-Israel border, and he blockaded the Straits of Tiran to prevent goods from reaching Israel. When Egypt and Syria mobilized their troops in preparation for war, Israel attacked. This war lasted a mere six days and resulted in Israel occupying Egyptian land all the way to the Suez Canal as well as Jordan's West Bank, Syria's Golan Heights, and East Jerusalem. In 1973, Egypt and Syria attempted to defeat Israel in yet another war, but failed again.

The failures showed that the Arab states were too weak to overcome Israel, which was far more advanced economically and militarily. A new entity, the nationalistic Palestinian Liberation Organization (PLO), stepped in to take up the war against Israel. Founded in 1964 by Arab states, the PLO was set up as an umbrella organization to bring together the many Palestinian groups that had formed in Arab lands. The PLO set two goals: destroying Israel and establishing a secular, democratic state in its place. It never favored an Islamist state. Initially, the PLO launched guerilla attacks on Israeli military targets. But then factions of it started using terrorism--kidnappings, shootings, bombings, and hijackings. The two most notorious attacks were probably the hostage-taking and murder of 11 Israeli athletes during the 1972 Munich Olympics and the 1985 hijacking of the Italian cruise ship Achille Lauro and murder of a disabled American tourist on board. In 1988, the PLO renounced its goal of destroying Israel. (The PLO has consistently denied it was ever involved in terrorism.)

EARLIER TERRORIST GROUPS

Al-Qaeda's Fluid organization, methods of recruitment, funding, and means of communication distinguish it as an advancement in twenty-first-century terrorist groups. Al-Qaeda is a product of the times. Yet it also echoes historical predecessors, expanding on such factors as the international links and ideological drive of nineteenth-century anarchists, the open-ended aims of Aum Shinrikyo, the brilliance in public communications of the early PLO, and the taste for mass casualty attacks of twentieth-century Sikh separatists or Hezbollah. Al-Qaeda is an amalgam of old and new, reflecting twenty-first century advances in means or matters of degree rather than true originality; still, most analysts miss the connections with its predecessors and are blinded by its solipsistic rhetoric. That is a mistake. The pressing challenge is to determine which lessons from the decline of earlier terrorist groups are relevant to al-Qaeda and which are not.

First, past experience with terrorism indicates that al-Qaeda will not end if Osama bin Laden is killed. There are many other reasons to pursue him, including bringing him to justice, removing his leadership and expertise, and increasing esprit de corps on the Western side (whose credibility is sapped because of bin Laden's enduring elusiveness). The argument that his demise will end al-Qaeda is tinged with emotion, not dispassionate analysis. Organizations that have been crippled by the killing of their leader have been hierarchically structured, reflecting to some degree a cult of personality, and have lacked a viable successor.

Al-Qaeda meets neither of these criteria: it has a mutable structure with a strong, even increasing, emphasis on individual cells and local initiative. It is not the first organization to operate in this way; and the demise of similar terrorist groups required much more than the death of one person. Unlike the PKK and Shining Path, al-Qaeda is not driven by a cult of personality;

despite his astonishing popularity, bin Laden has deliberately avoided allowing the movement to revolve around his own persona, preferring instead to keep his personal habits private, to talk of the insignificance of his own fate, and to project the image of a humble man eager to die for his beliefs. As for a viable replacement, bin Laden has often spoken openly of a succession plan, and that plan has to a large degree already taken effect. Furthermore, his capture or killing would produce its own countervailing negative consequences, including (most likely) the creation of a powerful martyr. On balance, the removal of bin Laden would have important potential benefits, but to believe that it would kill al-Qaeda is to be ahistorical and naive.

Second, although there was a time when the failure to transition to a new generation might have been a viable finale for al-Qaeda, that time is long past. Al-Qaeda has transitioned to a second, third, and arguably fourth generation. The reason relates especially to the second distinctive element of al-Qaeda: its method of recruitment or, more accurately, its attraction of radicalized followers (both individuals and groups), many of whom in turn are connected to existing local networks. Al-Qaeda's spread has been compared to a virus or a bacterium, dispersing its contagion to disparate sites. Although this is a seductive analogy, it is also misleading: the perpetuation of al-Qaeda is a sentient process involving well-considered marketing strategies and deliberate tactical decisions, not a mindless "disease" process; thinking of it as a "disease" shores up the unfortunate American tendency to avoid analysing the mentality of the enemy.

Al-Qaeda is operating with a long-term strategy and is certainly not following the left-wing groups of the 1970s in their failure to articulate a coherent ideological vision or the peripatetic right-wing groups of the twentieth century. It has transitioned beyond its original structure and now represents a multigenerational threat with staying power comparable to the enthonationalist groups of the twentieth century. Likewise, arguments about whether al-Qaeda is best described primarily as an ideology or by its opposition to foreign occupation of Muslim lands are specious: al-Qaeda's adherents use both rationales to spread their links. The movement is opportunistic. The challenge for the United States and its allies is to move beyond rigid mind-sets and paradigms, do more in-depth analysis, and be more nimble and strategic in response to al-Qaeda's fluid agenda.

The third and fourth models of a terrorist organization's end—achievement of the group's cause and transition toward a political role, negotiations, or amnesty—also bear little relevance to al-Qaeda today. It is hard to conceive of al-Qaeda fully achieving its aims, in part because those aims have evolved over time, variably including achievement of a pan-Islamic caliphate, the overthrow of non-Islamic regimes, and the expulsion of all infidels from Muslim countries, not to mention support for the Palestinian cause and the killing of Americans and other so-called infidels. Historically, terrorist groups that have achieved their ends have done so by articulating clear, limited objectives. Al-Qaeda's goals, at least as articulated over recent years, could not be achieved without overturning an international political and economic system characterized by globalization and predominant U.S. power. As the historical record indicates, negotiations or a transition to a legitimate political process requires feasible terms and a sense of stalemate in the struggle. Also, members of terrorist groups seeking negotiations often have an incentive to find a way out of what they consider a losing cause. None of this describes bin Laden's al-Qaeda.

This points to another issue. As al-Qaeda has become a hybrid or "virtual organization," rather than a coherent hierarchical organization, swallowing its propaganda and treating it as a unified whole is a mistake. It is possible that bin Laden and his lieutenants have attempted to cobble together such disparate entities (or those entities have opportunistically attached themselves to al-Qaeda) that they have stretched beyond the point at which their interests can be represented in this movement. Some of the local groups that have recently claimed an association with al-Qaeda have in the past borne more resemblance to ethnonationalist/separatist groups such as the PLO, the IRA, and the LTTE. Examples include local affiliates in Indonesia, Morocco, Tunisia, and Turkey. This is not to argue that these groups' aims are rightful or that their tactics are legitimate. Rather, because of its obsession with the notion of a monolithic al-Qaeda, the United States is glossing over both the extensive local variation within terrorist groups and their different goals; these groups have important points of divergence with al-Qaeda's agenda, and the United States does no one any favours by failing to seriously anneals and exploit those local differences (except perhaps al-Qaeda). The U.S. objective must be to enlarge the movement's internal inconsistencies and differences. Al-Qaeda's aims have become so sweeping that one might wonder whether they genuinely carry within them the achievement of specific local grievances. There is more hope of ending such groups through traditional methods if they are dealt with using traditional tools, even including, on a case-by-case basis, concessions or negotiations with specific local elements that may have negotiable or justifiable terms (albeit pursued through an illegitimate tactic). The key is to emphasize the differences with al-Qaeda's agenda and to drive a wedge between the movement and its recent adherents.

The historical record of other terrorist groups indicates that it is a mistake to treat al-Qaeda as a monolith, to lionize it as if it is an unprecedented phenomenon with all elements equally committed to its aims, for that eliminates a range of proven counterterrorist tools and techniques for ending it. It is also a mistake to nurture al-Qaeda's rallying point, a hatred of Americans and a resentment of U.S. policies (especially in Iraq and between Israel and the Palestinians), thereby conveniently facilitating the glossing over of differences within. Fifth, reducing popular support, both active and passive, is an effective means of hastening the demise of some terrorist groups. This technique has received much attention among critics of George W. Bush and his administration's policies, many of whom argue that concentrating on the "roots" of terrorism is a necessary alternative to the current policy of emphasizing military force.

This is a superficial argument, however, as it can be countered that a "roots" approach is precisely at the heart of current U.S. policy: the promotion of democracy may be seen as an idealistic effort to provide an alternative to populations in the Muslim world, frustrated by corrupt governance, discrimination, unemployment, and stagnation. But the participants in this debate are missing the point. The problem is timing: democratization is a decades-long approach to a short-term and immediate problem whose solution must also be measured in months, not just years. The efforts being undertaken are unlikely to have a rapid enough effect to counter the anger, frustration, and sense of humiliation that characterize passive supporters. As for those who actively sustain the movement through terrorist acts, it is obviously a discouraging development that many recent operatives have lived in, or even been natives of, democratic countries—the March 2004 train attacks in Madrid and 2005 bombings in London being notable examples.

The history of terrorism provides little comfort to those who believe that democratization is a good method to reduce active and passive support for terrorist attacks. There is no evidence that democratization correlates with a reduction in terrorism; in fact, available historical data suggest the opposite. Democratization was arguably the cause of much of the terrorism of the twentieth century. Moreover, democracy in the absence of strong political institutions and civil society could very well bring about radical Islamist governments over which the West would have little influence. There are much worse things than terrorism, and it might continue to be treated as a regrettable but necessary accompaniment to change were it not for two potentially serious developments in the twenty-first century: (1) the use of increasingly destructive weapons that push terrorist attacks well beyond the "nuisance" level, and (2) the growing likelihood that terrorism will lead to future systemic war. In any case, the long-term, idealistic, and otherwise admirable policy of democratization, viewed as "Americanization" in many parts of the world, does not represent a sufficiently targeted response to undercutting popular support for al-Qaeda.

There are two vulnerabilities, however, where cutting the links between al-Qaeda and its supporters hold promise: its means of funding and its means of communication. Efforts to cut off funding through traditional avenues have had some results. But not nearly enough attention is being paid to twenty-first-century communications, especially al-Qaeda's presence on the internet. The time has come to recognize that the stateless, anarchical realm of cyberspace requires better tools for monitoring, countermeasures, and, potentially, even control. Previous leaps in cross-border communication such as the telegraph, radio, and telephone engendered counteracting developments in code breaking, monitoring, interception, and wiretapping. This may seem a heretical suggestion for liberal states, especially for a state founded on the right of free speech; however, the international community will inevitably be driven to take countermeasures in response to future attacks. It is time to devote more resources to addressing this problem now. Western analysts have been misguided in focusing on the potential use of the internet for so-called cyberterrorism (i.e., its use in carrying out attacks); the internet is far more dangerous as a tool to shore up and perpetuate the al-Qaeda movement's constituency.

Preventing or interdicting al-Qaeda's ability to disseminate its message and draw adherents into its orbit is crucial. Countering its messages in serious ways, not through the outdated and stilted vehicles of government websites and official statements but through sophisticated alternative sites and images attractive to a new generation, is an urgent priority.

As for the opponent's marketing strategy, al-Qaeda and its associates have made serious mistakes of timing, choice of targets, and technique; yet the United States and its allies have done very little to capitalize on them. In particular, the United States tends to act as if al-Qaeda is essentially a static enemy that will react to its actions, but then fails to react effectively and strategically to the movement's missteps.

The Bali attacks, the May 2003 attacks in Saudi Arabia, the Madrid attacks, the July 2005 London attacks—all were immediately and deliberately trumpeted by al-Qaeda associates. Where was the coordinated counterterrorist multimedia response? There is nothing so effective at engendering public revulsion as images of murdered and maimed victims, many of whom resemble family members of would-be recruits, lying on the ground as the result of a terrorist act. Outrage is appropriate. Currently, however, those images are dominated by would-be family members in Iraq, the Palestinian territories, Abu Ghraib, and Guantanamo Bay.

The West is completely outflanked on the airwaves, and its countermeasures are virtually nonexistent on the internet. But as the RIRA, PFLP-GC, and ETA cases demonstrate, the al-Qaeda movement can undermine itself, if it is given help. A large part of this "war" is arguably being fought not on a battlefield but in cyberspace. The time-honored technique of undermining active and passive support for a terrorist group through in-depth analysis, agile responses to missteps, carefully targeted messages, and cutting-edge technological solutions is a top priority.

This is a crucial moment of opportunity. Polls indicate that many of al-Qaeda's potential constituents have been deeply repulsed by recent attacks. According to the Pew Global Attitudes Project, publics in many predominantly Muslim states increasingly see Islamic extremism as a threat to their own countries, express less support for terrorism, have less confidence in bin Laden, and reflect a declining belief in the usefulness of suicide attacks. In these respects, there is a growing range of commonality in the attitudes of Muslim and non-Muslim publics; yet the United States focuses on itself and does little to nurture cooperation. American public diplomacy is the wrong concept. This is not about the United States and its ideals, values, culture, and image abroad: this is about tapping into a growing international norm against killing innocent civilians—whether, for example, on vacation or on their way to work or school—many of whom are deeply religious and many of whom also happen to be Muslims. If the United States and its allies fail to grasp this concept, to work with local cultures and local people to build on common goals and increase their alienation from this movement, then they will have missed a long-established and promising technique for ending a terrorist group such as al-Qaeda.

There is little to say about the sixth factor, the use of military repression, in ending al-Qaeda. Even though the U.S. military has made important progress in tracking down and killing senior operatives, the movement's ability to evolve has demonstrated the limits of such action, especially when poorly coordinated with other comparatively underfunded approaches and engaged in by a democracy. Although apparently effective, the Turkish government's repression of the PKK and the Peruvian government's suppression of Shining Path, for example, yield few desirable parallels for the current counterterrorist campaign.

Transitioning out of terrorism and toward either criminality or full insurgency is the final, worrisome historical precedent for al-Qaeda. In a sense, the network is already doing both. Efforts to cut off funding through the formal banking system have ironically heightened the incentive and necessity to engage in illicit activities, especially narcotics trafficking. With the increasing amount of poppy seed production in Afghanistan, al-Qaeda has a natural pipeline to riches. This process is well under way. As for al-Qaeda becoming a full insurgency, some analysts believe this has already occurred. Certainly to the extent that Abu Musab al-Zarqawi and his associates in Iraq truly represent an arm of the movement (i.e., al-Qaeda in Iraq), that transition is likewise well along.

The alliance negotiated between bin Laden and al-Zarqawi is another example of an effective strategic and public relations move for both parties, giving new life to the al-Qaeda movement at a time when its leaders are clearly on the run and providing legitimacy and fresh recruits for the insurgency in Iraq.

As many commentators have observed, Iraq is an ideal focal point and training ground for this putative global insurgency. The glimmer of hope in this scenario, however, is that the foreigners associated with al-Qaeda are not tied to the territory of Iraq in the same way the local population is, and the tensions that will arise between those who want a future for the nascent Iraqi state and those who want a proving ground for a largely alien ideology and virtual organization are likely to increase—especially as the victims of the civil war now unfolding there continue increasingly to be Iraqi civilians.

The counter to al-Zarqawi's al-Qaeda in Iraq, as it is for other areas of the world with local al-Qaeda affiliates, is to tap into the long-standing and deep association between peoples and their territory and to exploit the inevitable resentment toward foreign terrorist agendas, while scrupulously ensuring that the United States is not perceived to be part of those agendas.

If the United States continues to treat al-Qaeda as if it were utterly unprecedented, as if the decades-long experience with fighting modern terrorism were totally irrelevant, then it will continue to make predictable and avoidable mistakes in responding to this threat. It will also miss important strategic opportunities. That experience points particularly toward dividing new local affiliates from al-Qaeda by understanding and exploiting their differences with the movement, rather than treating the movement as a monolith. It is also crucial to more effectively break the political and logistical connections between the movement and its supporters, reinvigorating time-honored counterterrorism tactics targeted at al-Qaeda's unique characteristics, including the perpetuation of its message, its funding, and its communications. Al-Qaeda continues to exploit what is essentially a civil war within the Muslim world, attracting alienated Muslims around the globe to its rage-filled movement. Al-Qaeda will end when the West removes itself from the heart of this fight, shores up international norms against terrorism, undermines al-Qaeda's ties with its followers, and begins to exploit the movement's abundant missteps.

ISLAMIC TERRORIST ORGANIZATIONS

ABU SAYYAF GROUP (ASG)

Description

The ASG is the smallest and most radical of the Islamic separatist groups operating in the southern Philippines. Some ASG members have studied or worked in the Middle East and developed ties to mjuahidin while fighting and training in Afghanistan. The group split from the Moro National Liberation Front in 1991 under the leadership of Abdurajik Abubakar Janjalani, who was killed in a clash with Philippine police on 18 December 1998. Press reports place his younger brother, Khadafi Janjalani, as the nominal leader of the group, which is composed of several factions.

Activities

Engages in bombings, assassinations, kidnappings, and extortion to promote an independent Islamic state in western Mindanao and the Sulu Archipelago, areas in the southern Philippines heavily populated by Muslims. Raided the town of Ipil in Mindanao in April 1995—the group's first large-scale action—and kidnapped more than 30 foreigners, including a US citizen, in 2000.

Strength

Believed to have about 200 core fighters, but more than 2,000 individuals motivated by the prospect of receiving ransom payments for foreign hostages allegedly joined the group in August.

Location/Area of Operation

The ASG primarily operates in the southern Philippines with members occasionally traveling to Manila, but the group expanded its operations to Malaysia this year when it abducted foreigners from two different resorts.

External Aid

Receives support from Islamic extremists in the Middle East and South Asia. Is partnered with Jemaah Islamiyah and Al-Qaeda.

Abu Sayyaf (1991-present; Islamic separatists; the Philippines) Based in the southern islands of Jolo, Basilan, and Mindanao. Branched off of the Moro National Liberation Front.

ARMY OF ISLAM (AOI)

aka Jaysh al-Islam; Jaish al-Islam

Description: Designated a Foreign Terrorist Organization on May 19, 2011, the Army of Islam (AOI) is a Gaza-based terrorist organization founded in late 2005 that has been responsible for numerous terrorist acts against the Governments of Israel and Egypt, as well as American, British, and New Zealander citizens. AOI is led by Mumtaz Dughmush, and operates in Gaza. It subscribes to a Salafist ideology together with the traditional model of armed Palestinian resistance. AOI has previously worked with Hamas and is attempting to develop closer al-Qa'ida contacts.

Activities: AOI's terrorist acts include a number of rocket attacks on Israel, the 2006 kidnapping of two journalists in Gaza (an American and a New Zealander), and the 2007 kidnapping of a British citizen, journalist Alan Johnston, in Gaza. AOI is also responsible for early 2009 attacks on Egyptian civilians in Cairo and Heliopolis, Egypt. AOI is alleged to have planned the January 1, 2011 Alexandria attack on a Coptic Christian church that killed 25 and wounded 100 . On May 7, 2011, the group released a eulogy for Usama bin Ladin via its Al Nur Media Foundation.

Strength: Membership estimates range in the low hundreds.

Location/Area of Operation: Gaza, with attacks in Egypt and Israel.

External Aid: AOI receives the bulk of its funding from a variety of criminal activities in Gaza.

AL-GAMA'A AL-ISLAMIYYA (ISLAMIC GROUP, IG)

Description

Egypt's largest militant group, active since the late 1970s; appears to be loosely organized. Has an external wing with a worldwide presence. The group issued a cease-fire in March 1999, but its spiritual leader, Shaykh Umar Abd al-Rahman, incarcerated in the United States, rescinded his support for the cease-fire in June 2000. The Gama'a has not conducted an attack inside Egypt since August 1998. Rifa'i Taha Musa-a hardline former senior member of the group-signed Usama Bin Ladin's February 1998 fatwa calling for attacks against US civilians. The IG since has publicly denied that it supports Bin Ladin and frequently differs with public statements made by Taha Musa. Taha Musa has in the last year sought to push the group toward a return to armed operations, but the group, which still is led by Mustafa Hamza, has yet to break the unilaterally declared cease-fire. In late 2000, Taha Musa appeared in an undated video with Bin Ladin and Ayman al-Zawahiri threatening retaliation against the United States for Abd al-Rahman's continued incarceration. The IG's primary goal is to overthrow the Egyptian Government and replace it with an Islamic state, but Taha Musa also may be interested in attacking US and Israeli interests.

Activities

Group specialized in armed attacks against Egyptian security and other government officials, Coptic Christians, and Egyptian opponents of Islamic extremism before the cease-fire.

From 1993 until the cease-fire, al-Gama'a launched attacks on tourists in Egypt, most notably the attack in November 1997 at Luxor that killed 58 foreign tourists.

Also claimed responsibility for the attempt in June 1995 to assassinate Egyptian President Hosni Mubarak in Addis Ababa, Ethiopia. The Gama'a has never specifically attacked a US citizen or facility but has threatened US interests.

Strength

Unknown. At its peak the IG probably commanded several thousand hard-core members and a like number of sympathizers. The 1998 cease-fire and security crackdowns following the attack in Luxor in 1997 probably have resulted in a substantial decrease in the group's numbers.

Location/Area of Operation

Operates mainly in the Al-Minya, Asyu't, Qina, and Sohaj Governorates of southern Egypt.

Also appears to have support in Cairo, Alexandria, and other urban locations, particularly among unemployed graduates and students. Has a worldwide presence, including Sudan, the United Kingdom, Afghanistan, Austria, and Yemen.

External Aid

Unknown. The Egyptian Government believes that Iran, Bin Ladin, and Afghan militant groups support the organization. Also may obtain some funding through various Islamic nongovernmental organizations.

AL-JIHAD

a.k.a. Egyptian Islamic Jihad, Jihad Group, Islamic Jihad

Description

Egyptian Islamic extremist group active since the late 1970s. Close partner of Bin Ladin's al-Qaida organization. Suffered setbacks as a result of numerous arrests of operatives worldwide, most recently in Lebanon and Yemen. Primary goals are to overthrow the Egyptian Government and replace it with an Islamic state and attack US and Israeli interests in Egypt and abroad.

Activities

Specializes in armed attacks against high-level Egyptian Government personnel, including cabinet ministers, and car-bombings against official US and Egyptian facilities. The original Jihad was responsible for the assassination in 1981 of Egyptian President Anwar Sadat.

Claimed responsibility for the attempted assassinations of Interior Minister Hassan al-Alfi in August 1993 and Prime Minister Atef Sedky in November 1993. Has not conducted an attack inside Egypt since 1993 and has never targeted foreign tourists there. Responsible for Egyptian Embassy bombing in Islamabad in 1995; in 1998, planned attack against US Embassy in Albania was thwarted.

Strength

Not known but probably has several hundred hard-core members.

Location/Area of Operation

Operates in the Cairo area. Has a network outside Egypt, including Yemen, Afghanistan, Pakistan, Sudan, Lebanon, and the United Kingdom.

External Aid

Not known. The Egyptian Government claims that both Iran and Bin Ladin support the Jihad. Also may obtain some funding through various Islamic nongovernmental organizations, cover businesses, and criminal acts.

AL-QA'IDA IN THE ISLAMIC MAGHREB (AQIM)

aka AQIM; Group for Call and Combat; GSPC; Le Groupe Salafiste Pour La Predication Et Le Combat; Salafist Group for Preaching and Combat

Description: The Salafist Group for Call and Combat (GSPC) was designated as a Foreign Terrorist Organization on March 27, 2002. After the GSPC officially merged with al-Qa'ida (AQ) in September 2006 and became known as al-Qa'ida in the Islamic Maghreb (AQIM), the Department of State amended the GSPC designation to reflect the change on February 20, 2008. AQIM remains largely a regionally-focused terrorist group. It has adopted a more anti-Western rhetoric and ideology and has aspirations of overthrowing "apostate" African regimes and creating an Islamic Caliphate. Abdelmalek Droukdel, aka Abu Mus'ab Abd al-Wadoud, is the group's leader.

AQIM factions in the northern Sahel (northern Mali, Niger, and Mauritania) conducted kidnap for ransom operations and conducted small-scale attacks and ambushes on security forces. The targets for kidnap for ransom are usually Western citizens from governments or third parties that have established a pattern of making concessions in the form of ransom payments for the release of individuals in custody.

In September 2010, AQIM claimed responsibility for the kidnapping of seven people working at a mine in Niger. AQIM released three of the hostages in February 2011, but at year's end, four French citizens remained in captivity. AQIM continued kidnapping operations throughout 2011.

In January, AQIM kidnapped two French civilians in Niamey, Niger. The kidnappers later killed both hostages during a failed rescue attempt. In February, AQIM conducted its first abduction of a foreigner in Algeria since 2003 when it kidnapped an Italian tourist in Alidena. In October, AQIM kidnapped two Spanish and one Italian aid worker from a refugee camp near Tindouf, Algeria.

In November, AQIM was responsible for the November 26 killing of a German man in Mali and the abduction of three men from the Netherlands, South Africa, and Sweden in Mali.

Strength: AQIM has under a thousand fighters operating in Algeria with a smaller number in the Sahel. AQIM is significantly constrained by its poor finances and lack of broad general appeal in the region. It is attempting to take advantage of the volatile political situation in the Sahel to expand its membership, resources, and operations.

Location/Area of Operation: Northeastern Algeria (including but not limited to the Kabylie region) and northern Mali, Niger, and Mauritania.

External Aid: AQIM members engage in kidnapping for ransom and criminal activitities to finance their operations. Algerian expatriates and AQIM supporters abroad, many residing in Western Europe, provide limited financial and logistical support.

AL-QAIDA'S TIES TO SOUTHEAST ASIA

Southeast Asia has become a major center of operations for Al-Qaida operatives for three primary reasons: the Afghan connection to Middle Eastern extremists, the growth of Islamic grievances within Southeast Asian states since the 1970s for socioeconomic and political reasons, and, most important, that Southeast Asian states are "countries of convenience" for international terrorists.

One of the aspects that made Southeast Asia so appealing to the Al-Qaida leadership in the first place was the network of Islamic charities, the spread of poorly regulated Islamic banks, business-friendly environments, and economies that already had records of extensive money laundering.

It is the contention of this book that Al-Qaida saw the region, first and foremost, as a back office for its activities (especially to set up front companies, fundraise, recruit, forge documents, and purchase weapons), and only later became a theatre of operations in its own right as its affiliate organization in Southeast Asia, the Jemaah Islamiya, developed its own capabilities.

Up to a thousand Southeast Asian Muslims fought with the mujahidin the 1980s, and there is an Afghan connection to most of the radical Islamic groups. Beginning in 1982, the Pakistani Intelligence Service began to "recruit radical Muslims from around the world to come to Pakistan and fight with the Afghan Mujahidin." Others disagree with this assertion. In the *Bear Trap*, the authors, senior ISI officials, contend that they simply tolerated the foreign jihadis. Between 1982 and 1992, some 35,000 Muslim radicals from thirtyfive countries joined the mujahidin—17,000 from Saudi Arabia alone. When bin Laden set up training camps in Afghanistan, he continued to recruit Islamic militants from around the world. Whether they returned home, or whether they joined Al-Qaida, the veteran mujahidin were able to rely on the network. One cannot underestimate how crucial the Afghan connection is: It was the basis for the Al-Qaida network around the world. As Peter Bergen wrote:

Still, in the grand scheme of things the Afghan Arabs were no more than extras in the Afghan holy war. It was the lessons they learned from the Jihad, rather than their contribution to it, that proved significant. They rubbed shoulders with militants from dozens of countries and were indoctrinated in the most extreme ideas concerning Jihad. They received at least some sort of military training, and in some cases battlefield experiences. Those who had their [tickets] punched in the Afghan conflict went back to their countries with the ultimate credential for later holy wars. And they believed their exertions had defeated a superpower.

Undeniably, the Afghanistan experience was the formative experience in the lives of Southeast Asian jihadis. In Indonesia, there was the Group 272 of returned veterans, and the key leaders of radical groups in the region are all veterans of the mujahidin: Jafar Umar Thalib, Riduan Isamuddin (Hambali), Mohammed Iqbal Rahman (Abu Jibril), Nik Aziz Nik Adli, Abdurajak Janjalani, and others. As one regional intelligence official recounted, they were miserably homesick, spoke poor Arabic, were unaccustomed to the harshness of their surroundings and the weather, hated the food, and experienced "diar-rhea as a way of life." Nonetheless, they were driven by the call to Jihad and their experience in

Afghanistan was the catalyst for radical activities in Southeast Asia.

By December 2001, there were an estimated 200 undocumented Filipinos in Afghanistan and 600 Islamic scholars in Pakistan. Of those scholars in Pakistan, only 70 percent were studying Islam and some 200 were "missing," according to the Philippine Embassy in Pakistan. The whereabouts of those students were unknown. According to a Russian report given to the Philippine government, "at least 50 Filipinos were recently trained in one of the 55 camps and bases being maintained in Afghanistan by Osama bin Laden" and who fought in the Taliban's 8th Division, which included fighters from across the Muslim world. With the rout of Taliban forces in November 2001, intelligence analysts estimated that some fifty Filipino militants had already returned to the southern Philippines.

More extensive and influential were the networks of *madrasas,* or Islamic schools, that were established in the 1980s by President Zia-ul-Haq to train refugees and young Pakistanis whose secular school system was beginning to crumble. The *madrasas* were the ideological front line against the Soviets, the primary socialization vehicle and recruitment organ for Jihad. The *madrasas* teach only Quranic studies and Arabic—no modern or secular studies. The products of *madrasas* are radical Muslims who believe that their life mission is Jihad. As Simon Reeve put it, "They leave the schools with only a rudimentary knowledge of the world, but a fanatical belief in the supremacy of Islam and their responsibility to fight and ensure its spread." Once the Soviets were defeated, the *madrasas* stayed open, often funded by radical political parties or wealthy patrons. And as Pakistan slumped into economic malaise, the *madrasas* filled an important void in the country's crumbling educational system. By 2000 there were some 10,000 *madrasas* that had almost 1.5 million students. During the 1980s, up to 100,000 foreigners attended *madrasas* in Pakistan where they came into contact with the jihad and established transnational networks. The World Bank found that 15 to 20 percent of Pakistani *madrasas,* to some degree, had a military training component. In early 2002, Pakistani president Pervez Musharraf announced that he would implement new policies to oversee the 10,000 *madrasas,* which "propagate hatred and violence" and "produce semi-literate religious scholars." Pakistan has recently pledged to reduce the number of foreign students attending Pakistani *madrasas* by 60 percent.

Most Southeast Asians returned and set about committing themselves to running jihads at home, recruiting followers, in an attempt to create Islamic states governed by *sharia* law. Since the mujahidin, tens of thousands of Southeast Asian Muslims have travelled to the Middle East to study in Islamic universities, including those in Egypt, Syria, Yemen, and Pakistan.

Thousands of Southeast Asians have studied in the Pakistani *madrasas* that gave rise to the radical Taliban regime. In the 1990s the CIA tried to keep track of some 700 to 1,500 Indonesian students who went to Egypt, Syria, and Iran for study. According to a retired CIA officer, "We figured 30–40 percent of them never showed up. We don't know where they went."

None of the countries in Southeast Asia has an accurate fix on how many of their nationals studied in *madrasas* in the past or are currently studying now. There are an unknown number of Malaysian students studying in other Islamic universities and *madrasas* in Pakistan, as the government keeps no records on privately funded students studying abroad. One Malaysian official recounted to me how its embassy in Islamabad, Pakistan, believed there were 5 to 10 Malaysians studying at a certain *madrasa* in Pakistan; there turned out to be 150.

In the Philippines, some 1,600 *madrasas* have been established, unsupervised by state educational authorities, and almost entirely funded by contributions from the Middle East. Forty-four Indonesian students were expelled from Yemeni *madrasas* in February 2002 alone. The Indonesian government has no idea how many Indonesians are studying in Egypt, Pakistan, or elsewhere. In addition to the Pakistani *madrasas,* many Southeast Asians have attended Egypt's Al-Azhar University, the foremost Islamic university in the world, and Yemen's Al Imam University, both of which teach rigid Wahhabi interpretations of Islam and have produced the most radical firebrands in the Muslim world, such as Abdel Meguid al Zindani, and have been key recruiting grounds for Al-Qaida.

At Egypt's Al-Azhar University, there are some 6,000 Malaysian students alone. Each of the nine state governments on the Malaysian peninsula rents a block of apartments for the students that it sponsors. Although most of these students will return and join the government's Islamic bureaucracy, and not turn militant, some students return committed to turning Malaysia into an Islamic state. This was brought to the government's attention in February to March 2002, when twelve Malaysian students were arrested in Yemen in a crackdown on radical Islamic *madrasas*. Though released after they were found to not have terrorist connections, Malaysia agreed to repatriate the 250 to 300 privately funded students in Yemen.

The very strict and orthodox Wahhabi brand of Islam is a literal interpretation of the Quran. This puritanical sect was founded by Muhammad Ibn al-Wahhab (c. 1703–1791) and rejects all Islamic practices adopted after the third century of the Muslim era (approximately 950 C.E.). Wahhab considered it a duty to conquer all other "heretical" sects of Islam practiced among the Saudi tribes.

He allied himself with one clan, the Saud, in 1744. In the mid-1760s the Saud completed their conquest of Saudi Arabia, and ever since, there have been close links between the House of Saud and the Wahhabi sect. The growth of the Wahhabi sect around the world can be explained by two reasons. First, the sect markets itself as the "purest" brand of Islam. Second, it has been patronized by the Saudi royal family, the Saudi Arabian government, and especially Saudi-based charities, which have financed thousands of Islamic schools around the world as well as new mosque construction.

The financial power of Saudi Arabia has ensured that its predominant Islamic sect has been able to propagate itself, including in places like Southeast Asia that have always had very tolerant and undoctrinaire interpretations of Islam. Even in devoutly Buddhist Cambodia nearly 15 percent of Cham Buddhists are Wahhabi, the result of Saudi aid and scholarships.

The Pakistani *madrasas* blended rigid Wahhabism with Deobandism, an authoritarian and pan-Islamic sect that emerged in the subcontinent in the nineteenth century. Deobandists wanted to create a pan-Islamic movement to combat British and other European colonial rule. This is noteworthy because if one studies the language of bin Laden, he evokes the idea of the caliphate. As Gerecht explained, "For many fundamentalists, as least sentimentally, the ideal geopolitical expression of Muslim universalism [is] an empire free of Westernized nation-states, where the sharia, the holy law, reigns supreme, thus guaranteeing the union of the church and state and the brotherhood and strength of the faithful." This is important because increasingly in Southeast Asia, radical groups, such as the Kampulan Mujahidin Malaysia and the JI, are beginning to reconceive precolonial notions of pan-Islamicism. *Madrasas* are not just a Middle Eastern phenomenon. In their pursuit of the creation of Islamic states, many Southeast Asian jihadis established Islamic schools to indoctrinate, propagate, and recruit. The leaders of many militant groups in Southeast Asia, including the Laskar Jihad, Kampulan Mujahidin Malaysia, and Jemaah Islamiya, returned from Afghanistan and established a network of *madrasas* as the base of their operations and recruitment. And *madrasas* are increasingly beyond state control. Of the 37,362 *madrasas* in Indonesia, only 3,226 (8.6 percent) are run by the state; and 81 percent of the 5.6 million students enrolled in *madrasa* attend privately funded and run Islamic schools. In the Philippines only thirty-five of 1,600 are controlled by the state, with alarming consequences. As one education official put it, the privately funded *madrasas* "tailor their curricula to the wishes of whoever subsidizes them."

The *madrasas* and *pesentren,* or Muslim boarding schools, in Southeast Asia that have been set up since the late 1980s, have advocated a stricter, more intolerant brand of Islam and condemn the secular nation-state. They are the core of a growing and powerful radical Islamic movement and have established networks within the region and with the Middle East. There is now a critical mass of students studying in Islamic universities and *madrasas* who are reinforced in their conviction that Malaysia, Indonesia, and Mindanao must become Islamic states in order to overcome the myriad socioeconomic and political woes that secularism has wrought. They believe that in Islam there is no separation between church and state, that Islam is a complete way of life, and that *sharia*, not man's positive laws, can be the only ordering principle in society. This radical fringe will continue to grow, as modernization leaves people more isolated and the political process leaves people more disenfranchised. The Islamists and their supporters will continue to gain in power unless the more secular Muslim community again provides a successful model of tolerant and modernist Islam that it has done fairly successfully for forty years.

The vast majority of Southeast Asian Muslims do not attend *madrasas* and *pesentren;* they are the products of secular education. Yet they are attending prayers at mosques in increasing numbers, more children are being educated in Islamic schools, and there has been a surge in interest in Arabic studies. Many parents lament that their children are unable to read the Quran in Arabic. *Pesentren* also provide room and board, in addition to education, which is not insignificant in the context of a prolonged economic downturn and declining public investment in public education in the region. But parents are increasingly sending their children to *pesentren* because of their discipline, the failure of states to provide adequate schooling, and the protection of their children from the vices of secular, urban education: the decline of Islamic values, drug use, and teenage pregnancy. In Malaysia's Kelantan State, for example, there are some 40,000 students enrolled in ninety-two *madrasas;* 50 percent of those come from other states. Moreover, since 1994, the passing rate for the government's secondary school examination for students in Kelantan's *pesentren* has been 90 percent, higher than the national average. *Madrasas* in Pakistan and elsewhere in the Middle East are increasingly appealing to Malaysians, Moro Filipinos, and Indonesians for several reasons: They were a cheap source of education that gave the student and their family status in their communities; they were a hedge against the growing political clout of Islamic hardliners; and finally, in uncertain economic times, graduates of *madrasas* could always find work as clerks in mosques or *sharia* courts.

Although many of the recruits into the ranks of militant Islamic groups in Southeast Asia came from *madrasas*, one of the hallmarks of Al-Qaida is its ability to recruit and radicalize students from Western secular education, especially those with technical training. In Southeast Asia, many of the leading operatives in Jemaah Islamiya were trained or teachers in technical universities, notably the University of Technology Malaysia and Bandung Institute of Technology.

Both have traditionally been hotbeds of radical Islamic activities. In addition to prayers, which are shown on TV in Malaysia, Indonesia, Singapore, and the southern Philippines five times a day, there are Arabic language lessons on television focusing solely on the reading of the Quran across the region.

There is also the Yemeni connection. The traders who spread Islam to Indonesia and Southeast Asia from the Arabian Peninsula hailed in particular from what is now Yemen. Osama bin Laden, though formerly a Saudi national, is actually from a south Yemeni clan from Hadramaut.

Hadramauts were seafaring traders who migrated en masse to Southeast Asia and were instrumental in spreading Islam. The British actively encouraged Yemeni and Arab migration to their colonies in Singapore and Malaya. Even in the predominantly Muslim states of Malaysia and Indonesia, there were distinct Arab minorities who constituted a powerful economic and social force.

The fact that they came from the land of the Prophet accorded them special status: "As nominal countrymen of the prophet, Arabs came to be respected as scholars of the writ and as judicial authorities in matters of the Islamic faith." As Peter H. Riddell put it, "Their influence as traders and authorities in the religious sphere should be seen as inextricably interlinked; it is likely that the authority accorded to them in the religious domain at times seemed to provide them with preferential trading circumstances."

And there continued to be considerable flows between the communities throughout the twentieth century. Riddell notes considerable Malay Arab and Singaporean Arab communities in Hadramaut and Mecca. Both Indonesia and Malaysia have sizeable

Arab minority communities. The vast network of Yemenis in the region is not a tangential point.

Bin Laden, as with Al-Qaida, relies on personal networks, and Yemen's clan-based society transcends the oceans and has spread to Southeast Asia. The single largest Yemeni industrialist, Hail Saeed, had extensive investments throughout the region, as does the Binladen Group itself. These corporate conglomerates have always relied on the vast network of Yemeni traders and businessmen in the region as business partners. And Yemen itself has become a key operational base for Al-Qaida agents as well as a site for attacks, such as the bombing of the USS *Cole* or the French oil tanker in October 2002. Yemenis are major investors in Southeast Asia, and they operate many joint ventures that we now know were fronts for Al-Qaida.

The second reason that Al-Qaida has looked to Southeast Asia is that the Islamic resurgence in the region has occurred because of long-standing disputes with the secular governments. Many of the Islamic movements in Southeast Asia have legitimate grievances, whether they have been repressed or whether they clamor for autonomy or simply greater religious freedom.

Economically speaking, in all Southeast Asian countries, the Muslim *pribumi* or *bumiputera* communities are less well off. Indeed, Malaysia had to implement a reverse-affirmative action program in the early 1970s following race riots in 1969 to give the ethnic majority a greater share of the nation's wealth. The goal of the New Economic Policy (NEP), as it was titled, was to ensure that Malays (who make up two-thirds of the population) were able to account for one-third of economic assets.

Now, more than thirty years later, the original goals of the NEP still have not been met, despite significant improvements in the socioeconomic position of Malays. There are considerable socioeconomic inequalities that exist across the region between the different religious communities that have only been exacerbated by the Asian economic crisis since 1997. In Indonesia, anti-Chinese riots in May 1998, though provoked by a faction within the military, were the clearest manifestation of popular grievances toward the commercially advantaged Chinese community. In Indonesia, there is a stronger sense that the economy has still not recovered than in any other Southeast Asian state: 58 percent argued that it is harder to find work, 56 percent believed that working conditions are getting worse, 74 percent believed that the gap between the rich and poor is getting worse, and 44 percent attributed that to globalization.

The growth of Islamic extremism around the world since the Iranian Revolution of 1979 has less to do with theology and a lot to do with the failure of the domestic political economies of their respective countries. Increasing gaps between the rich and poor, unemployment, corruption, a lack of economic diversity, and the lack of a viable political alternative have all given rise to Islamic extremism. People literally become so desperate that they have nowhere to turn but to extremist religious politics. The Iranian Revolution, which took place in the most secular state in the region, was clearly a catalyst.

The most secular governments in the Muslim world were Malaysia and Indonesia, two of the fastest growing economies from the mid-1970s to the mid-1990s. Once their economies slowed and became mired in the Asian economic crisis, which saw the value of their currencies collapse and public and private debt soar, causing mass unemployment, Islamic extremism was able to take hold and enter the mainstream, whereas before it was on the fringes of society. Clerics were able to veil their political criticisms in Friday prayer sermons.

In some countries, notably Malaysia and Indonesia, rather than being aggrieved by minority status, Islam became more radical because authoritarian secular governments repressed it for so long. Secular leaders never gave political space to religious elites and religious-based political parties, even when they relied on them in their own ascension to power. Religious elites and parties felt that they had been, at best, ignored or marginalized, and, at worst, repressed by governments who feared the Islamization of politics. The jailed former Malaysian deputy prime minister, Anwar Ibrahim, contends that the lack of democracy and civil society is the root cause of Islamic fundamentalism in the country. Without a free press and a truly democratic system where people can blow off steam, radical Islamists provide one of the only viable alternatives to the ruling coalition. In a well-publicized essay entitled "Who Hijacked Islam?" Anwar made a compelling, though implicit, argument that the government's authoritarian policies and the lack of democracy were only going to serve as a catalyst for Islamic fundamentalism: Bin Laden and his protégés are the children of desperation; they come from countries where political struggle through peaceful means is futile. In many Muslim countries, political dissent is simply illegal. Yet, year by year, the size of the educated class and the number of young professionals continues to increase. These people need space to express their political and social concerns....

The need for Muslim societies to address their internal social and political development has become more urgent than ever. Economic development alone is clearly insufficient: it creates its own tensions in the social and political spheres, which must be addressed.

At the same time, these governments have often turned to religion as a legitimizing force for their rule. For example, the Malaysian and Indonesian governments began to actively facilitate the *haj*, the pilgrimage to Mecca. By the 1980s, more than 80,000 Indonesians and 15,000 Malays went to Mecca annually, all with the support of their governments. In short, across the region, socioeconomic and political issues have created a large body of people who are turning to Islam to change the status quo, which they believe has kept them poor and disenfranchised. Governments often turn to religion in times of political and economic crisis to shore up their domestic legitimacy, as Indonesian president Suharto did in the early 1990s. Although governments try to keep religion in check, this is never easy to do. For example, the mosques are often the focal points of antigovernment resistance and propaganda, as the Iranian Revolution drove home in 1979.

The growth of radical groups in Southeast Asia must also be seen in the context of religious and political leaders who were kept out of an elite status and used Islam to manipulate sectarian issues for their own political purpose. As Michael Davis said in his study of the Laskar Jihad in Indonesia, radical groups must be militant and confrontational: "This derives from basic selfinterest: No conflict, no Laskar Jihad—only the maintenance of hostilities legitimates the group's position." In part, Islamic hardliners have been able to do this because of the spread of democracy in the region.

This is the irony of the "illiberal democracy." On the one hand, the lack of democratic institutions (political parties, freedom of assembly, and free speech) permitted Islamic extremism to spread. Only in the mosques in veiled language could there be political dissent. Yet the spread of democracy has now sanctioned the extremists, giving them political platforms to express their pent-up grievances. For example, in Indonesia, since the fall of Suharto in May 1998, nearly 25 percent of the political parties have an Islamic affiliation or identity. There is a crisis in the belief of democracy's efficacy in Indonesia. The percentage of people who believed that Western-style democracy works in Indonesia fell from 64 percent in 2002 to 41 percent in 2003, a trend that favours the less democratic Islamic parties. The fact is, we have to let this run its course.

The breakdown of secular institutions, especially the educational and legal systems in the wake of the Asian economic crisis, has created a vacuum in which nonsecular institutions emerge to fill the void. Increasingly parents are turning to *pesentren* and *madrasas* to educate their children as state funding for the educational sector collapses. Likewise, in a recent column, the Malaysian intellectual Farish Noor contended that *sharia* courts were becoming more prominent because of the absolute failure of the secular court system in adapting itself to changes in the political-economy of a "globalized" world.

Finally, we cannot underestimate the influence of the ongoing conflict in the Middle East, which has a surprisingly large impact on popular opinion in the region. While the Palestinian issue is primarily a national struggle cloaked in religion, it strikes a chord in Southeast Asia. The injustices suffered by the Palestinians become a metaphor for the injustices of all Muslims, while the Americans, already scapegoats for the region's economic woes, are implicated again. It does not help matters that Singapore, whose Chinese population is mistrusted and maligned by the larger populations of Indonesia and Malaysia, is a very close ally of Israel.

What is so evident is that radical Islam is spreading very quickly across the region, and the once secular states are becoming more Islamic as a result. Moderate Muslims who embrace tolerance and cohabitation with ethnic and religious minorities are still the majority of the population, but they are being overshadowed by a more radical and outspoken group that is bent on establishing Islamic states. The radical right is dictating the national agendas and forcing the governments to adopt policies to protect themselves against the accusation of not protecting the rights and interests of the Muslim communities. What is more, secular politicians in the region are increasingly unwilling to confront the Islamic parties; to do so now is becoming a political liability.

ARMED ISLAMIC GROUP (GIA)

Description

An Islamic extremist group, the GIA aims to overthrow the secular Algerian regime and replace it with an Islamic state. The GIA began its violent activities in 1992 after Algiers voided the victory of the Islamic Salvation Front (FIS)—the largest Islamic opposition party—in the first round of legislative elections in December 1991.

Activities

Frequent attacks against civilians and government workers. Between 1992 and 1998 the GIA conducted a terrorist campaign of civilian massacres, sometimes wiping out entire villages in its area of operation. Since announcing its campaign against foreigners living in Algeria in 1993, the GIA has killed more than 100 expatriate men and women—mostly Europeans—in the country. The group uses assassinations and bombings, including car bombs, and it is known to favour kidnapping victims and slitting their throats. The GIA hijacked an Air France flight to Algiers in December 1994. In late 1999 several GIA members were convicted by a French court for conducting a series of bombings in France in 1995.

The Salafi Group for Call and Combat (GSPC) splinter faction appears to have eclipsed the GIA since approximately 1998 and is currently assessed to be the most effective remaining armed group inside Algeria. Both the GIA and GSPC leadership continue to proclaim their rejection of President Bouteflika's amnesty, but in contrast to the GIA, the GSPC has stated that it limits attacks on civilians. The GSPC's planned attack against the Paris-Dakar Road Rally in January 2000 demonstrates, however, that the group has not entirely renounced attacks against high-profile civilian targets.

Strength

Unkown; probably several hundred to several thousand.

Location/Area of Operation

Algeria.

HAMAS (ISLAMIC RESISTANCE MOVEMENT)

Description

Formed in late 1987 as an outgrowth of the Palestinian branch of the Muslim Brotherhood. Various HAMAS elements have used both political and violent means, including terrorism, to pursue the goal of establishing an Islamic Palestinian state in place of Israel.

Loosely structured, with some elements working clandestinely and others working openly through mosques and social service institutions to recruit members, raise money, organize activities, and distribute propaganda. HAMAS's strength is concentrated in the Gaza Strip and a few areas of the West Bank. Also has engaged in peaceful political activity, such as running candidates in West Bank Chamber of Commerce elections.

Activities

HAMAS activists, especially those in the Izz el-Din al-Qassam Brigades, have conducted many attacks—including large-scale suicide bombings—against Israeli civilian and military targets. In the early 1990s, they also targeted suspected Palestinian collaborators and Fatah rivals. Claimed several attacks during the unrest in late 2000.

Strength

Unknown number of hard-core members; tens of thousands of supporters and sympathizers.

Location/Area of Operation

Primarily the occupied territories, Israel. In August 1999, Jordanian authorities closed the group's Political Bureau offices in Amman, arrested its leaders, and prohibited the group from operating on Jordanian territory.

External Aid

Receives funding from Palestinian expatriates, Iran, and private benefactors in Saudi Arabia and other moderate Arab states. Some fundraising and propaganda activities take place in Western Europe and North America.

HARAKAT-UL JIHAD ISLAMI (HUJI)

aka HUJI, Movement of Islamic Holy War; Harkat-ul-Jihad-al Islami; Harkat-al-Jihad-ul Islami; Harkat-ul-Jehad-al-Islami; Harakat ul Jihad-e- Islami; Harakat-ul Jihad Islami

Description: Designated as a Foreign Terrorist Organization on August 6, 2010, Harakat-ul Jihad Islami (HUJI) was founded in 1980 in Afghanistan to fight against the Soviet Union. Following the Soviet withdrawal from Afghanistan in 1989, the organization re-focused its efforts on India. HUJI seeks the annexation of Indian Kashmir and expulsion of Coalition Forces from Afghanistan. It also has supplied fighters for the Taliban in Afghanistan. In addition, some factions of HUJI espouse a more global agenda and conduct attacks in Pakistan as well. HUJI is composed of militant Pakistanis and veterans of the Soviet-Afghan war. HUJI has experienced a number of internal splits and a portion of the group has aligned with al-Qa'ida (AQ) in recent years, including training its members in AQ training camps. Mohammad Ilyas Kashmiri, one of HUJI's top leaders who also served as an AQ military commander and strategist, was killed on June 3, 2011.

Activities: HUJI has been involved in a number of terrorist attacks in recent years. On March 2, 2006, a HUJI leader was the mastermind behind the suicide bombing of the U.S. Consulate in Karachi, Pakistan, which killed four people, including U.S. diplomat David Foy, and injured 48 others. HUJI was also responsible for terrorist attacks in India including the May 2007 Hyderabad mosque attack, which killed 16 and injured 40, and the March 2007 Varanasi attack, which killed 25 and injured 100. HUJI claimed credit for the September 7, 2011 bombing of the New Delhi High Court, which left at least 11 dead and an estimated 76 wounded. HUJI sent an email to the press stating that the bomb was intended to force India to repeal a death sentence of a HUJI member.

Strength: HUJI has an estimated strength of several hundred members.

Location/Area of Operations: HUJI's area of operation extends throughout South Asia, with its terrorist operations focused primarily in India and Afghanistan. Some factions of HUJI conduct attacks within Pakistan.

External Aid: Unknown.

ISLAMIC JIHAD UNION (IJU)

aka Islamic Jihad Group; Islomiy Jihod Ittihodi; al-Djihad al-Islami; Dzhamaat Modzhakhedov; Islamic Jihad Group of Uzbekistan; Jamiat al-Jihad al-Islami; Jamiyat; The Jamaat Mojahedin; The Kazakh Jama'at; The Libyan Society

Description: Designated as a Foreign Terrorist Organization on June 17, 2005, the Islamic Jihad Union (IJU) is a Sunni extremist organization that splintered from the Islamic Movement of Uzbekistan (IMU).

Activities: The IJU, based in Pakistan, primarily operates against Coalition Forces in Afghanistan and continues to pose a threat of attacks in Central Asia. The group claimed responsibility for attacks in March and April 2004, targeting police at several roadway checkpoints and at a popular bazaar, killing approximately 47 people, including 33 IJU members, some of whom were suicide bombers. In July 2004, the group carried out near-simultaneous suicide bombings of the Uzbek Prosecutor General's office and the U.S. and Israeli Embassies in Tashkent. In September 2007, German authorities disrupted an IJU plot by detaining three IJU operatives, including two German citizens. Foreign fighters from Germany, Turkey, and elsewhere in Europe continued to travel to the Afghan-Pakistan border area to join the IJU to fight against U.S. and Coalition Forces.

Strength: 100-200 members .

Location/Area of Operation: IJU members are scattered throughout Central Asia, Europe, Pakistan, and Afghanistan.

External Aid: Unknown.

JAISH-E-MOHAMMED (JEM) (ARMY OF MOHAMMED)

Description

The Jaish-e-Mohammed (JEM) is an Islamist group based in Pakistan that has rapidly expanded in size and capability since Maulana Masood Azhar, a former ultrafundamentalist Harakat ul-Ansar (HUA) leader, announced its formation in February. The group's aim is to unite Kashmir with Pakistan. It is politically aligned with the radical, pro-Taliban, political party, Jamiat-i Ulema-i Islam (JUI-F).

Activities

The JEM's leader, Masood Azhar, was released from Indian imprisonment in December 1999 in exchange for 155 hijacked Indian Airlines hostages in Afghanistan. The 1994 HUA kidnappings of US and British nationals in New Delhi and the July 1995 HUA/Al Faran kidnappings of Westerners in Kashmir were two of several previous HUA efforts to free Azhar.

Azhar organized large rallies and recruitment drives across Pakistan throughout 2000. In July, a JEM rocket-grenade attack failed to injure the Chief Minister at his office in Srinagar, India, but wounded four other persons. In December, JEM militants launched grenade attacks at a bus stop in Kupwara, India, injuring 24 persons, and at a marketplace in Chadoura, India, injuring 16 persons.

JEM militants also planted two bombs that killed 21 persons in Qamarwari and Srinagar.

Strength

Has several hundred armed supporters located in Azad Kashmir, Pakistan, and in India's southern Kashmir and Doda regions.

Following Maulana Masood Azhar's release from detention in India, a reported three quarters of Harakat ul-Mujahedin (HUM) members defected to the new organization, which has managed to attract a large number of urban Kashmiri youth.

Supporters are mostly Pakistanis and Kashmiris and also include Afghans and Arab veterans of the Afghan war. Uses light and heavy machineguns, assault rifles, mortars, improvised explosive devices, and rocket grenades.

Location/Area of Operation

Based in Peshawar and Muzaffarabad, but members conduct terrorist activities primarily in Kashmir. The JEM maintains training camps in Afghanistan.

External Aid

Most of the JEM's cadre and material resources have been drawn from the militant groups Harakat ul-Jihad al-Islami (HUJI) and the Harakat ul-Mujahedin (HUM). The JEM has close ties to Afghan Arabs and the Taliban. Usama Bin Ladin is suspected of giving funding to the JEM.

Jama'at al-Tawhid wa'al - Jihad-Abu Musab al-Zarqawi's network, operating in Iraq on U.S. State Department list of Foreign Terrorist Organizations

Jemaah Islamiyah -Southeast Asia

JKLF Jammu and Kashmir Liberation Front -Pakistan and Kashmir

LASHKAR-E-TAYYIBA (LT) (ARMY OF THE RIGHTEOUS)

Description

The LT is the armed wing of the Pakistan-based religious organization, Markaz-ud-Dawa-wal-Irshad (MDI)—a Sunni anti-US missionary organization formed in 1989. One of the three largest and best-trained groups fighting in Kashmir against India, it is not connected to a political party. The LT leader is MDI chief, Professor Hafiz Mohammed Saeed.

Activities

Has conducted a number of operations against Indian troops and civilian targets in Kashmir since 1993. The LT is suspected of eight separate attacks in August that killed nearly 100, mostly Hindu Indians. LT militants are suspected of kidnapping six persons in Akhala, India, in November 2000 and killing five of them. The group also operates a chain of religious schools in the Punjab.

Strength

Has several hundred members in Azad Kashmir, Pakistan, and in India's southern Kashmir and Doda regions. Almost all LT cadres are foreigners—mostly Pakistanis from seminaries across the country and Afghan veterans of the Afghan wars. Uses assault rifles, light and heavy machineguns, mortars, explosives, and rocket propelled grenades.

Location/Area of Operation

Based in Muridke (near Lahore) and Muzaffarabad. The LT trains its militants in mobile training camps across Pakistan-administered Kashmir and Afghanistan.

Maktab al-Khadamat -Afghanistan

Moroccan Islamic Combatant Group -Morocco and Spain

Muslim Brotherhood -international

TEHRIK-E TALIBAN PAKISTAN (TTP)

Aka: Pakistani Taliban; Tehreek-e-Taliban; Tehrik-e-Taliban; Tehrik-e Taliban Pakistan; Tehrik-i-Taliban Pakistan; TTP

Description: Designated as a Foreign Terrorist Organization on September 1, 2010, Tehrik-e Taliban Pakistan (TTP) is a Pakistan-based terrorist organization formed in 2007 in opposition to Pakistani military efforts in the Federally Administered Tribal Areas. Previously disparate militant tribes agreed to cooperate and eventually coalesced into TTP under the leadership of now deceased leader Baitullah Mehsud. The group officially presented itself as a discrete entity in 2007. TTP has been led by Hakimullah Mehsud since August 2009. Other senior leaders include Wali Ur Rehman, the TTP emir in South Waziristan, Pakistan. TTP's goals include overthrowing the Government of Pakistan by waging a terrorist campaign against the civilian leader of Pakistan, its military, and NATO forces in Afghanistan. TTP uses the tribal belt along the Afghan-Pakistani border to train and deploy its operatives, and the group has a symbiotic relationship with al-Qa'ida (AQ). TTP draws ideological guidance from AQ, while AQ relies on TTP for safe haven in the Pashtun areas along the Afghan-Pakistani border. This arrangement gives TTP access to both AQ's global terrorist network and the operational experience of its members. Given the proximity of the two groups and the nature of their relationship, TTP is a force multiplier for AQ.

Activities: TTP has carried out and claimed responsibility for numerous terrorist acts against Pakistani and U.S. interests, including a December 2009 suicide attack on a U.S. military base in Khowst, Afghanistan, which killed seven U.S. citizens, and an April 2010 suicide bombing against the U.S. Consulate in Peshawar, Pakistan, which killed six Pakistani citizens. TTP is suspected of being involved in the 2007 assassination of former Pakistani Prime Minister Benazir Bhutto. TTP claimed to have supported the failed attempt by Faisal Shahzad to detonate an explosive device in New York City's Times Square on May 1, 2010. TTP's claim was validated by investigations that revealed that TTP directed and facilitated the plot.

Throughout 2011, TTP carried out attacks against the Government of Pakistan and civilian targets, as well as against U.S. targets in Pakistan. Attacks in 2011 included: a March bombing at a gas station in Faisalabad that killed 31 people; an April double suicide bombing at a Sufi shrine in Dera Ghazi Khan that left more than 50 dead; a May bombing of an American consulate convoy in Peshawar that killed one person and injured twelve; a May siege of a naval base in Karachi; the May assassination of the PNS Mehran Saudi diplomat in Karachi; and a September attack against a school bus that killed four children and the bus driver.

Strength: Several thousand.

Location: Federally Administered Tribal Areas (FATA), Pakistan

External aid: TTP is believed to raise most of its funds through kidnapping for ransom and operations that target Afghanistan-bound military transport trucks for robbery. Such operations enable TTP to steal military equipment, which they then sell in Afghan and Pakistani markets.

THE PROLIFERATION OF JIHADIST ORGANIZATIONS IN PAKISTAN

The proliferation of jihadist organizations in Pakistan over the previous two decades had been the result of a militant culture espoused by radical madrasas like Darul Uloom Haqqania. Thousands of madrasas across the country became hubs for militancy and religious extremism, having a spill-over effect and presenting a serious threat to Pakistan's internal security. Pakistani madrasas were once considered centres for basic religious learning, mostly attached to local mosques.

The more formal ones were used for educating clergy. The development of simple, sparse religious schools into training centres for Kalashnikov-toting religious warriors was directly linked with the rise of militant Islam. Many of the religious parties operating the madrasas turned to militancy courtesy of the US-sponsored Jihad in Afghanistan. From waging Jihad against infidels in that foreign land, taking on perceived enemies of Islam at home was just a small step away. The influx of huge sums of money and a growing sense of power transformed the mullah's image from that of a docile and humble man to a mafia thug with a four-wheel-drive Jeep and armed bodyguards.

The influence of mullahs with local Pakistani leaders had also become formidable. Successive governments ignored their activities out of political expediency and also because most of the foreigners supporting them were 'brotherly Muslim' countries. The Islamic revolution in Iran in 1979 opened up the first wave of foreign funding for madrasas in Pakistan. Fearful of growing Iranian influence and the spread of revolution, Kuwait, Saudi Arabia, Iraq and some other oil-rich Muslim countries started pumping money into hardline Pakistani Sunni religious organizations willing to counter the supposed Shia threat. Millions of dollars were poured into setting up madrasas across the country, particularly in Balochistan province, bordering Iran. The Islamization process started by General Zia ul-Haq's regime in 1979 also contributed to the mushrooming of madrasas. For the first time in Pakistani history, the state started providing financial support for the expansion of religious education from Zakat and Ushr funds. The Islamization of education and levying of Islamic taxes had a profound long-term effect.

Zakat, one of the five pillars of Islam, had been treated as a private matter in most Muslim states. General Zia's regime broke with that tradition by deducting it from bank accounts each year during the Islamic holy month of Ramadan. The substantial amount raised by Zakat was used to finance the traditional religious schools, most of them belonging to the Deobandi movement, which is akin to Saudi Wahabism. Zakat did little to improve the lot of millions of Pakistanis living in abject poverty. The only visible consequence was the transformation of the religious landscape of the nation. The foreign and government-funded madrasas also became the main centres for spreading sectarian hatred. Saudi Arabian patronage, especially of more radical Ahle Hadith madrasas, played a major role in worsening the situation.

Madrasas also had a key place in Pakistani religious and social life. Most of the seminary students came from the poorest sections of Pakistani society and were provided with free religious education, lodging and meals. The influx of the impoverished rural population to the madrasas was a major reason for their growth, with Punjab and the North West Frontier Province having the highest number of religious seminaries. Divided along sectarian and political lines, religious seminaries were largely controlled by the two main branches of Sunni Islam in South Asia – the Deobandi and the Barelvi. Ahle Hadith or Wahabi Muslims had their own schools, as did the Shias. The religious doctrinal differences among these sects were irreconcilable. Most of the madrasas were centuries apart from the outside world. Generally the students were poor, from broken homes, or were orphans. Conditions in schools were regularly condemned by human rights groups as crowded and inhumane. The students were often subjected to a regimen as harsh as any jail, and physical abuses were commonplace. In many schools, students were put in chains and iron fetters for the slightest violation of the rules. There were almost no extracurricular activities and television and radio were banned. Teaching was rudimentary and students were taught religion within a highly rigorous and traditional perspective, giving them a deeply retrograde world-view.

At the primary stage, madrasa pupils learnt to read, memorize and recite the Qur'an. Exegeses of the holy script and other branches of Islamic studies were introduced at the higher stages of learning. Though the focus was on religious learning, some institutions also taught elementary mathematics, science and English. The most dangerous consequence of the content and style of teaching in religious schools was that the people that emerged could do nothing apart from guide the faithful in rituals that demand no experts. Job opportunities for madrasa graduates were few and narrow. They could only work in mosques, madrasas, the parent religious sectarian party, or its affiliate businesses or organizations.

The education imparted by traditional madrasas often spawned factional, religious and cultural conflict. It created barriers to modern knowledge, stifled creativity and bred bigotry, thus laying the foundation on which fundamentalism – militant or otherwise – was based. Divided by sectarian identities, these institutions were, by their very nature, driven by their zeal to outnumber and dominate rival sects. Students were educated and trained to counter the arguments of opposing sects on matters of theology, jurisprudence and doctrines. Promoting a particular sect inevitably implied the rejection of other sects, sowing the seeds of extremism in the minds of the students. The literature produced by their parent religious organizations promoted sectarian hatred and was aimed at proving the rival sects as infidels and apostates. The efforts by the successive government to modernize madrasa curricula and introduce secular subjects failed because of stiff resistance from the religious organizations controlling the religious schools.

The rise of Jihad culture since the 1980s gave madrasas a new sense of purpose. As a result, their numbers multiplied and the clergy emerged as a powerful political and social force. At independence in 1947, there were only 137 madrasas in Pakistan; in the next ten years their number rose to 244. After that, they doubled every ten years. A significant number remained unregistered and therefore it was hard to know precisely how many there were. Government sources put the figure at 13,000, with total enrolment close to 1.7 million. The vast majority of students were between five and 18 years old. Only those advancing into higher religious studies were older. According to the government's own estimates, ten to 15 per cent of the madrasas had links with sectarian militancy or international terrorism. The trail of international terror often led to the madrasas and mosques.

Madrasas were basically conservative institutions before they were radicalized during the 1980s Afghan Jihad. The growing army of extremists fought the anti-Soviet Afghan Jihad alongside Arabs and Afghans. They later served the cause of Jihad from Kashmir to Chechnya to Bosnia, Egypt and Yemen. At the height of the Afghan Jihad – 1982–1988 – more than 1,000 new madrasas were opened in Pakistan, mostly along the borders with Afghanistan in the North West Frontier Province and Balochistan. Almost all belonged to hardline Sunni religious parties like Jamiat-e-Ulema Islam (JUI) and Jamaat-i-Islami (JI), which were Zia's political allies as well as partners in the Afghan Jihad.

Their location in the two border provinces, which had close cultural, linguistic and sectarian affinities with Afghan Pashtuns, made it easier to motivate the pupils to fight for their brethren in distress. These madrasas did not conduct military training or provide arms to students, but encouraged them to join the 'holy war'. The purpose was to ensure a continued supply of recruits for the Afghan resistance. The message was simple: all Muslims must perform the duty of Jihad in whatever capacity they could. It was the responsibility of the Pakistani military, particularly the ISI, to provide training to the recruits in camps inside Afghanistan and Pakistan's tribal region. As the Afghan Jihad progressed, so did the influence of the jihadists coming out of these madrasas. The USA indirectly – and sometimes directly – promoted militancy, the culture of Jihad and supported the clergy in its war against communism.

Special textbooks were published in Dari and Pashto by the University of Nebraska-Omaha and funded by USAID with an aim to promote jihadist values and militant training. Millions of such books were distributed at Afghan refugee camps and Pakistani madrasas, where students learnt basic maths by counting dead Russians and Kalashnikov rifles. The same textbooks were later used by the Taliban in their madrasas.

As General Zia attempted to consolidate his authority through Islamization at home and Jihad in Afghanistan, the madrasa system was profoundly transformed. The Islamization process nurtured many, often mutually hostile, varieties of fundamentalism. In a society where many sects coexisted, the measures representing the belief of the dominant sect acted as an identity marker, heightening sectarian divisions and promoting sectarian conflicts. As a result, sectarian divisions were militarized. The zealots began to look inwards and fight a new Jihad against sectarian rivals, particularly Shias. The madrasa phenomenon drew international attention, particularly following the rise of the conservative Taliban regime in Afghanistan. The movement was largely the product of hundreds of seminaries in the Pashtun belt on the border with Afghanistan.

The link between madrasas and the Afghan Jihad is exemplified by the Darul Uloom Haqqania madrasa. Founded in 1947 by Haq's father, Maulana Abdul Haq, a well-respected Islamic scholar belonging to the Deobandi order, Darul Uloom Haqqania developed into a centre for pan-Islamism with the beginning of the Afghan war. It saw a huge expansion with the support of the government and funds from abroad. Like other Deobandi institutions, Darul Uloom was controlled by a faction of JUI, a mainstream religio-political party that was part of a six-party conservative alliance known as Muttehida Majlis Amal (MMA). The party became an important part of the Afghan Jihad. The seminary traditionally had a large number of students from Afghanistan, but they increased considerably with the influx of Afghan refugees.

By 1985, about 60 per cent of the students in the seminary were Afghans. It also attracted students from Tajikistan, Uzbekistan and Turkmenistan. From the beginning of the Afghan Jihad, the school had relaxed the rules concerning attendance, allowing the students to take time off to participate in the 'holy war'. The seminary, however, drew immense international attention in the 1990s with the emergence of the conservative Taliban movement. Thousands of Afghan, as well as Pakistani students crossed the border into Afghanistan to join the Islamic militia. In 1997 the school was closed for several months to allow the students to participate in the Taliban's war to capture Afghanistan's northern province of Mazar-i-Sharif. Such a large-scale cross-border movement would not have been possible without the collusion of Pakistani intelligence agencies.

Just months before the 11 September terrorist attacks in New York and Washington, the school hosted a conference of Islamic parties and militant groups to express solidarity with bin Laden and the Taliban regime. Masked gunmen in camouflage guerrilla outfits stood guard as Islamic leaders from Pakistan and Afghanistan congregated at the sprawling auditorium on 9 January 2001, vowing to defend bin Laden and to launch a holy war against the West. Besides the 300 leaders representing various radical Islamic groups, the meeting was also attended by a former army chief, General Aslam Beg, and a former ISI chief, General Hamid Gul. They declared it a religious duty of Muslims all over the world to protect the Saudi dissident whom they described as a 'great Muslim warrior'. One of the objectives of the assembly was to press Islamabad not to comply with UN sanctions against the Taliban. Interestingly, the military government, which had banned political parties holding public rallies, did not try to stop the conference. No action was taken against the militants for the public display of weapons. They obviously had the backing of the intelligence agencies. Islamic seminaries and clerics had never been as numerous and so powerful in Pakistan.

Islamic seminaries also became a transit point for foreign militants aspiring to join al-Qaeda and the Taliban forces in Afghanistan. Very few people had heard about the primitive fundamentalist Madrasa-i-Arabia outside the remote corner of north-west Pakistan until its name sprung on the international scene in connection with the American Taliban, John Walker Lindh. The young American was wounded in battle and captured by US-supported Northern Alliance forces in the Afghan northern province of Kunduz in December 2001.

It was in this isolated and spartan school where there were no amenities that the 19-year-old American learnt his lesson in Islamic sharia and Jihad. A new convert to Islam, he spent some six months in this austere madrasa housed in a one-storey building before leaving for Afghanistan in May 2001 to join the Taliban. Lindh, who had grown up in upper-middle-class surroundings in California, chose the school to properly understand Islam. Mufti Mohammed Iltimas, the white-bearded head of the school, remembered him as a hard-working student who was determined to memorize every word of the Qur'an. He slept on a rope bed in a place where there was no hot water and no electricity after 10 pm. Lindh's introduction to the madrasa came through a Pakistani missionary he met in California in 1998. A Pashtun, Khizar Hayat, who had travelled to America on a preaching mission, was closely linked with the local militant organizations. Even though he was much older than the other boys, Lindh was granted admission to the school. Lindh, who went by the name Suleyman al-Faris, was not in Pakistan to engage solely in scholarly pursuits. During his stay in the madrasa, he frequently met visiting Taliban activists. In May 2001, Hayat took him to the office of a pro-Taliban Islamic militant group, HuM, where he enrolled for guerrilla training.

Lindh was sent to a HuM camp near Islamabad. After learning the use of firearms, he was dispatched to Afghanistan to work with the Taliban. He was not the only American and not the only westerner to have joined al-Qaeda and the Taliban. Many western men, a lot of them Afro-American, were recruited by the Tablighi Jamaat and its front organizations and sent to Afghanistan after receiving basic religious training in Pakistani madrasas and guerrilla training at the camps run by militant groups, closely affiliated with the religious institutions. Some of the madrasas had links with international Islamist organizations like Egypt's Akhwan-ul Muslimeen (Muslim Brotherhood), Indonesia's Jemmah Islamiyah, Algeria's Islamic Salvation Front (FIS) and the Philippines' Abu Sayyaf group, all of whom extended support to alQaeda.

Radical madrasas were not restricted to the remote border region in northern Pakistan. In fact, the country's largest city and its main financial centre Karachi, became the hub of militant seminaries. According to one estimate, more than 200,000 students were enrolled in around one thousand madrasas in the city. Not all, but many of them, had links with sectarian or Islamic militant groups. The largest among them was the Jamia Ulumia Islami or Jamia Binoria. The sprawling red-brick campus, with tall minarets right in the heart of the city, served as the backbone of militant Islam and was the breeding ground for 'Islamic warriors'. The country's premier institution for Islamic learning had also become the citadel of Sunni extremist groups. The main campus and eight other affiliated madrasas enrolled more than ten thousand students from Pakistan as well as 30 other countries including China, Central Asia, Chechnya, Malaysia, the Philippines and Britain. Students were taught the concept of Jihad as a special subject to prepare them to fight for the cause of Islam. Many of the Taliban leaders were graduates and took guidance from their former teachers for running the fundamentalist Islamic state. The students were sent regularly to Afghanistan for training and orientation during Taliban rule. At the main gate stood a huge banner exhorting Muslims to join Taliban forces in Afghanistan. Over the last two decades, thousands of its students fought in Afghanistan and Kashmir.

Dozens of other smaller and relatively low-profile madrasas spread across Karachi became the base for al-Qaeda 'sleeper' cells in Pakistan. A lean and shy Ahmed Hadi was an ordinary student at Jamia Abu Bakr and the last person one would suspect of being an important cog in the international terrorist network. It was only after Pakistani security forces raided the seminary in Karachi's middle-class neighbourhood of Gulshan-e-Iqbal in September 2003 that his real identity was revealed. Gun Gun Rusman Gunawan was a leading member of Indonesia's Jemmah Islamiyah and the brother of Hambali, the mastermind of the 2002 bombing in the Indonesian holiday resort of Bali in which more than 200 people died. The Indonesian, who was captured along with 11 other Southeast Asian students, had spent four years at the seminary under a fake identity.

Hambali, who was arrested in Thailand in 2003, had contacts with alQaeda's top leaders Ramzi bin al-Shibh and Khalid Sheikh Mohammed, both of whom were apprehended in Pakistan. It was the first indicator of a terrorist sleeper cell operating in Pakistan's main commercial hub. Gunawan was granted admission to the Jamia Abu Bakr Islamia in 1999. He was among 15,000 students from Muslim countries who came to Pakistan to study in Pakistani madrasas during the 1990s. Founded in 1978, the seminary had a large number of foreign students mainly from Thailand, Indonesia, Malaysia and African countries. The arrest of Gunawan provided some indication of the strong links between Islamic seminaries and the international terrorist network. His arrest was followed by a series of raids less than a kilometre away from the Abu Bakr seminary. Another eight Southeast Asian students were arrested from the Jamia Darasitul Islamia, a seminary run by Jamaatud Da'awa, the political wing of Lashkar-e-Taiba. This connection compelled investigators to explore Jemmah Islamiyah's links with Pakistan's militant groups. Pakistani intelligence agencies suspected that Gunawan was instrumental in channelling funds provided by al-Qaeda to the Jemmah Islamiyah. Despite the government's crackdown, many madrasas continued to provide safe haven to al-Qaeda sleeper cells.

Over the past several years, there had been a visible rise in the number of madrasa students belonging to families of the expatriate Pakistani community, particularly those living in the USA and Britain. Fired by the desire to become 'true Muslims', hundreds of second-generation expatriates joined Pakistani seminaries each year. Most of them from prosperous middle-class families, they took time off from their schools to learn about their faith. While the majority of the boys confined themselves to Islamic learning, dozens of them got involved in jihadist activities under the influence of militant groups that operated inside some of the madrasas.

It was one such radical madrasa where Shehzad Tanweer, one of the suicide bombers involved in the 7 July 2005 terror attacks in London, spent time during his last visit to Pakistan. Twenty-two-yearold Shehzad, who blew himself up on a subway train near Aldgate station in East London, was the eldest son of Mohammed Mumtaz Tanweer, who had migrated to England in the 1960s. He grew up in the Beeston area of Leeds, but remained connected with Pakistan through his extended family members who lived in a farming village in Faisalabad district. In December 2004, Shehzad went to Manzoor ul Islamia madrasa in Lahore, which was linked with JeM. He intended to stay there for nine months of religious education, but left just a week later.

There are strong suspicions that Shehzad might have met the mastermind of the London bombings during his brief stay there. The suspected Pakistani connection to the 7/7 attacks brought Musharraf under a renewed pressure to act against militant madrasas. As in the past, he responded this time by ordering a nationwide crackdown on Islamic extremist groups. The police again stormed a number of madrasas and arrested hundreds of suspected extremists. But the entire operation appeared merely superficial; most of them were released after a few weeks. In his new role as a key ally in the US-led war on terror, Musharraf toned down many policies that had previously fostered militancy and religious extremism. But most of the measures, particularly against the home-grown jihadists, were taken under external pressure and lacked conviction. Very little was done to rein in the militant madrasas, despite their continuing involvement in jihadist politics. While talk about reform went on, fresh batches of volunteers ready to confront what they perceived as enemies of their faith continued to graduate from madrasas.

Even after the ousting of the Taliban regime, many madrasas in parts of Balochistan continued to preach Jihad to Afghan students. A major part of Musharraf's anti-extremism drive was to regulate and transform those madrasas whose role in promoting Jihad had come under increasing international scrutiny. The move was stalled because of the administration's failure to stop their funding from Pakistanis working abroad, as well as from foreign Muslim charities.

The biggest source of financing for madrasas was external – from Muslim countries as well as private donors and Pakistani expatriates. A report by the Brussels-based International Crisis Group (ICG) revealed that Pakistani madrasas and religious centres had received more than 90 billion rupees ($1.5 billion) every year through charitable donations. The amount was almost equal to the government's annual direct income tax revenue. Most of the madrasas, which had in the past received government funding, now relied solely on private charity. Ninety-four per cent of charitable donations made by Pakistani individuals and business corporations went to the religious institutions. Though most donors did not support the politics of religious parties, they felt that Islamic education and the preservation of Islam were the most worthy choice for their donations. Many religious leaders who ran the Islamic seminaries had strong links in Arab countries that went back to the Afghan Jihad. For many it had become a 'status symbol' to receive funding from foreign sources.

Muslims in Britain had been one of the largest donors to the Pakistani Islamic institutions and Muslim militant groups, some of whom had been declared terrorists and outlawed by Pakistan's military government. UK-based charities were the main financiers for Islamic groups. Diversion of funds for educational and humanitarian projects to the Islamic militant groups had become a normal practice. 'It is difficult to separate finances for terror from those for charity,' said the ICG report. LeT and JeM, reportedly collected more than £5 million each year in mosques in Britain. Although both the groups were banned in Britain, the Kashmiri diaspora continued to make donations to them. While Islamabad had repeatedly downplayed the link between extremism and the madrasas, most religious schools continued to preach Jihad. After the failed attempts on Musharraf's life in December 2003, the administration launched raids on some extremist madrasas, but such half-hearted and piecemeal measures could hardly help improve the situation.

Pakistan's failure to curb extremism owed less to the difficulty of implementing reforms than to the administration's own unwillingness. Musharraf had promised to ban the use of mosques and madrasas for spreading religious and sectarian hatred. However, all those pledges remained largely rhetorical and seemed to have been made under international pressure. The sectarian groups continued to challenge the authority of the state in different ways. Pakistan's failure to strictly enforce laws against the preaching of religious hatred and reining in of the extremist madrasas had largely been responsible for the rise in sectarian-based violence.

The failure to deliver to any substantial degree on pledges to reform madrasas and contain the growth of jihadist networks had not only given rise to religious extremism in Pakistan, but also continued to present a threat to domestic, regional and international security. Several madrasas continued to provide recruits for Taliban insurgents in Afghanistan. Run by JUI, part of the coalition government in the western Balochistan province, the seminaries not only provided the Taliban with ideological training, but also extended material help. Pashtunabad, a congested slum district in the provincial capital, Quetta, had a large concentration of former Taliban activists. A stronghold of radical Islamic groups, it looked more like a Kandahar neighbourhood under the former Taliban regime, and several former Taliban leaders were believed to have taken refuge there. The main madrasa in the neighbourhood was run by Maulana Noor Mohammed, a MMA member of the National Assembly. He appeared convinced that the Taliban would re-establish their control over Afghanistan. 'They will ultimately triumph,' declared the 75-year-old cleric.

3

Religion, Politics and Terrorism in Pakistan

During the 1950s, if one were to attempt to predict which of the new Muslim states that emerged during the 20th century would pose a major threat to global peace and security, Pakistan would be very much at the bottom of the list. Pakistan was then widely regarded as a beacon of moderation: a highly tolerant secular state and a strong ally of the West in its conflict with the Soviet Union. Since the attacks on the United States on 11 September 2001, however, Pakistan has come to be regarded as the world's epicentre of terrorist activity committed in the name of Islam. Currently, the Pakistan state is waging a bitter war with terrorist groups many of whom are also actively supporting the Taliban in fighting the US and its allies in neighbouring Afghanistan. Pakistani nationals have been involved in terrorist attacks on India, Britain and the United States. In Pakistan itself, sectarian violence between extremists from the majority Sunnis perpetrated against the minority Shia sect has involved assassinations, attacks on religious processions and places of worship, and, most deadly of all, suicide bombings.

The major precondition for the emergence of terrorism during the 1980s has been the ongoing structural weaknesses of Pakistan. Ever since its formation in 1947, Pakistan has been ruled either by weak ineffectual civilian governments or military dictators both of whom have failed to address Pakistan's problems particularly relating to good governance and the maintenance of law and order. Weak governments, both civilian and military, have had a poor record in combating terrorism. Indeed, some politicians and elements within the armed forces have supported extremists for political advantage.

In addition, three specific major political developments provide an explanation for the terrorist phenomenon. The first is the long-standing bitter dispute between India and Pakistan over control of the Kashmir Valley that had been partitioned between India and Pakistan in 1947. Ever since, Pakistan has felt threatened by its much more powerful neighbor India and the countries have waged two major and one localized war over Kashmir. Pakistan governments – both civilian and military – have trained, financed and used terrorist groups to fight a proxy war in Indian–ruled Kashmir. This policy backfired after Pakistan was coerced by the United States into supporting the disastrous highly unpopular invasion of Afghanistan in October 2001 which is regarded throughout the Islamic world as an attack on Islam itself. As a consequence, many of the jihadi groups turned on the Pakistani government and security forces which previously had nurtured them.

The second major development was the military dictatorship of General Zia ul-Haq who ruthlessly governed Pakistan from 1977 to 1988. In part because of his religious zealotry but also to build his legitimacy and power, Zia attempted to Islamize Pakistan according to his own narrow interpretation of Sunni Islam. Under Zia the tolerance so long characteristic of Pakistani Islam began to break down. The most damaging consequence of Zia's Islamization policy was the outbreak of on-going sectarian violence between the majority Sunnis and the minority Shias, who had been threatened by Zia's attempts to impose Sunni law on the country. These sectarian terrorist organisations were the forerunners of many other terrorist groups that have plagued Pakistani society since the 1980s.

The final, and, in many ways, the most critical factor was the impact of the Soviet invasion of Afghanistan in 1979. The spontaneous uprising of the Afghans assumed the form of a holy war or jihad which was strongly supported by Pakistan. The

Pakistan military, particularly its intelligence service, the Inter-Services Intelligence (ISI), channeled lavish funds and weapons, supplied largely by the United States and Saudi Arabia, to the most extremist groups of the mujahedin or holy warriors who fought the Soviets. After the Soviets had left Afghanistan in 1989, the numerous well trained and well armed jihadists were recruited, with the tacit support of Pakistani governments, by the many terrorist groups active in Pakistan and in Indian-ruled Kashmir. In addition, Saudi Arabia used the Afghanistan jihad to promote its narrow Wahhabi ideology within Afghanistan and Pakistan itself. Wahhabism is implacably hostile both to Shias and to Sufism, the mystical more tolerant form of Islam that is widely practised in Pakistan. Many of the Sunni extremists engaged in anti-Shia and anti-Sufi acts of terrorism have drawn upon Wahhabi doctrines to justify violence whose roots lie in political, economic and social rivalries.

The historical analysis demonstrates clearly that Islam as a belief system played little or no role in the rise of terrorism in Pakistan. Although dubious interpretations of Islamic teachings, which have been rejected by mainstream Islamic scholars, have been used to justify terrorist actions, the history of terrorism in Pakistan refutes the belief held by many Western political leaders, the media and a great many Western academics that 'Islamic extremism' is one of the primary drivers of contemporary terrorism and that Islam is a prime security threat facing Western countries. Unfortunately, the mainstream Western media continues to report and explain acts of terrorism largely in terms of their roots in religious extremism without reference to the political and historical contexts. Researchers also need to challenge the assumption held by many Western politicians and the media that Muslims engaged in terrorist actions are irrational religious fanatics whose repression justifies the abuse of human rights through torture, extrajudicial killings and other violent forms of counter-terrorism. Finally, contrary to the popular view held in non-Muslim countries, the major victims of terrorism in Pakistan committed in the name of Islam have been other Muslims – not outsiders. The major struggle today is not between Islam and the West but rather within Islam itself between the majority of Muslims who desire to live at peace with their neighbors and the small but powerful minority who want to impose their extremist forms of Islam on their fellow Muslims and non-Muslims alike. More in-depth studies of Pakistan and other Islamic states are needed in order to understand the complex social, economic and political problems that have nurtured violence that has been committed in the name, if not the essential spirit, of Islam.

TOWARD A LOOSIAN THEORY OF RELIGION IN MODERNITY

If we look back over the century of modernity, we can re-read it as a Loosian battle where religion comes to be viewed as a form of ornament. Contemporary religious fundamentalism is another form of Loosian-like move against ornament, but it is an inverted move, whereby the modern unornamented world is seen as a form of unnecessary ornamentation. In response, modern religious fundamentalism often retreats to what Loos or a secular modern would see as a world of ornamentation, a costume of literalism which draws on pre-modern belief – but for very modern purposes:

O ye who believe! When ye meet a force, be firm, and call Allah in remembrance much (and often); That ye may prosper. God, who sent the book unto the prophet, who drives the clouds, and who defeated the enemy parties, defeat them and make us victorious over them. Our Lord! Give us good in this world and good in the Hereafter and save us from the torment of the Fire! [Koranic verse]. May God's peace and blessings be upon Prophet Muhammad and his household.

The New Age, seen from a secular modern Loosian viewpoint, can be understood as the return of unnecessary ornamentation. In a physical manner, buildings, lives and bodies became newly unnecessarily ornamented – all are costumed, tattooed, decorated. In a manner similar to modern religious fundamentalism, the interior *Raumplan* of spirituality became inverted over and against the white walls of modernity. Religion and secularity are now both seen as forms that the necessary ornamentation of postmodern spirituality and the New Age reacted against. Conversely, the return of conservative religious movements signals a reaction against such decoration. Viewing both the inverted interior spirituality of the New Age and the lingering late modern secularity as forms of unnecessary ornamentation, modern (and postmodern) religious conservatism attempts to both banish what is seen as unnecessary and, paradoxically, enforce a modernist-derived order of necessary ornamentation. This "soft modernism" can hold together both Peter Berger's desecularization and Steve Bruce's continued secularization theses. Both can view the other as forms of costume that limit the Loosian pursuit of the expression of "our time" – they are types of "bad form". Therefore, what sits at the heart of the modern condition (whether modern, postmodern, anti-modern or soft modern) is the question of the necessity or otherwise of ornament; and the continuing, debatable, contestable question of what exactly constitutes ornament when, as Loos demanded, we "think and feel in the spirit of our time".

THE GROWING RELIGIOUS FUNDAMENTALISM IN PAKISTAN

The religious fundamentalists in Pakistan are once again on the full swing. They are very much encouraged by the outcome of the general elections in Pakistan. In overall, they have got over 16% of the total votes caste in the elections. But in the national assembly, they have emerged the second largest parliamentary group leaving behind Pakistan Peoples Party. Thanks to the support of the conservative Muslim League Nawaz MLN that their nominee for the prime minister Fazal Rehman got 86 votes while PPP trailed behind with 71 votes. The pro military Muslim League Q group was able to fetch the needed 172 votes for the Prime Minister lot.

The upsurge in the fundamentalist support was witnessed on 19th November 2002 when over 70,000 turned up for the funeral of Aimal Kansi in Quetta Baluchistan. This was the largest ever funeral in the whole history of Baluchistan. Aimal, body was brought from US where was awarded the death sentence after found guilty of killing two CIA officers in 1993. Till his last breath, he was very much proud of what he has done to the American imperialism. He has become another hero of the fundamentalists after Assama Bin Laden.

Another sign of the growth in religious fundamentalism was seen on 24th November when activists of Lashkar Tayaba, the banned religious group in Pakistan took over for six hours two temples in Jammu district of Indian held Kashmir. The incident resulted killing of the two and 10 more in the struggle to re-hold the temples by the Indian forces. There have been more incidents like this during the week in Kashmir resulting over 20 deaths mainly of Indian army men. This is no incident. The leader of Lashkar Tayaba Hafiz Saeed was released last week in Pakistan. The Pakistan authorities would not accept at Lahore High Court only a month before that he is held up with them. ? Withdraw your writ petition if you want your husband to be released? Was the message of the intelligence agencies to the wife. Later the wife of Hafiz Saeed was forced to withdraw her write petition. Hafiz Saeed as brought to his hometown after being held for over a year and was house arrested. Lahore High Court declared the move as illegal. Since his release on 18th November, he has addressed many thousands in several cities of Punjab. At Faisalabad, the third largest city of Pakistan, he spoke to over 50,000 who came to greet him after his release. Many women threw their children in the air and begged him to take them for Jihad. ? Jihad can not be stopped by any mean,? he declared at the meeting.

Lashkar Tayaba was the main religious group promoted by the military intelligence of Pakistan during the nineties to carry on jihad in the Indian held Kashmir. Many youth were provided the military training at camps set up by the group in different parts of Pakistani held Kashmir. "Suicidal missions are the only way forward to further the message of Jihad" was the main philosophy of the group training. The 11th September 2001 changed the priorities of the military intelligence. The Lashkar Tayaba was asked to wind up the camps. The leader was kidnapped. The military intelligences thought that it would be all over by these actions. That is been proved all wrong. The ghost of religious fundamentalist propped up by the military intelligence is out of control and is in a process of changing its colour. From pro military group, it is fast becoming an anti military group in Pakistan.

In the eighties, the religious fanatics were very closely linked with American imperialism. In the nineties, they left them on their own. From the beginning this century, the fanatics have taken roots among the general consciousness of the masses in Pakistan as an anti imperialist force. ?It is war between Islam and American infidels,? says Samee-ul-Haq, one of the main leaders of MMA, the religious political alliance in Pakistan. He was also the main supporter of the Talban regime.

While in the nineties, the American imperialism has left them on their own but not the major part of the establishment in Pakistan. They wanted to use them against their traditional rival Indians. They had also the illusions that a stable regime in Afghanistan would give them access to the markets of the Central Asia. So the formation and the support for Talban were the main priorities. All that changed with 11th September. The crushing of Talban in Afghanistan by bombing of US imperialism has not curbed the spread of religious fundamentalism. It has spread in a different form in Pakistan at present. Leon Trotsky, the architecture of the Soviet revolution of 1917 in Russia, once quoted ?You can not crush the will of the masses to change the society?. The will of the most of the masses to change the society has not emerged, as was the case in the past, through the left forces in the region. Rather through the religious sentiment. The general elections in Pakistan held on 10th October gives some glimpse how they have emerged as a serious political force in Pakistan. The fundamentalist united in one main group called Mutehida Majlas Ammal MMA (United Action Forum) won the most seats in two provinces. They took considerable votes in all other constituencies. But the most alarming fact was their support in the two major cities, Lahore and Karachi. At Lahore, they won three national assembly seats out of 13 and in Karachi, a neck-to-neck fight against the MQM, the immigrant mass force. MMA got 5 out of 20 seats in Karachi but it was very closely defeated in all the other 15 seats. MQM fetched 12 in the end. The MMA anti US rhetoric, which played a seminal role in wooing voters elsewhere in the country, played important part in their victory. But their campaign in Karachi was also centered on the issues like health and education. Mayer belonging to MMA already rules the local government in Karachi. MMA captured 29 out of 35 National and 52 out of 99 provincial assembly seats in North West Frontier Province (NWFP).

In Baluchistan, it got 6 out of 13 National and 14 out of 51 provincial seat. In over all, MMA got nearly 3.2 millions votes. While the main bourgeoisie party MLQ got 7.3 millions. PPP fetched the most votes, nearly over 7.4 million votes. The total vote caste in Pakistan was over 28.9 millions. MMA got over 52 per cent of its seats in the low turnout areas. The fragmentation and disenchantment of the secular vote coupled with increased mobility and motivated election campaign by the MMA are definitely factors that cannot be ignored.

The conservative Muslim League, the main bourgeoisie party in Pakistan was split on the question of the support for military. A large part of it went to support the military rule while the rest under MLN supported the religious fundamentalist on the name of seat adjustment in many parts of Pakistan.

MLN was taking revenge from the military as their leader Nawaz Sharif was ousted from power in October 1999. Later he was forced to leave Pakistan and now reside in Saudi Arabia. In the process, the MMA got more votes and seats than the MLN.

MLN strategy made the fundamentalist stronger and is now no more close associates of the MLN. In fact MLN is fast becoming a tail end of the fanatics in Pakistan. MMA took more advantage of the lowering of the vote age from 21 to 18 than another political group. The Pakistan Talban from the Madrasas, the religious schools, over 70,000 of them in Pakistan, energetically worked for the successful campaign of the MMA. ? He who has the youth has the future,? Lenin said once. The majority of the youth is fed up with the system. "They are all corrupt", is the argument presented in most of the discussion among youth. ?Only Islamic revolution is the answer? you hear very often.

After the general election, the strategy of MMA was to give an impression to the masses of Pakistan that they are ready to shares the power but it has to be on their principal position. To attract and enlarge their support among the petty bourgeoisie, the MMA in words at least has become champions of the democracy and defendant of the 1973 constitutions.

The constitution, unanimously passed by parliament under Bhutto government, is a combination of capitalist democratic values and religious norms. The MMA also opposed the constitutional amendments by General Pervaiz Musharaf regime to give him more dictatorial powers as president. The Legal Framework Order (LFO) was announced on 21st August 2002, giving powers to president to sack the government anytime he likes and also powers for important postings in the establishment. This strategy has earned MMA some more respect and they are not seen as power hungry as was the impression of them in the past. The religious fanatics have supported most of the military regimes in Pakistan history. Only this time, they opted to remain in opposition in the center. They are more likely to form the provincial government in North West Frontier Province (NWFP) which is next to Afghanistan and could be part of the government in Baluchistan. They have not gone to share the government at the center because of their perspective to become a mass force at national level. ? Had Punjab been awoke like the other province, the Islamic revolution in Pakistan would have been complete in this elections? cried Qazi Hussain Ahmed, the main leader of the most organized Jamaat-i-Islami; JI is a decisive component of MMA. It is JI successful political strategy of forming political alliance of all the religious forces that has won the mass support for the MMA. ?They are never united and can never be united? was the main arguments of the some of the Left intellectuals during the past years. MMA has at least made these intellectuals think twice before they bring this argument against them.

The unity process of the religious forces started long before the 11th September realizing the political vacuum after the failure of the successive civilian regimes to solve any of the basic problems of the masses in Pakistan. The 10 years of successive failed regimes of PPP and MLN after the fall of the last military regime in 1988, has provided the opportunity to the religious forces to exploit the opportunity.

In 1993, the JI formed a Pakistan Islamic Front with some minor Islamic groups to contest the general elections. The PIF failed badly and fetched less than 3 per cent of the total votes. In 1995, Mutehida Jakjehti Council (United Solidarity Council) was formed mainly to address the question of sectarian killings. In 2000, almost 29 religious groups formed the Islamic Mutehida Inqilabi Mehaz IMAM (Islamic United Revolutionary Front. This was mainly to deal with the Western ideas spread by the NGOs in the NWFP and Baluchistan. Jamiat Ulemai Islam under Fazal Rehman played the main role in this group. In June 2001, MMA was founded at the initiative of Jamaat-i-Islami. After 11th September, over 40 different religious groups formed Pak Afghan Defense Counsel. The MMA all eyes are on Punjab, the most populated province with over 64% of the total inhabitants living in this rather prosperous area of Pakistan. Many villages in Punjab particularly in Southern Punjab have young martyrs. Those who have been killed Kashmir or Afghanistan. These ?sacrifices? are laying a strong foundation for the possible growth of the religious political influence on those areas where MMQ is yet to become a majority. MMA activists unlike the main bourgeoisie parties are not driven by careers or greed. They are from the middle and working class background committed for a change. Most of the elected members of MMA from NWFP are from poor background and are seen by many all the time on cycles. This is contrary to elected members of rich parties who are on land cruisers and Mitsubishi Pajeros. The class question is very much in the mind of many who have gone to support the MMA in the recent elections. In the absence of the any significant left force in Pakistan MMA have echoed the class sentiments mixed with religion.

Would the American imperialism tolerate the growing influence of religious fundamentalism in Pakistan? The Americans has so for relied on the military generals to do the dirty job. Musharaf has done it very happily. But the political situations are getting out of control. The formation of the MMA government in NWFP will bring new contradictions between the new government in he center with the provincial government. The under ground Talban will feel easier in surfacing in NWFP under a religious government. Already new social tensions have emerged in the area. Women rights, human rights advocated in the province are under attack. ?NGO, s in these fields must wind up their offices? is the hidden message by the fanatics. The Sunday regular weekly off day will be once again replaced by Friday by the new provincial government. ?Beard is a must,? the new young elected leaders of MMA are advocating for every Muslim. ?Women must obey the Islamic norms and must cover themselves?. It is Talbanisation of Pakistani society in a different form. It is not yet advocating an open Jihad like the Alqaida did. But it is in the oven.

So NWFP and Pakistan could be the next target of all the propaganda of the US imperialism after Iraq. Any attempt by the center to dissolve or suspend the provincial government at NWFP will result in more civil war like situation. In 1974, the united government of the nationalist and religious fundamentalist was dissolved by Bhutto under the pressure of Shah if Iran, a guerilla war started in Baluchistan. Many were killed and many went to Afghanistan in exile. Now nationalist have diminished to large extent for the time being in this election, as they were seen as pro imperialists force. Many of these nationalists supported the American bombing in the false hope that it will crush the religious threat at home as well.

More dark period is heading Pakistan unless new initiatives is been taken by the Left and progressive forces to stop the onslaught of the fanatics.

The handing over the recorded message of Asama Bin Laden in Islamabad to Algezeera tele network shows how things can develop in Pakistan. The possibility of the presence of Asama Bin Laden in Pakistan, the pro Talban provincial government in NWFP, the growing influence of religious fundamentalism in Punjab and Sind can force the newly elected pro Musharaf regime to take drastic actions against them. This in return will make the life of ordinary Pakistani more difficult. And it will make the ideas of religious fundamentalism more popular. Labour Party Pakistan had foreseen the recent growth of religious fundamentalism. It has declined to side with them on any issue. It has opposed the American bombing alongside with the condemnation of religious terrorism. It is adopting the policy to oppose the recently formed new civil pro Musharaf regime. The new civil regime is no change for the masses. It is the continuation of the Musharaf regime in civilian cloths. It will carry the IMF; World Bank dictated policies on the name of reform agenda. The religious fundamentalist will also oppose the reform agenda but only in words. Initially they are showing a very liberal face to the West. They have already said that privatization is a must. But under the pressure of the masses, they can make big noise against the economic exploitation of the people by the Multi nationals alongside with the social and political repressions. The hypocrisy of the fundamentalist can only be exposed with a united action of the trade unions, Left and progressive forces.

RETHINKING TERROR, RELIGION AND MODERNITY

To respond to the *religare* of terror in modernity, we could turn to the Loosian response to the roadside shrine: the confrontation with that which posits an alternative to secular modernity. Unfortunately, we tend to respond like the revolutionary and see it (the *religare* of terror) as an affront. Rather, we could view it for what is actually is, the survival of religion *as a provocation* to the modern world, seeking affirmation in and from the attempt to destroy it. An alternative for secular modernism is to remember what Nietzsche claimed caused the death of God: not the frontal attacks and dismissals, but rather, in the end, the turn of indifference. Thus, instead of the current ongoing exchange of affirmation in which both the fundamentalist terrorist and those who respond symbolically affirm each other, we could seek to adopt a position of indifference. This of course does not mean fundamentalist terror will fade away completely, but it could lead to its marginalization from the everyday, whereby terror is located as sectarian. Every response to terror actually affirms the destruction that takes place as being necessary for it and its claimants to be noticed.

Here we can look to what Brian Tamaki has done with a small (7000 strong) sectarian religious movement, Destiny Church, in New Zealand. Understanding the importance of the mass media to articulate (a media-derived) legitimacy – to be seen is to exist

– he moved into the public media, creating a deliberately provocative presence on both television and the internet , by opposing the proposed extension of civil unions to homosexuals and the reform of prostitution laws. His central message decries moral and spiritual decay, calling the nation back to a proposed theocracy of the kingdom, allied with a strongly protestant gospel of prosperity. What makes Tamaki important is his recognition that public appearance is, in a postmodern-inflected world of image and spectacle, *itself* an act of self-legitimacy. To appear on television, in a localized version of American televangelism, even if within the early-morning dead-zone of church-funded "infomercial" preaching, is to recognize that it is the *appearance* on television that creates the real for those uninitiated in post-structuralist semiotics. For those able to decode such action, his infomercial televangelism is a simulacra; but for those who do not decode, this becomes a form of "real presence". He "made real" his presence, in what was a carefully stage-managed "return to the real" – but as simulacra that was based – albeit vigorously denied – in good modernist, futurist fashion, on the hyper-real mythic history of Mussolini's act of legitimacy: his fascist march on Rome of 28 October 1922.

Tamaki's simulacrum of this occurred on 23 August 2004 with a rally of his Destiny Church followers down the main street of the capital, Wellington, culminating in a march on Parliament, accompanied by body-guards and lead by a crowd of predominantly Maori and Pacific-island men, in black t-shirts, waving their fists and chanting "enough is enough". This courting of public notice by partaking in what was a pseudo-event, a spectacle, was an act of public terror with its fascistic overtone and black-shirted associations of masculinity, power and the war-dance confrontation of a mass haka. It worked – the indifference of the general public and the media to Brian Tamaki lasted only as long as he and his cult were *not* a pseudo-event, were *not* a public spectacle, as long as they did *not* evoke a response of fear that was out of all proportion to the size of his organization.

In the months since his pseudo-spectacle he has become a form of alternative legitimate voice of religion in New Zealand –

the one that the media turn to because of the "terror" of his provocative stance. To counter the hyper-real terror of Bin-laden or Tamaki is actually to seek to control the reproduction of the hyper-real – the circulation and mass-media production of the image. Mass-media provides a hyper-real "*religare*" – a binding together, a communal presentation and affirmation as to the efficacy and indeed legitimacy not only of the circulation and presentation of the event, but of the event itself. Yet conversely, to seek to limit the spectacle is to enforce the control of image and truth that is sought by the terrorist.

In effect, terrorism occurs and is "justified" when the spectacle is reported and repeated. This is because it is in the *religare* of the mass media that terrorism really occurs. It frees the act of terror and intimidation from its physical location in the event and makes it national – and increasingly transnational. This means we now "believe" in terror because we respond to its representation: that is, to its image.

It has actually become a form of *religare* that binds us all together – "we believe in terror" – and in our belief we give it a form of efficacy and legitimacy. Yet is important that we remember that a *religare* binds different groups together in different ways. Therefore, if religion arises in a multiplicity of ways from *religare* (that which binds us together) then terrorism itself has become a cause of – and expression of – a new global religion that is basing itself on a theory of exchange and sacrifice to institute an alternative modernity.

Or rather, to institute alternative forms of modernity that challenge what is seen as the chaos occasioned not only by secular modernity but also the conversant multiplicity of chaos that arose out of postmodernism and its turn to the multiplicities of others and the pluralism of truth and identity. Terrorism is a hyper-real apocalyptic event that provides an alternative teleology. In fact, *after* the event we now live in terror of the "pseudo-event": not that which *has* occurred, but rather something that we believe *may* or *will* "occur". In many ways we are living in our own version of millennial apocalyptic cults, seeking an *eschaton* that will affirm that our hopes and fears are correct.

TERRORISM ACTS IN PAKISTAN

Numerous terrorist acts also took place in Pakistan some of them are as under:-

a. In Pakistan, sporadic acts of terrorism can be traced back from the assassination of Mr. Liaqat Ali Khan.

b. Indian sponsored "Mukhti Bahni" in East Pakistan can also be termed one of the organized terrorist movements resulting in creation of Bangladesh. Insurgency in Baluchistan was yet another event involving Pakistan Army to such an environment

c. Pakistan was subjected to foreign sponsored terrorism for its moral support to afghan Mujahedeen against Russian Intervention.

d. The activities of RAW in collaboration with other anti Pakistan elements/ agencies worked on Afghan refugees in particular to create harassment and lawlessness in various parts of the country.

e. Recently the assassination of the Benzair Bhutto is one of the brutal act of terrorism in Pakistan

Post 9/11 Environment

After 9/11 the direction of terrorism in the world changed its face some salient aspects are:-

a. The environment of 9/11 was a direct confrontation between America and the Forces against America/ America interests. Non state actors mainly Al Qaeda worked as a magnet for all those who were In search of an allying point/ base. This was future compound by direct onslaught of Americans forces in Afghanistan. Iraq and Afghanistan played major role in dragging Pakistan onto this quagmire. Interests of extra regional forces compounded the situation further. Subsequent event drew Pakistan into international lime light due to its geographical location bordering Afghanistan and Iran.

b. Since Taliban who were Pashto speaking residing mostly in southern part of Afghanistan adjacent to FATA, were the target of American forces, hence on Pakistan side of Pak Afghan border, Sympathies with them rose to the highest point among the locals. Afghan militants were welcomed and assisted by locals. However, international environment were against this nexus. American President remarked on the rubbles of World Trade Center "America today is on the bended knee in prayers for people whose lives were lost here.... The rest of the world hears you. And the people, who knocked these buildings down, will hear all of us soon". They declared Taliban responsible for the tragedy because Al Qaeda's main leadership in Afghanistan, which according to USA was organizing, planning and initiating anti American activities from the soil state ruled by Taliban.

c. Pakistan, due to its own compulsions, having recognized Taliban regime was justifying its stance at various international forums. However 9/11 surprised the whole world including Pakistan and this blatant act of terrorism could not be justified. Pakistan principally condemns terrorism in all its forum and manifestations. It was the need of the hour to work with international community to rid the world of this peril.

d. The government of Pakistan took a considered decision to support Global War against Terrorism, safeguarding own national interests. Revenging attack on World Trade Center, USA retaliated and because of its operation in Afghanistan (Tora Bora), Pakistan Army was deployed on the western border to seal it and prevent influx of militants into Pakistan. It was a golden opportunity to open "No Go areas" in FATA and bring it par with the rest of the country.

APPROACH TO THE WAR ON TERROR IN PAKISTAN

Although Pakistan has been a frontline state in the war on terror since the tragic events of September 11, 2001, there is no doubt that General Musharraf initially cast his lot with the United States mainly as a result of deep fears about what U.S. enmity might imply for Pakistan's long-standing rivalry with India, its efforts at economic revival, its nuclear weapons program, and its equities in the conflict over Kashmir.

Desirous of protecting Islamabad's interests in these areas and to avoid Pakistan becoming a target in the campaign against terrorism, Musharraf reluctantly cut loose Islamabad's ties with the Taliban— a force it had nurtured, trained, and equipped for almost a decade in its effort to secure control over Afghanistan— and stood aside as the U.S.-led coalition assisted its detested antagonist, the Northern Alliance, to rout its own clients and their al- Qaeda accomplices and seize power in Kabul.

Because the al- Qaeda elements in Afghanistan during the 1990s were never directly dependent on the Pakistani Inter-Services Intelligence Directorate (ISID) for their success (despite maintaining a significant liaison relationship), the ejection of their Arab, African, and Central Asian mercenaries was viewed with fewer misgivings than the flight of the Pashtun- dominated Taliban, who were tied to Pakistan directly in terms of both patronage and ethnicity.

Islamabad's ties to the Taliban were so strong and so important that throughout the initial phase of Operation Enduring Freedom, General Musharraf and his cohort implored the United States to desist from decisively destroying Mullah Muhammad Omar's regime in Afghanistan. When this objective could not be secured, Pakistani leaders argued against all coalition military operations that would result in ejecting the Taliban's foot soldiers from their traditional bases in the southeastern provinces of the country. When these entreaties were also disregarded by the United States and the comprehensive defeat of the Taliban appeared inevitable as a result of joint U.S. and Northern Alliance military operations, Islamabad responded by covertly exfiltrating its army and intelligence personnel seconded to the movement— along with some key Taliban operatives, if Indian intelligence sources are accurate— while permitting the defeated stragglers to cross over to safety across the frontier and into Pakistani territory.

Taliban forces and their al- Qaeda guests thus found their way across the highly porous Afghanistan- Pakistan border into the FATA. While Pakistani border patrols concentrated their efforts against the latter group, resulting in the seizure of numerous low-level al- Qaeda elements, these operations nonetheless were never rigorous or watertight enough and were, in any event, frustrated by other factors: the old tribal tradition of extending succor to strangers who ask for protection; the region's history of providing foot soldiers, first, for the anti- Soviet jihad and, later, for the war against the Northern Alliance in Afghanistan; the absence of a strong Pakistani state presence in this area; and the utterly hostile topography consisting of remote and difficult mountain terrain with poor lines of communication, all of which combined to bestow on the defeated remnants a substantial measure of sanctuary and assistance.

The U.S. inauguration of the "global war on terror" soon compelled General Musharraf to make good on his "principled" decision to join the U.S.-led coalition. This inevitably required Musharraf to confront the sources of terrorism that had developed internally in Pakistan, most of which ironically resulted from his own army's previous decisions to nurture radical Islamist organizations because of their utility to Islamabad's military campaigns in Kashmir and Afghanistan.

Four different terrorist groupings were implicated in this regard. The first were the domestic sectarian groups like the Sunni Sipah- e- Sahaba and its offshoot the Lashkar- e- Jhangvi and the Shia Tehrik- e- Jafria Pakistan and its offshoot the Sipah- e- Muhammad, which were engaged in violent bouts of bloodletting within the country. Although many of these groups had enjoyed the support of the Pakistani government, the military, and the intelligence services previously, their unexpected growth in power over time had become not only an embarrassment to their sponsors but also a serious challenge to domestic order.

As Christine Fair has summarized it, "The scale of sectarian violence in Pakistan is staggering, with hundreds of people killed or injured in such attacks each year." The New Delhi–based Institute for Conflict Management has documented sectarian violence alone as claiming close to 5,000 lives in Pakistan since 1989, with incidents involving everything from targeted killings of high-profile civilians, to bombings of mosques and drive- by shootings of innocents, to pitched gun battles in major population centers. In one incident, for example, sectarian hostility in the town of Parachinar in the Kurram Agency involved a five- day war, where small arms, mortars, rocket launchers, and antiaircraft missiles were all used in a convulsive spasm that claimed hundreds of lives and injured many more.

Confronted by such challenges to the writ of his state, Musharraf was only too happy to exploit the opportunities offered by the war on terror to crack down on these groups and suppress them once and for all. He did so, however, only selectively. Focusing the government's energies primarily on those Deobandi and Shia groups whose objectives were out of sync with the military's perception of the national interest, he targeted Sunni groups such as the Lashkar- e- Jhangvi, the Sipah- e- Sahaba Pakistan, the Harkat- ul- Mujahideen al- Alami, the Jundullah, and to a much lesser degree the Harkat- ul- Jihad- e- Islami, as well as Shia threats such as the Sipah- e- Muhammad, primarily because they were engaged in "anti- national" jihadi violence within Pakistan rather than in support of Islamabad's external ambitions vis-à- vis India and Afghanistan.

Using the entire panoply of coercive state capabilities, these entities were therefore put down with a heavy hand through arrests, targeted assassinations, and aggravated intergroup massacres. Although many of the tools used to defeat these perpetrators of sectarian violence were often unconstitutional, Musharraf shrewdly judged that the aggressive dismemberment of these groups would not evoke either domestic or international condemnation. He was right.

Using the opportunities therefore afforded by the global war on terror, the Pakistani security services systematically eliminated many sources of sectarian violence within two years of the campaign's initiation, even though they have been unable to conclusively eradicate the cancer of sectarian bloodshed within Pakistan itself. In part, this is due to the selectivity of Musharraf's antisectarian campaign. But the continuing fragmentation of these violent groups; their links to the wider networks of international terrorism now resident in Pakistan, various foreign sponsors abroad, and the flourishing madaris within the country; and the continuing utility of their gun- toting membership to different political parties and occasionally to governmental organs themselves imply that sectarian threats will be impossible to extinguish so long as "state policies of Islamisation and [the] marginalization of secular democratic forces" continue to persist in Pakistan.

The second set of groups, the terrorist outfits operating with Pakistan Army and ISID support against India in Kashmir, was treated in a remarkably different way compared with the anti-national sectarian militants inside Pakistan. These groups, such as the Lashkar- e- Toiba, the Jaish- e- Muhammad, and the Harkat-ul- Mujahideen, for example, were the long lances in the Pakistani campaign to wrest the disputed state of Jammu and Kashmir from India. Since the late 1980s, the Pakistani military has financed, trained, armed, and launched these cadres on their murderous missions into Kashmir and elsewhere inside the Indian union. Because the struggle for control over the disputed Himalayan state was fully under way by the time the global war on terror was inaugurated, these terrorist groups were more or less exempted from Musharraf's domestic campaign against violence and extremism.

This exclusion was justified both on the strategic rationale that Pakistan's participation in the war on terror was intended, among other things, to protect its freedom of action in Kashmir and on the repeated, though fraudulent, assertion that these groups, far from being terrorists, only personified the legitimate Kashmiri struggle for self- determination against India. In fact, of all the Pakistani- sponsored Deobandi terrorist groups operating against India in Kashmir and elsewhere, only one entity— the Hizbul Mujahideen— began life as an indigenous Kashmiri insurgent group; the others, including the most violent organizations such as the Lashkar- e- Toiba, the Jaish- e- Muhammad, and the Harkat-ul- Mujahideen, are all led, manned, and financed by native Pakistanis. This reality notwithstanding— and perhaps because of it— Islamabad continued to sustain the operations of these groups against India but, in an effort to maintain the consistency of its commitments to the global war on terror, now began to emphasize that its support took only the form of moral, and not material, encouragement.

This charade was rudely interrupted by the December 13, 2001, terrorist attack on India's parliament when, in response to New Delhi's subsequent military mobilization, Pakistan was compelled by U.S. diplomacy to initiate a series of measures to restrict the activities of its terrorist clients. The implementation of these actions, however, was at best halfhearted and inconsistent. Far from seeking to extirpate these terrorist groups permanently, Musharraf sought mainly to defang India's threats of military action and to alleviate Washington's fears of an inconvenient Indo-Pakistani war. His overarching objective consisted of protecting these terrorist assets to the extent possible because they represented national investments— a "strategic reserve"—in Islamabad's subconventional war against New Delhi. Consequently, to this day, Musharraf has not sought to eliminate the Deobandi terrorist groups operating against India in Kashmir and elsewhere; he has instead sought only to modulate their activities, depending on the extent of satisfaction he derives from the prevailing state of diplomatic relations with New Delhi and the progress secured in the ongoing Indo- Pakistani peace process.

Although the Pakistani- supported infiltration of terrorist groups into Kashmir— but not into the rest of India— appears to have abated in recent years, most observers conclude that this phenomenon is linked either to Musharraf's desire not to provide India with any excuses to abandon the generally fragile peace process or to domestic crises within Pakistan. In any event, it is agreed that Musharraf simply has not made the decisive decision to abandon or eliminate the terrorist groups operating against India in the manner witnessed, for example, in the case of the more virulent anti- national sectarian entities operating within Pakistan.

The third group relevant to the Pakistani decision to join the U.S.-led coalition against terrorism consisted of the Taliban, that is, the Pashtun remnants of the regime ejected from power in Kabul as a result of the initial success of Operation Enduring Freedom. After their defeat at the hands of the Northern Alliance, the Taliban cadres hastily returned to the regions whence they originated. Many in the rank and file withdrew to their villages in the southern Afghan provinces of Helmand, Kandahar, Oruzgan, and Zabol as well as along the border areas on the western side of the Durand Line separating Afghanistan from Pakistan, that is, in the eastern Afghan provinces of Paktika, Paktia, Khowst, Nangarhar, and Konar.

Given their significance as high- value targets, the core Taliban leadership— along with those Pakistani Pashtuns who had joined their movement— crossed over the Afghanistan-Pakistan border into the relative safety of the FATA. Because most of the Taliban's fighters originally mobilized by the Pakistani ISID were drawn from the Ghilzai confederation of Pashtuns, which dominates eastern and southeastern Afghanistan, and from the other Pashtun tribes inhabiting the FATA, their return to these ancestral lands was not surprising. In fact, all the evidence relating to the incidence of terrorist attacks since 2001 suggests strongly that the war- fighting cadres of the Taliban continue to remain bivouacked in these areas.

The exact location of the supreme leadership of the Taliban movement, however, cannot be established with any self- evident clarity. Irrespective of where the rahbari shura (leadership council) centered on Mullah Omar and his closest associates found shelter in the immediate aftermath of their defeat, Afghan military and civilian intelligence officials as well as NATO commanders today believe that this coterie eventually found refuge in Quetta, the largest city and capital of Pakistan's Baluchistan Province, from where they continue to operate to this day.

As Col. Chris Vernon, NATO's chief of staff for southern Afghanistan, declared forthrightly, "The thinking piece of the Taliban [operates] out of Quetta in Pakistan. It's the major headquarters— they use it to run a series of networks in Afghanistan." These networks, in turn, are judged to be directed by four subsidiary shuras based in Quetta, Miran Shah, Peshawar, and Karachi: the first three actually control or coordinate most of the ongoing terrorist operations occurring, respectively, along the southern, central, and northern "fronts" in Afghanistan, whereas the fourth is believed to connect the Taliban with the logistics, financial, and technical assistance conduits emanating from the wider Islamic world. The pattern of terrorist attacks occurring in Afghanistan from 2002 to 2007, again corroborates this judgment.

Because the Pakistani state was most intimately involved in the creation of the Taliban before their fall, Musharraf's antiterrorism campaign after September 11, 2001, deliberately avoided any concerted targeting of this group and, in particular, its senior leadership. No other explanation is consistent with the fact that, although Pakistani military, intelligence, and paramilitary forces apprehended scores of al- Qaeda operatives, including numerous key individuals in the al- Qaeda hierarchy, the senior Taliban leaders killed or captured in southern Afghanistan or in the FATA have numbered literally a handful in comparison. This asymmetry in seizures is all the more odd because, prior to Operation Enduring Freedom, Pakistani military and ISID liaison elements were deeply intertwined with all levels of the Taliban mand structure and its war fighters in the field. In contrast, the Pakistani intelligence relationship with al- Qaeda in Afghanistan was more tenuous, yet Pakistan's military forces were able to apprehend far more al- Qaeda cadres than Taliban operatives. These successes in regard to al- Qaeda have invariably been attributed by Pakistanis, including General Musharraf, to the fact that it was always easier to identify the ethnically alien al- Qaeda elements along the frontier in comparison with the Taliban who, being ethnically Pashtun, were able to disguise their identities by assimilating into the larger tribal population.

While this explanation is only partly true— non- native fighters have lived in and become amalgamated into the social structures of the Afghan- Pakistani frontier since at least the anti-Soviet jihad of the 1980s— it is also disingenuous because the Pakistani ISID was not only deeply involved in the recruitment, training, arming, and operations of Taliban fighters at multiple bureaucratic levels, but it also maintained an intense liaison relationship with the Ghilzai tribes whose population has been disproportionately represented in the Taliban. Since protecting these relationships was deemed to be especially critical for Pakistan's national security interests in the aftermath of the Northern Alliance victory in Kabul, the large number of Taliban foot soldiers who made their way into the FATA were largely ignored by Pakistani counterterrorism operations so long as they did not engage in any untoward activities that either called attention to their presence or magnified the troubles confronting the Pakistani state. All told, then, the Taliban network, just like the Pakistani- aided terrorist groups operating in Kashmir and elsewhere in India, was deliberately permitted to escape the wrath of General Musharraf's counterterrorism operations in the initial phase of the war on terror.

Such an approach, however, could not be extended to the fourth group, al-Qaeda, which had also taken up sanctuary in the FATA, particularly in South Waziristan initially. Although al- Qaeda continued to have sympathizers within the extreme fringes of Pakistani society even after the terrible events of September 11 were conclusively attributed to its operations, the Pakistani military establishment did not enjoy the luxury of slackening its campaign against this target because of the consequences for U.S.-Pakistani relations at a time when bilateral ties were just recovering after a decade of U.S. disfavor and when Washington had just embarked on a ferocious campaign against al- Qaeda worldwide. Most senior Pakistani military officers at the corps command level were also genuinely horrified by the destruction that al- Qaeda wreaked in New York and Washington and, fearing for their country's own future in the face of the monster now present in their midst, supported Musharraf's decision to engage and destroy this terrorist organization of global reach.

Pakistan's military, accordingly, began to prosecute the war against al- Qaeda with great vigor, if not always with finesse, through multiple instruments. These included providing the United States and its military with facilities and access for the prosecution of Operation Enduring Freedom in Afghanistan, and conducting various law enforcement and internal security operations (sometimes in cooperation with their U.S. counterparts) aimed at interdicting terrorist financing and apprehending and rendering terrorist targets for prosecution abroad. Most important, however, the Pakistani military initiated Operation Al Mizan, a large- scale effort that involved moving major military formations from the Army's XI Corps and elite Special Services Group (SSG) battalions into the FATA, an area where regular army units had not ordinarily been deployed for decades. These infantry forces joined the Frontier Corps regiments— the paramilitary formations usually located in the region— as a show of force in order to both reassert the strong state presence that historically was lacking and apprehend the al-Qaeda elements that had taken shelter within the area.

This military campaign, which took the form of a gigantic cordon- and- search operation, had several consequences. First, it resulted in the capture of numerous al- Qaeda and other extremist operatives— some 700 at last count— who have since been turned over to the United States. Because these individuals are mostly foreigners— non–South Asian arrivals living in what are essentially Pashtun lands— detecting their presence, while not easy because of the local support they receive from the natives for ideological reasons and sometimes simply out of greed or fear, was certainly easier.

Second, it forced some though by no means all senior al-Qaeda operatives— for example, Khalid Sheikh Muhammad and Ramzi Binalshibh— to leave the relatively secure FATA sanctuary and disperse further inward into Pakistan, where their insertion into less ideologically congenial surroundings and their need to rely on more complex means of communication increased their susceptibility to detection and arrest.

Third, the dramatic irruption of the Pakistani state into the FATA, through a significant military presence of the kind not seen in more than a century, resulted in making conditions sufficiently inhospitable for al- Qaeda such that its senior leadership and cadres were compelled to relocate under fire from South to North Waziristan and beyond, where they operate to this day. This forced displacement, which unfortunately remains at continuous risk of reversal, nonetheless had the beneficial effect of disrupting many planned terrorist operations, but the dispersal of the organization's leadership in the northern FATA, especially in the Bajaur Agency where the terrain is inhospitable, the population is violently pro-Taliban, and the presence of the Pakistan Army is thin, has inadvertently made the task of destroying the al- Qaeda core all the more difficult.

In any event, these outcomes suggest that although Pakistan began as a reluctant entrant into the global war on terrorism, it has since become an active participant in the struggle. More than 85,000 Pakistani troops remain garrisoned along the Afghanistan-Pakistan border— a deployment that predates the initiation of the global war on terror. A significant fraction of these forces, however, is engaged today in counterterrorism operations in the border areas, and more than 600 soldiers have already sacrificed their lives in this effort. Further, Islamabad itself has now become a victim of terrorism as a variety of groups, ranging from those previously nurtured and now discarded by the Pakistani state, such as the al-Alami faction of the Harkat- ul- Mujahideen, to more distant beneficiaries of past Pakistani policies, such as al-Qaeda, seek to wreak an orgy of revenge against institutions and individuals whom they had previously counted among their sponsors and friends.

That Pakistan has made significant contributions to defeating various terrorist groups is therefore undeniable, yet its larger campaign against terrorism has also been conspicuously selective and perhaps self- serving. While it has secured major gains in eradicating some domestic anti- national sectarian terrorist groups and has contributed disproportionately to the ongoing campaign against al- Qaeda, it has been much more reluctant to conclusively eliminate those terrorist entities operating against India in Kashmir and elsewhere and against Afghanistan both in the FATA and in transit back and forth to the southern and eastern Afghan provinces. Further, the protection of the terrorist infrastructure that supports these groups has produced undesirable blowback because the actors traditionally involved in perpetrating terrorism in Kashmir increasingly either coordinate with or directly assist the Taliban and al- Qaeda in operations against not only Afghanistan but also the United States and even Pakistan itself.

Clearly, strategic and geopolitical calculations play an important part in accounting for this segmented Pakistani response. Islamabad, for example, has long viewed the terrorist groups operating in Kashmir and now in other Indian states as useful instruments for executing its policy of "strategic diversion" against

New Delhi. For this reason, Pakistan has been reluctant to target and eliminate these groups conclusively, preferring instead to alternately tighten and loosen control over their operations depending on how much satisfaction it receives from India at any given moment.

The decision to avoid targeting the Taliban was born of similar calculations. Initially, it was owed simply to the inclinations of senior Pakistani military commanders who were just not prepared to add insult to injury by physically eliminating the very forces they had long invested in, especially because they had now suffered the ignominy of having to consent to their client's defeat. Over time, however, the reasons for protecting the Taliban only grew stronger: India's growing prominence in Afghan reconstruction, its increased influence and presence in Afghanistan more generally, the weakening of the Hamid Karzai government in Kabul, the progressive souring of Pakistani- Afghan relations (including those between Karzai and Musharraf personally), and the disquiet about a possible U.S. exit from Afghanistan (a prospect inferred from the mid-2005 announcement that the United States would divest full command of Afghan combat operations to NATO) once again increased Pakistan's paranoia about the prospect of a hostile western frontier. It was exactly the desire to avert this outcome that led to the initial Pakistani decision to invest in sustaining the Taliban. And with fear of the wheel turning full circle gaining strength in Islamabad since at least 2005, the temptation to hedge against potentially unfavorable outcomes in Kabul— by protecting the Taliban as some sort of a "force- in- being"—only appeared more and more attractive and reasonable to Pakistan.

Although Pakistan's discriminative approach to fighting terrorism was shaped and implemented by General Musharraf in his dual capacity as president and previously chief of army staff, it would be erroneous to conclude that this prevailing strategy is owed simply to the whim of one man. This is particularly relevant today when Musharraf's hold on power has become progressively weaker and the future of his political status and effectiveness increasingly clouded. Rather, Musharraf's decisions in regard to counterterrorism strategy since 2001, although publicly perceived as personal dicta, invariably reflected the consensus among the corps commanders of the Pakistan Army and, hence, represent the preferences of Pakistan's military- dominated state. In other words, even if Musharraf were to suddenly exit the Pakistani political scene at some point, Islamabad's currently disconsonant counterterrorism strategy would still survive so long as the men on horseback continue to be the principal guardians of national security policy making in Islamabad. Because it is unreasonable to expect that the uniformed military will give up its privileges in this regard anytime soon— even if a civilian regime were to return to the helm in the future— the internally segmented counterterrorism policy currently pursued by Pakistan will likely persist for some time to come.

Even if it could be imagined that a civilian dispensation could wrest some control of Pakistan's national security policy from the military, it is not at all certain that the current strategic direction would change dramatically: a civilian regime would probably have greater incentives to combat all sectarian terrorist groups more evenhandedly, but that too is uncertain. After all, both the Pakistan People's Party led by the late Benazir Bhutto and the Pakistan Muslim League led by Nawaz Sharif have had problematic Islamist political allies in the past and, depending on the political exigencies of the moment, could harbor incentives to give even sectarian or otherwise radical entities a breather from prosecution, although that would likely be justified as only a temporary expedient. Both civilian parties historically also permitted the Pakistani military and intelligence services to aid, abet, and arm the terrorist groups operating in Kashmir and elsewhere in India, sometimes because they were simply powerless to prevent it but at other times with their full knowledge and consent. It also ought not to be forgotten that even a radically atavistic Islamist group such as the Taliban was raised, promoted, and unleashed by the civilian government of the late Benazir Bhutto (during her second term in office from 1993 to 1996) with the full collaboration of the Pakistani military and intelligence services— and that the Taliban continued to receive complete moral and material support under her civilian successor, the then prime minister, Nawaz Sharif.

Both the principal civilian political alternatives in Pakistan would likely continue to prosecute the current antiterrorist operations against al- Qaeda because there seems to be a fragile consensus among Pakistani political elites that this group remains a grave threat to both their country and the international community. This fact, however, only underscores the continuity that is likely to persist in Pakistan's approach to counterterrorism even if a civilian government were to ascend to power in Islamabad. Although there are likely to be differences in style, nuance, and emphasis, the weaknesses of Pakistan's moderate political parties, Islamabad's enduring interests vis- à- vis Afghanistan and India, and the likely inability of any civilian government to exercise comprehensive control over the Pakistani military and intelligence services all combine to suggest that dramatic changes in attitude and performance toward the Taliban and the terrorist groups operating on Indian soil may not be forthcoming. And, although sectarian groups within Pakistan may be pursued more uniformly and hopefully just as resolutely as the war against al- Qaeda, the net deviation from Musharraf's currently segmented antiterrorism policies may be either too subtle or too insignificant to really matter.

Ironically, the Bush administration itself bears some responsibility for reinforcing Musharraf's original instincts and entrenching what has now become the enduring Pakistani calculus. Although President Bush affirmed in the aftermath of the September 11 attacks that his war on terrorism would be total and that states supporting terrorist groups would be required to divest themselves of these entanglements decisively or face America's wrath, his own government never implemented his stirring vision in regard to Pakistan. Rather, during the Indo- Pakistani crisis of 2001–2002—a key moment of truth for Pakistan and its future course in the war on terror— successive U.S. intermediaries visiting the subcontinent pursued an approach that only permitted Islamabad to conclude that the war on terrorism was in fact eminently "divisible." By not pressing Pakistan to relinquish all its terrorist clients once and for all during that crisis— as Washington had previously compelled Islamabad to forsake the Taliban on September 13, 2001[36]—the United States lost a momentous opportunity to help Pakistan rid itself of its long addiction to terror. Instead, the administration's diplomacy, by declining to hold Musharraf accountable for breaching his serial promises to end Pakistani support for terrorism, enabled Islamabad to infer that so long as operatives belonging to "terrorist groups of global reach"—meaning al- Qaeda— were being regularly apprehended by Pakistan, the ISID's links to, and protection of, other regional terrorist organizations would not become a critical liability in U.S.-Pakistan relations.

The liberties thus afforded Pakistan in regard to sustaining its ties with local Kashmiri terrorist groups during the initial phase of the global war on terror consequently reinforced Pakistan's inclination to treat the Taliban remnants similarly. This blunder had few consequences as long as the Taliban movement was in remission, but it has proved to be a most costly lapse on the part of the United States because the sanctuary afforded by Pakistan to the Taliban— and especially its leadership— since 2002 has only permitted the group to rejuvenate and, once again, to begin offensive operations in Afghanistan that, in effect, threaten to undo the gains secured by the early victories in Operation Enduring Freedom.

The U.S. neglect of the early Pakistani decision to ignore the Taliban as a target of counterterrorism operations can be explained only by the administration's single- minded concentration on the war with al- Qaeda. This obsession was no doubt justified at the time, but its inadvertent consequences have now come back to haunt the United States, NATO, Afghanistan, and the ongoing military operations associated with Operation Enduring Freedom more generally. By failing to recognize that the early immunity provided to the Taliban would eventually complicate the effort to defeat al- Qaeda— if for no other reason than that these two groups remain geographically commingled and because Taliban endurance in southern and eastern Afghanistan and in the FATA is an essential precondition for al- Qaeda's survival— the administration lost an opportunity to consolidate its political and military gains in Afghanistan while simultaneously compelling Pakistan to hasten its march away from extremism.

The Bush administration has now begun to press Musharraf to actively interdict the Taliban — an issue that did not become the subject of high- level U.S. demarches before 2005–2006—but it is not certain that, even if responsive Pakistani counterterrorism actions were to be mounted today, they would be as effective as they could have been had they been pursued in the administration's first term. This is because Pakistan's own current intelligence capabilities with respect to the Taliban are probably not as strong as they were when Mullah Omar and his associates were first ejected from Kabul.

Although it is certain that Pakistani information about the Taliban and their leadership is still better than that possessed by other intelligence agencies, including those of the United States, the probable atrophy of Islamabad's connections during the past several years of the war on terror, the strong and growing antagonism within Pakistan toward Musharraf's counterterrorism policies in the FATA, and the increasing opposition from Pakistan's fundamentalist political parties and their social bases of support toward Musharraf's domestic and foreign policies all viciously interact to increase the risk that belated Pakistani actions against the Taliban, including its leadership, may end up being far less successful than they otherwise might have been if executed a few years earlier. And that, in turn, implies not only that the challenges of defeating the Taliban are from a historical perspective rooted in fateful U.S. decisions to treat the Kashmiri terrorists differently when the administration should have done otherwise, but also that Washington ignored the Taliban until it was too late.

RELIGION, TERROR AND SACRIFICE

To disenchant terrorist discourse also means, in a multi-religious and multicultural society, the necessity of disenchanting the state and public rhetoric. The turn to talk of religion and spirituality, that talk of re-enchantment and desecularization, not only serves to act as public space for religious diversity to state their claims of communal legitimacy, it also provides a public space for the religion of terror and terror discourse. To disenchant is not to dismiss the various religious claims or affiliations, but to effectively seek to secularize them into the realm of privatism. Yet in order to do this we need to be also aware of the claims of the sacred, especially in claims of sacrifice and transgression that *exist still* within our society – and which are repositioned into the public sphere by acts of terror.

Georges Bataille offers a provocative take on the challenges of sacrifice and transgression, in which the sacred unleashes itself in acts of passion which are contrary to reason. He notes the links of horror, terror and the sacred and how, in the contemporary world, with the reduction to symbolic passion in our religion we have attempted to domesticate our fascination with death and destruction that sits at the heart of religion. This is the basis of the *religare* of terror – our fascination with death as *sign and symbol* of the sacred. Therefore the challenge of terror is the return of the sacred as transgressive in a world seeking to limit and contain it, to reduce it. The problem is that we fail to see acts of terror as acts of exaltation and intoxication in the sacred, failing to acknowledge Bataille's claim for the transgressive eroticism of terror:

> The inner experience of eroticism demands from the subject a sensitiveness to the anguish at the heart of the taboos no less great than the desire which leads him to infringe it. This is religious sensibility, and it always links desire closely with terror, intense pleasure and anguish.

This is why terror has become the new global religion. It reflects and provides the religious sensibility in the contemporary world – it transgresses the space given to religion in the postmodern turn and rejects both the restraints of controlled plurality and the turn away from plurality in the turn back to a new modernity. Today, terror is a religion that acts as transgression and taboo to *both* modernity and postmodernity. In a sense, following the Nietzschean nihilism of *Beyond Good and Evil* we now exist in a world of taboo and transgression, a world of sacred violence. As Bataille notes: "the transgression does not deny the taboo but transcends and completes it". In this we need to now view the transgression of terror as that *which transcends and completes* both taboos – those of death and of religion/sacred in public space –

in the modern world. As "the taboo is there to be violated" and is "at the very least...the threshold beyond which murder is possible", our taboos on public death and public religion are in fact those which paradoxically issue a form of demand *for* the transgression of terror – and the terror of transgression. In effect, notes Bataille, for our profane world to exist we require the complementary acts of transgression that exceed its limits but do not destroy it: "the profane world is the world of taboos. The sacred world depends on limited acts of transgression".

This means that acts of terror are acts of transgression for the expression of the reality of the sacred world. In other worlds, acts of terror are a form of sacrifice. What the act of sacrifice does is not a killing but rather a relinquishing and a giving. What is sacrificed is what is useful – it "restores a lost value by relinquishment of that value". As bin Laden would have it:

When you talk about the invasion of New York and Washington, you talk about the men who changed the face of history and went against the traitors....These great men have consolidated faith in the hearts of believers and undermined the plans of the crusaders and their agents in the region. Terrorism against America deserves to be praised because it was a response to injustice, aimed at forcing America to stop its support for Israel, which kills our people.

The acts of terror are, from a religious viewpoint, acts of sacrifice: they give up what is useful – the life of the terrorist, the life of the believer, the sacrifice of people in the profane world – in a manner of transgressive action that seeks to transcend the taboo on violence, death and the sacred. As Bataille notes: "The sacrificer declares ...I call you back to the *intimacy* of the divine world, of the profound immanence of all that is...".

The spectacle of terror is therefore on one level the intimacy of sacrifice in the intimacy of our daily lives, in the intimacy of our living rooms, in the intimacy of our public and private spaces. It is on one level, as Bataille states of sacrifice, "the communication of anguish". So what is this anguish? Perhaps it is as Slavoj Zizek notes, the cry of anguish of sacrifice, of terror, of violence. Furthermore, that our transgressive avidity for these is our passion for the "Real" – that which he notes Alain Badiou as claiming is "the key feature of the twentieth century". This passion for the Real is what sits at the heart of Loos' call for the overthrow of unnecessary ornamentation; this passion for the Real sits at the heart of the Futurist worship of the cleansing effect of technology, war and death; this passion for the Real is what lies in modernity's rejection of transcendence – and in Postmodernity's rejection of modernity's secularity. In effect, the dualistic battle in modernity between what is seen as order and what is seen as chaotic *is* this battle over what is Real and where the Real is located. Violence, taboo, transgression and sacrifice are those acts that serve as both statements of the Real – and the rejection of what is perceived to be non-Real. Acts of terror, made possible by the space given in postmodernity for the articulation of varieties of transcendent "Real", are an act of the rejection of these possibilities in a challenge of what is seen as the Real. Yet in their symbolic intention, they participate in the postmodern spectacle as an attempt to evangelize by effect. The passion for the Real and the attempt to represent it are actually transgressive to modern world where we attempt to keep the Real controllable by not confronting it. The response to the rise of transcendence as the location of the Real was not to confront it but rather to seek to splinter it by postmodern tolerance. Yet all this did was to give consent to those who sought to destroy even the possibilities of competing Reals.

In effect, contemporary terrorism is the Real of modernity (a battle beyond good and evil, of order and chaos) confronting itself with the non-reality of terror and spectacle that act as transgressive to that which we seek to hold as Real. The effect is not concerned with the reality of the chaotic act, but rather with the chaos that is the response to the reality of the act. In effect we say "we cannot believe this act has occurred" and this stating of our inability to believe in the Real is the chaos that the act of terror seeks. We then search to ascribe a meaning to the event that may mean *we claim to see the reason behind the act*, the "cry of anguish" that caused this act. To ascribe meaning to the act is to order it, in effect to attempt to "make it real" – and in making it Real paradoxically giving a form of inverted value and meaning to the actions and beliefs of those who undertook it.

Yet often what happens in response is the turn away from the liberal tolerance of dissenting beliefs that (perhaps) marks off a Western sense of the Real: a form of order that exists by ordering chaotic elements within pluralism. Yet the act of terror is a rejection of Western liberal pluralism, a rejection of the type of Western order that secularizes its taboos and transgressions.

CONFLICTS WITH THE OTHER SUNNI MILITANT GROUPS

The first reports of a split and even armed clashes between AQI/MSC and other insurgent Sunni groups date back to 2005. In the summer of 2006, local Sunni tribes and insurgent groups, including the prominent Islamist-nationalist group Islamic Army in Iraq (IAI), began to speak of their dissatisfaction with al-Qaeda and its tactics, and openly criticized the foreign fighters for their deliberate targeting of civilians. In September 2006, thirty Anbar tribes formed their own local alliance called the Anbar Salvation Council (ASC), directed specifically at countering al-Qaeda-allied ("terrorist") forces in the province, openly siding with the government and the U.S. troops.

By the beginning of 2007, Sunni tribes and nationalist insurgents had begun battling with their former allies in AQI in order to retake control of their communities. In early 2007, forces allied to al-Qaeda in Iraq committed a series of attacks against Sunnis critical of the group, including the February 2007 attack in which scores of people were killed when a truck bomb exploded near a mosque in Fallujah. Al-Qaeda also supposedly played a vital role in the assassination of the leader of the Anbar-based insurgent group 1920 Revolution Brigade (military wing of the Islamic Resistance Movement). In April 2007, the IAI spokesman accused the ISI of killing at least 30 members of the Islamic Army, as well as members of the Jamaat Ansar al-Sunna and Mujahideen Army insurgent groups, and called on Osama bin Laden to personally intervene to rein in al-Qaeda in Iraq. The following month, the government stated that AQI leader al-Masri was killed by ASC fighters. Four days later, AQI released an audio tape in which a man claiming to be al-Masri warned Sunnis not to take part in the political process (later in May the U.S. forces announced the release of dozens of Iraqis who were tortured by AQI as a part of the group's intimidation campaign), but also said that reports of internal fighting between Sunni militia groups were "lies and fabrications".

By June 2007, the growing hostility between foreign-influenced religious extremists and Sunni nationalists led to open gun battles between the groups in Baghdad. The Islamic Army, however, soon reached a ceasefire agreement with AQI (yet still refused to sign on to the ISI). There were also reports that Hamas of Iraq insurgents were involved in assisting U.S. troops in their Diyala Governorate operations against al-Qaeda in August 2007. In September 2007, AQI claimed responsibility for the assassination of three people including Sunni sheikh Adbul-Sattar Abu Risha (leader of the Anbar "Awakening council"). That same month, a suicide attack on a mosque in the city of Baqubah killed 28 people, including members of Hamas of Iraq and the 1920 Revolution Brigade, during a meeting at the mosque between tribal, police and guerilla leaders. Meanwhile, the U.S. military began arming moderate insurgent factions on the promise to fight al-Qaeda in Iraq instead of the Americans.

By December 2007, the strength of the "Awakening" movement irregulars (also called "Concerned Local Citizens" and "Sons of Iraq") was estimated at some 65,000-80,000 fighters. Many of them were former insurgents (including even alienated former AQI supporters), now being armed and paid by the Americans specifically to combat al-Qaeda's presence in Iraq. As of July 2007, this highly controversial strategy proved so far to be effective in helping to secure the Sunni districts of Baghdad and the other hotspots of central Iraq and route out al-Qaeda-aligned militants.

Al-Qaeda, an international terrorist network led by Osama bin Laden, remains "the most serious terrorist threat" to the United States according to the July 2007 National Intelligence Estimate (NIE). The report assessed that the organization was regrouping and regaining strength in Pakistan's tribal areas along the border with Afghanistan. The group is wanted by the United States for its September 11, 2001, attacks on the World Trade Center and the Pentagon, as well as a host of lesser attacks. To escape the post-9/11 U.S.-led war in Afghanistan, al-Qaeda's central leadership is believed to have fled eastward into Pakistan, securing a safe haven in loosely governed areas there. Director of National Intelligence J. Michael McConnell told the Senate Armed Services Committee in his February 2008 annual threat assessment report that al-Qaeda's "central leadership based in the border area of Pakistan is its most dangerous component."

Al-Qaeda is an international terrorist network led by Osama bin Laden. It seeks to rid Muslim countries of what it sees as the profane influence of the West and replace their governments with fundamentalist Islamic regimes. After al-Qaeda's September 11, 2001, attacks on America, the United States launched a war in Afghanistan to destroy al-Qaeda's bases there and overthrow the Taliban, the country's Muslim fundamentalist rulers who harbored bin Laden and his followers. "Al-Qaeda" is Arabic for "The Base."

What are Al-Qaeda's Origins?

Al-Qaeda grew out of the Services Office, a clearinghouse for the international Muslim brigade opposed to the 1979 Soviet invasion of Afghanistan. In the 1980s, the Services Office—run by bin Laden and the Palestinian religious scholar Abdullah Azzam—recruited, trained, and financed thousands of foreign mujahadeen, or holy warriors, from more than fifty countries. Bin Laden wanted these fighters to continue the "holy war" beyond Afghanistan. He formed al-Qaeda around 1988.

4

Motivations and Islamic Terrorism

MOTIVATION: A CONNECTION UNEXPLORED

The idea for this project grew out of the observation that the relationship between Palestinian Islamism and transnational jihadism remains understudied despite figuring prominently in informal discussions about the causes of Islamist terrorism. In the years after 9/11 we both found that the issue of "al-Qaida and Palestine" regularly came up at dinner conversations or in question-and-answer sessions after public talks about jihadism. The past decade has also seen a substantial number of opinion pieces staking out various claims about the Palestine-al-Qaida connection. The issue clearly has important policy implications, both for counterterrorism and for third countries' approaches to the Israeli-Palestinian conflict.

Yet, academics have largely shied away from exploring the Palestineal-Qaida relationship systematically. A review of the literature reveals no books and only a few peer-reviewed articles that tackle the issue in depth. Of these, almost all pertain to a limited subset of descriptive topics, especially the recent bickering between Hams and al-Qaida and the fighting between Hams and Salafa grouplets in Gaza. The larger causal question of whether and how the Palestinian-Israeli conflict may have fuelled transnational jihadism has yet to be addressed head-on. Moreover, an invisible fence has long separated the academic subfields of

"Palestine studies" and "Jihad studies". With a few exceptions, Middle East specialists who study al-Qaida and its affiliates have tended not to study Hamas or Palestinian Islamic Jihad, and vice versa. Each of the two subfields has made important advances in recent decades, but they have mostly not overlapped.

One reason why the intersection remains understudied seems to be its politicization. Issues such as the Hamas-al-Qaida connection or the Palestine factor in Jihad recruitment are sensitive because they can potentially affect the moral standing of the main parties to the conflict. Naturally, Palestinian activists do not want to be associated with the perpetrators of 9/11 any more than Israelis want to be blamed for the rise of global jihadism. As a result, pro-Palestinian observers—who happen to be strongly represented in the academic Middle East Studies community in the West—have tended to view inquiries into al-Qaida connections with scepticism because they might be used by Israel to smear the entire Palestinian resistance.

Conversely, pro-Israeli commentators have been quick to counter suggestions that al-Qaida might be genuinely motivated by Palestine, presumably because it could lead Western governments to pressure Israel for political concessions or tactical restraint in the latter's conflict with the Palestinians. In other words, this is a thorny topic and a risky specialization, especially for untenured academics.

Another reason why the subject has not been widely studied is that it is really quite complex. The "relationship between the Palestinian issue and the al-Qaida phenomenon" is a conceptually vague formulation that encapsulates a broad range of different research questions, each of which requires separate treatment. One way to start disaggregating the notion of "relationship" is to think of ideal-type mechanisms by which events in the Palestinian theatre might affect the occurrence of transnational Islamist violence. We see at least three such ideal types of mechanisms: "organizational", "motivational", and "historical".

In the first, the Palestinian conflict affects transnational jihadism through organizational links between local and international organizations. In the second, events in Palestine create solidarity-based grievances in non-Palestinians that inspire them to take up arms. In the third, the conflict or its by-products, affected the early development of transnational jihadism at critical junctures in its history. This leads to three somewhat more specific questions: 1) What is the organizational relationship between Palestine-focused and transnational militant Islamists? 2) To what extent does the Palestinian conflict motivate transnational jihadists? And 3) what has been the effect of the Palestinian-Israeli conflict on the historical evolution of transnational Jihad networks? This is but one of several possible ways to parse the problem, but the general point is that we are dealing with a messy set of distinct questions, not a single one.

Moreover, each of these inquiries requires good data, most of which have been inaccessible in open sources until recently. To study group connections, for example, we need information about the inner workings of clandestine organizations, which is by definition hard to acquire. To analyse motivations of al-Qaida recruits we need detailed biographical data on a decent sample of non-leaders as well as a relevant control group, which is also very difficult to collect. Tracing the historical impact of the Israeli-Palestinian conflict on transnational jihadism may require primary sources from decades past that may not be available on the Internet, only through interviews and archival work. Given these obstacles it is no wonder that some of these questions have been left unanswered.

It is worth recalling that these challenges are not specific to the study of militant Islamism, and that transnational dimensions of sub-state armed conflict remain under-researched in the social sciences more generally. It is arguably only in the past decade that scholars of civil war and insurgency have begun exploring the issue in depth. Social movement scholars and some international relations specialists began studying transnationalism earlier, in the 1990s, but their empirical focus was largely on non-violent protest movements in the West. In fact, the recent upsurge in transnationalism studies has also yielded new insights into the global connections of the leftist Palestinian resistance of the 1960s and 1970s. In light of this, we should perhaps not expect to have all the answers to the questions about Palestine and transnational jihadism already, but it is time to start working on them.

What We Know

So far, the literature that does exist on the Palestine-al-Qaida connection has mostly focused on the first two problem sets (connections and motivational effects). Some preliminary answers have emerged. Studies of the Hamas-al-Qaida relationship suggest that organizational links have been very limited, and that the ideological relationship is one of competition and hostility. A rare contact point was the ideologue Abdallh Azzm, who was in touch with Hamas from

Pakistan and remains popular in Palestine, but the interaction occurred back in the 1980s, and Azzm (d. 1989) never advocated international terrorism the way al-Qaida does today. Throughout the 1990s and 2000s Hamas-al-Qaida interactions were negligible, and in recent years, the rise of Salafa groups in Gaza has brought the tension between Hamas's pragmatic Muslim Brotherhood ideology and the intransigent Salafism of the transnationalists into very sharp relief.

However, Palestinian militants and transnational jihads are not in two different worlds. They have kept a close eye on, and learned from, one another over the years. Al-Qaida, for instance, adopted some of Hamas's tactics—notably suicide bombings and the practice of recording martyrdom videos—after observing them from afar in the 1990s. Mutual sympathies and respect also exist; for example, many Hamas supporters are fiercely anti-American and have expressed respect for Usma bin Ldin, although this has not translated into military operations against Western targets. It is worth noting here that reliable polls long showed levels of Palestinian popular support for Usma bin Ldin to be among the highest in the Muslim world. In 2003 no less than 72 percent of Palestinians expressed "some" or "a lot of" confidence in the al-Qaida leader. So far it is only among the relatively small—but growing—Jihad-Salafi community in Gaza that we see explicit attempts to associate organizationally with al-Qaida and a willingness to attack Western targets in the territories. However, these groups have yet to be declared formally a part of the al-Qaida franchise by the latter's leaders.

Regarding Palestine as a motivation for al-Qaida, we know that the cause features prominently in the group's ideological statements. Top leaders Usma bin Ldin and Ayman al-'awhir have both spoken regularly and extensively about Palestine since at least the late 1980s. The claim that bin Ldin only invoked Palestine after 9/11 when it was opportune to do so is patently false. As one of us (Hegghammer) noted in 2007:

A search for the word Palestine in a compilation of al-Qaida texts between 1990 and 2002 that I made for the Norwegian Defence Research Establishment (FFI), produces no less than 158 hits. Most al-Qaida recruitment videos, including the first such production from early 2001, include images from Palestine. In short, Palestine is all over al-Qaida's propaganda and has been so for over a decade. Usma bin Ldin remained substantially and consistently higher in Palestine than in the six other Muslim countries polled (Egypt, Jordan Lebanon, Turkey, Pakistan and Indonesia).

Similarly, Matthew Levitt of the Washington Institute for Near East Policy noted: Palestine has featured prominently in al-Qaeda's statements and propaganda from the early outset of the group's founding. In fact, nearly every public statement made by Usama bin Ladin since 1990 has mentioned the Palestinian cause, often represented through references to the al-Aqsa Mosque in Jerusalem that strike both religious and political chords among Muslims and Arabs worldwide.

The list of quotes by al-Qaida leaders and Jihad ideologues on Palestine is too long to include here, so we shall content ourselves with a few key observations. One is that al-Qaida's arguably most important ideological statement, the "Declaration of the World Islamic Front for Jihad against the Jews and the Crusaders" (February 1998), lists Palestine as number three on a list of reasons why Jihad against America is justified (after the US military presence in Saudi Arabia and the sanctions regime against Iraq).

Another is that al-Qaida's favoured term for its enemy— "*the Jews* [our emphasis] and the Crusaders" (and variants thereof)—

implicates Israel. Yet another observation is that the mastermind of 9/11, Khalid Sheikh Mohammed, cited American support for Israel as his principal motivation for undertaking the attack. Furthermore, his nephew Ramzi Yousef, who masterminded the first World Trade Centre bombing in February 1993, also appears to have been motivated by the

Israeli-Palestinian issue. Yousef later said he chose New York City because of its large Jewish population, and in letters sent to newspapers before the attack he stated three demands, the first two of which were an end to all US aid to Israel and an end to US diplomatic relations with Israel. Yousef was not an al-Qaida member, but he had fought in Afghanistan in the 1980s and was the nephew of Khalid Sheikh Mohammed. Of course we cannot know the true motivation of all these individuals, but there is good reason to believe that the Israeli-Palestinian conflict has loomed relatively large in their worldview.

However, the emphasis placed on Palestine has varied over time and between individuals. Global Jihad ideologues have tended to invoke the plight of the Palestinians more often in times of tension in the territories, for example during the second Palestinian intifada (2000–ca. 2005) or operation Cast Lead in Gaza (2008–2009). Moreover, quantitative content analysis has shown that bin Ldin's statements cite political grievances such as Palestine more often than religious arguments, but also that he invoked political grievances relatively more often in speeches addressed to Westerners than in speeches addressed to Muslims.

In addition, when Jihad ideologues speak about Palestine, it is not always to lament the Israeli oppression of Palestinians; it can also be to comment on internal Palestinian politics. For instance, in the largest online library of Jihad texts, *Minbar al-Tawhid wa-l-Jihd*, there are more texts devoted to criticizing Hamas than to the Israeli-Palestinian conflict as such.

Finally, we face a major analytical problem in that Palestine is only one of several political challenges invoked in al-Qaida's statements to persuade Muslims to take up arms. Measuring the motivating effect of Palestine *relative to that of other issues*—such as the Russian repression in Chechnya, the US-led invasion of Iraq, or any other of the many grievances invoked—is a difficult exercise indeed.

Some argue that targeting preferences might be a better proxy for leader motivations and point to the relatively few al-Qaida attacks on Israeli or Jewish targets as evidence that al-Qaida's brass are not particularly concerned with Palestine. It appears to be true that Jews and Israelis have not been *preferred* targets of al-Qaida, but there have been too many attacks on such targets to infer that al-Qaida and its affiliates avoid them. Even before 9/11 there were several attacks on Jewish/Israeli targets by non-Palestinian jihads of various affiliations—albeit not by core al-Qaida—such as:

- The killing of Rabbi Meir Kahane by Egyptian Islamist El Sayyid Nosair in New York in November 1990
- The car-bombing of a Jewish school in Lyon, France, in September 1995, by the Algerian GIA
- The killing of 17 Greek tourists—mistaken for Israelis—in Cairo in April 1996 by the Egyptian Islamic Group
- The "Millennium Plot" by al-Qaida linked operatives to attack Israeli and American tourists in Jordan in December 1999.
- Another important anecdote is that Richard Reid, known as the "shoe bomber" for his attempt to down a transatlantic plane in December 2001 with explosives concealed in his shoe, travelled to Israel in mid2001, reportedly to scout targets for al-Qaida.

The post-9/11 period saw even more al-Qaida-linked plots and attacks against Jewish/Israeli targets, the most prominent of which include:

- The plot by al-Qaida linked militants (the so-called "Tawhid Cell") to attack Jewish targets in Germany in the spring of 2002
- The bombing of the Ghriba synagogue on the Tunisian island of Djerba in April 2002
- The attacks on an Israeli-owned hotel and airliner in Mombasa, Kenya, in November 2002

- The bombing of a Jewish cultural centre, a Jewish cemetery and a Jewish-owned restaurant in Casablanca, Morocco, in May 2003
- The bombing of two synagogues in Istanbul, Turkey, in November 2003
- The rocket attack against Eilat in southern Israel in August 2005, claimed by al-Qaida in Iraq
- The rocket attacks against Northern Israel in October 2009 and November 2011, claimed by the "Abdallah Azzam Brigades"

Two observations are worth noting here. One is that several of these attacks were against soft Jewish targets outside Israel, i.e., relatively "lowhanging fruit" from a terrorist's perspective. Another is that the connection to al-Qaida Central is unclear or absent in several of these operations, so we do not really know the extent to which the top al-Qaida leadership prioritized them.

Thus, once again we are faced with evidence that al-Qaida leaders appear neither consumed with nor despondent to the Palestinian issue, but care about it to some intermediate extent. In the absence of rigorous quantitative studies of al-Qaida's attempted plots, we cannot say exactly how much resources al-Qaida has devoted to Jewish/Israeli targets. Even if we did, it is debatable whether targeting preferences would reveal underlying motivations. It is perfectly possible for a militant group to be concerned with a problem in one part of the world and pursue a military strategy in another. Just as al-Qaida's attacks against the United States can be interpreted as an instrumental strategy to undermine secular regimes in the Muslim world, so anti-Western targeting could reflect resentment against Western support for Israel.

As far as low-level al-Qaida recruits or sympathisers are concerned, the evidence is somewhat more suggestive of a Palestinian motivation effect, but uncertainties remain. For a start, many surveys indicate that Muslims in general feel quite strongly about the Palestinian issue. The *9/11 Report* remarked: "it is simply a fact that American policy regarding the Israeli-Palestinian conflict and American actions in Iraq are dominant staples of popular commentary across the Arab and Muslim world." More important, several studies of al-Qaida recruits have found the Palestinian issue to be a frequently declared motivation for joining. According to the *9/11 Report*, several of the plotters and operatives involved in the 9/11 attacks were preoccupied with the Palestinian issue in the years leading up to the operation. However, the issue is not mentioned by all recruits, and it is not always the sole motivation for those who do mention it. Besides, these studies tend to have many missing values, since declared motivations are not always available for every profile.

There is also some evidence to suggest a correlation between chronological variation in aggregate recruit supply and tensions in the territories. For example, the flow of recruits to al-Qaida's training camps in Afghanistan in the 1996–2001 period seems to have reached its highest level in early to mid-2001, after the outbreak of the second Palestinian intifada. Similarly, British government officials reported increased recruitment to radical Islamist networks during and after operation "Cast Lead" in Gaza. However, this evidence is sparse and not controlled against other factors.

Thus, aside from ruling out the most extreme positions—i.e., that Palestine does not matter at all, or, conversely, that it is al-Qaida's overriding motivation—the evidence is inconclusive. The picture is probably even less clear-cut today because the transnational Jihad movement is more fragmented and decentralised than it was in the 1990s and early 2000s, which makes it harder to generalise about what the typical transnational Jihad thinks about Palestine.

There is every reason to believe that the various affiliates—such as al-Qaida in the Islamic Maghreb, al-Qaida on the Arabian Peninsula, and Jabhat al-Nucra—differ with respect to the prevalent motivations of their recruits.

Another point worth noting is that some of the most prominent American advocates of the view that Palestine helps al-Qaida recruitment are former senior CIA officials and military commanders. These include Michael Scheuer (former head of the bin Ladin unit in the CIA), Bruce Riedel (veteran CIA analyst and former Deputy Secretary of Defense), Paul Pillar (former head of the CIA's Counterterrorism Centre), and General David Petraeus (former Commander of US Central Command and former Director of the CIA). It must count for something when those who have been at the forefront of the war against al-Qaida —and who have had access to better primary sources than most of us will ever see—reach this conclusion.

The bottom line is that the Palestinian cause does appear to motivate al-Qaida recruits to at least some extent. The best evidence for this is found in the now substantial number of internal documents that have been captured in raids on al-Qaida safe houses and compounds over the years. These documents tell us that leaders talked about Palestine when they thought nobody was listening. In several documents, al-Qaida leaders instruct their propagandists to highlight the Palestinian issue more often, on the grounds that it will increase popular support for al-Qaida. For example, the documents captured by US Special Forces from bin Ldin's compound in Abbottabad in the lethal raid on 1 May 2011 show that in the years before his assassination, bin Ldin wanted his lieutenants to focus more on Israel/Palestine in their statements and operations.

There are two equally valid ways to interpret these instructions: One is that bin Ldin cared so much about the Palestinian cause that he was willing to devote resources to it. The other is that bin Ldin believed potential recruits cared so much about Palestine that they might be persuaded to support or join al-Qaida on account of it. Either way, Palestine matters. The argument that al-Qaida leaders opportunistically "exploit" the Palestinian cause is an implicit admission that the same cause motivates recruits. There can only be opportunism if there is something to exploit.

MUSLIM ATTITUDES TOWARD TERRORISM

Muslim popular opinion on the subject of attacks on civilians by Islamist groups varies. Fred Halliday, a British academic specialist on the Middle East, argues that most Muslims consider these acts to be egregious violations of Islam's laws. Muslims living in the West denounce the September 11th attacks against United States, while Hezbollah contends that their rocket attacks against Israeli civilian targets are defensive Jihad by a legitimate resistance movement rather than terrorism. Subsequently, however, on Osama Bin Laden's death, many Muslims in the UK came out on streets in support of Osama, announcing him as an Islamic hero and condemned the role of US and west in killing him. The protest against Bin Laden's death was organised by controversial preacher Anjem Choudary – who praised both 7/7 and the September 11 attacks. Statistics compiled by the United States government's Counterterrorism Center present a complicated picture: of known and specified terrorist incidents from the beginning of 2004 through the first quarter of 2005, slightly more than half of the fatalities were attributed to Islamic extremists but a majority of over-all incidents were considered of either "unknown/unspecified" or a secular political nature. The vast majority of the "unknown/ unspecified" terrorism fatalities did however happen in Islamic regions such as Iraq andAfghanistan, or in regions where Islam is otherwise involved in conflicts such as the West Bank, the Gaza Strip, southern Thailand and Kashmir.

View of Islamic law

Although the murder of Muslims is always forbidden in Islam, the murder of non-Muslims is also prohibited in certain circumstances. Many Muslim scholars have presented subjective evidence against the religious justification of terrorism against certain non-Muslims, a notable example being that of Muhammad ibn al Uthaymeen who states regarding killing a non-Muslim who is living in an Islamic state or with whom Muslims have a peace treaty: "As for a non-Muslim living under Muslim rule and a Mu'âhid (a Non-Muslim ally with whom Muslims have a treaty, trust, peace, or agreement), the prophet said: "Whoever kills a Mu'âhid will not even smell the fragrance of paradise and its fragrance can be smelled from the distance of forty years away." and he also said: "Certainly, one of the most difficult situations for which there is no turning back for whomever casts himself into it - shedding sacred blood without right." However this does not address the killing of non-Muslims living outside the Islamic world who do not have a specific treaty with Muslims.

Another example is that of late scholar Abd al-Aziz Ibn Baz who stated: "It is well-known to anyone with the slightest amount of common sense that hijacking planes and kidnapping embassy officials and similar acts are some of the greatest universal crimes that result in nothing but widespread corruption and destruction. They place such extreme hardships and injuries upon innocent people, the extent of which only Allâh knows."

Numerous fatwâs (rulings) condemning terrorism and suicide bombing as *haram* have been published by Islamic scholars worldwide, one of the most extensive being the 600-page ruling by Sheikh Tahir-ul-Qadri, whose fatwa condemned them as *kufr*. On 2 March 2010, Qadri's fatwa was an "absolute" condemnation of terrorism without "any excuses or pretexts." He said that "Terrorism is terrorism, violence is violence and it has no place in Islamic teaching and no justification can be provided for it, or any kind of excuses or ifs or buts." Qadri said his fatwa, which declares terrorists and suicide bombers to be unbelievers, goes further than any previous denunciation. Iranian Ayatollah Ozma Seyyed Yousef Sanei issued a fatwa (ruling) that suicide attacks against civilians are legitimate only in the context of war. The ruling did not say whether other types of attacks against civilians are justified outside of the context of war, nor whether jihad is included in Sanei's definition of war.

An influential group of Pakistani scholars and religious leaders declared suicide attacks and beheadings as un-Islamic. 'Ulema' (clerics) and 'mushaikh' (spiritual leaders) of the Jamaat Ahl-e-Sunnah, who gathered for a convention, declared suicide attacks and beheadings as un-Islamic in a unanimous resolution. Chairman of the Pakistani Ruet-e-Hilal Committee, Mufti Muneeb-ur-Rehman, said in his address that those who were fighting in the name of implementing Shariah or Islamic law must first abide by these same laws and killing minors is contrary to the teachings of Islam.

Some contemporary scholars who have followed a textual based approach to the study of the Qur'an with an emphasis over the coherence in the Book and the context of situation offered a radical interpretation on the verses and prophetic narratives that are usually quoted by the militants to promote militancy. According to Javed Ahmad Ghamidi(his booklet on Jihad is considered one of his most important contribution towards understanding the religion according to the principles of interpreting the Qur'an introduced byFarahi and Islahi) the Qur'an does not allow waging war except for against oppression under a sovereign state. He holds that jihad without a state is nothing but creating nuisance in the land when hijacked by the individuals and groups independent of the state authority defeats the purpose. The principle behind this study of the issue in the basic sources is the principle that there are divine injunctions in the Qur'an which are specific to the age of the Messenger. He says that nobody can be punished for apostasy or being non-Muslim after the Prophet who acted as the divine agent when he punished the disbelievers by sword who had rejected the message of God and his messenger even after the truth was made manifest to them. Ghamidi and his associates have written extensively on the topics related to these issues. In his book Meezan Ghamidi has concluded that:

1. Jihad can only waged against persecution Islamic jihad has only two purposes : putting an end to persecution even that of the non-Muslims and making the religion of Islam reign supreme in the Arabian peninsula. The latter type was specific for the messenger of God and is no more operative .
2. Under a sovereign state.
3. There are strict ethical limits for jihad which do not again allow fighting for example non-combatants.
4. Seen in this perspective acts of terrorism including suicide bombing becomes prohibited.

Opinion Surveys

- Gallup conducted tens of thousands of hour-long, face-to-face interviews with residents of more than 35 predominantly Muslim countries between 2001 and 2007. It found that more than 90% of respondents condemned the killing of non-combatants on religious and humanitarian grounds.

- A 2004, a year after the invasion of Iraq, Pew Research Center survey found that suicide bombings against Americans and other Westerners in Iraq were seen as "justifiable" by many Jordanians (70%), Pakistanis (46%), and Turks (31%). At the same time, the survey found that support for the U.S.-led War on Terror had increased.
- A 2005 Pew Research study that involved 17,000 people in 17 countries showed support for terrorism was declining in the Muslim world along with a growing belief that Islamic extremism represents a threat to those countries. A *Daily Telegraph* survey showed that 88% of Muslims said the July 2005 bombings in the London Underground were unjustified, while 6% disagreed. However it also found that 24% of British Muslims showed some sympathy with the people who carried out the attacks.
- Polls taken by Saudi owned Al Arabiya and Gallup suggest moderate support for the September 11 terrorist attacks within the Islamic world, with 36% of Arabs polled by Al Arabiya saying the 9/11 attacks were morally justified, 38% disagreeing and 26% of those polled being unsure. A 2008 study, produced by Gallup, found similar results with 38.6% of Muslims questioned believing the 9/11 attacks were justified. Another poll conducted, in 2005 by the Fafo Foundation in the Palestinian Authority, found that 65% of respondents supported the September 11 attacks.
- In Pakistan, despite the recent rise in the Taliban's influence, a poll conducted by Terror Free Tomorrow in Pakistan in January 2008 tested support for al-Qaeda, the Taliban, other militant Islamist groups and Osama bin Laden himself, and found a recent drop by half. In August 2007, 33% of Pakistanis expressed support for al-Qaeda; 38% supported the Taliban. By January 2008, al-Qaeda's support had dropped to 18%, the Taliban's to 19%. When asked if they would vote for al-Qaeda, just 1% of Pakistanis polled answered in the affirmative. The Taliban had the support of 3% of those polled.

- Pew Research surveys in 2008 show that in a range of countries – Jordan, Pakistan, Indonesia, Lebanon, and Bangladesh – there have been substantial declines in the percentages saying suicide-bombings and other forms of violence against civilian targets can be justified to defend Islam against its enemies. Wide majorities say such attacks are, at most, rarely acceptable. The shift of attitudes against terror has been especially dramatic in Jordan, where 29% of Jordanians were recorded as viewing suicide-attacks as often or sometimes justified (down from 57% in May 2005). In the largest majority-Muslim nation, Indonesia, 74% of respondents agree that terrorist attacks are "never justified" (a substantial increase from the 41% level to which support had risen in March 2004); in Pakistan, that figure is 86%; in Bangladesh, 81%; and in Iran, 80%.
- A poll conducted in Osama bin Laden's home country of Saudi Arabia in December 2008 shows that his compatriots have dramatically turned against him, his organisation, Saudi volunteers in Iraq, and terrorism in general. Indeed, confidence in bin Laden has fallen in most Muslim countries in recent years.

CRITICISM OF ISLAMIC TERRORIST IDEOLOGY

Although "Islamic" terrorism is commonly associated with the Salafis (or "Wahhabis"), the scholars of the group have constantly attributed this association to ignorance, misunderstanding and sometimes insincere research and deliberate misleading by rival groups.

Following the September 11 attacks, Abdul-Azeez ibn Abdullaah Aal ash-Shaikh, the Grand Mufti of the Kingdom of Saudi Arabia, made an official statement that "the Islamic Sharee'ah (legislation) does not sanction" such actions. A Salafi Committee of Major Scholars"in Saudi Arabia has declared that "Islamic" terrorism, such as the May 2003 bombing in Riyadh, are in violation of Sharia law and aiding the enemies of Islam.

Criticism of Islamic terrorism on Islamic grounds has also been made by Abdal-Hakim Murad (Timothy Winter):

> *Certainly, neither bin Laden nor his principal associate, Ayman al-Zawahiri, are graduates of Islamic universities. And so their proclamations ignore 14 centuries of Muslim scholarship, and instead take the form of lists of anti-American grievances and of Koranic quotations referring to early Muslim wars against Arab idolaters. These are followed by the conclusion that all Americans, civilian and military, are to be wiped off the face of the Earth. All this amounts to an odd and extreme violation of the normal methods of Islamic scholarship. Had the authors of such fatwâs followed the norms of their religion, they would have had to acknowledge that no school of mainstream Islam allows the targeting of civilians. An insurrectionist who kills non-combatants is guilty of baghy, "armed aggression," a capital offense in Islamic law.*

Colonel Eikmeier points out the "questionable religious credentials" of many Islamist theorists, or "Qutbists," which can be a "means to discredit them and their message":

> *With the exception of Abul Ala Maududi and Abdullah Yusuf Azzam, none of Qutbism's main theoreticians trained at Islam's recognized centers of learning. Although a devout Muslim, Hassan al-Banna was a teacher and community activist. Sayyid Qutb was a literary critic. Muhammad Abd al-Salam Faraj was an electrician. Ayman al-Zawahiri is a physician. Osama bin Laden trained to be a businessman.*

Fethullah Gülen, a prominent Turkish Islamic scholar, has claimed that "a real Muslim," who understood Islam in every aspect, could not be a terrorist.

There are many other people with similar points of view such as Karen Armstrong, Prof. Ahmet Akgunduz, Harun Yahya and Muhammad Tahir-ul-Qadri. Huston Smith, an author on comparative religion, noted that extremists have hijacked Islam, just as has occurred periodically in Christianity, Hinduism and other religions throughout history. He added that the real problem is that extremists do not know their own faith.

Ali Gomaa, former Grand Mufti of Egypt, stated not only for the Islam but in general: "Terrorism cannot be born of religion. Terrorism is the product of corrupt minds, hardened hearts, and arrogant egos, and corruption, destruction, and arrogance are unknown to the heart attached to the divine."

Identity-based Frameworks for Analyzing Islamist-based Terrorism

Islamist-based fundamentalist terrorism against Western nations and the U.S. in particular, has numerous motivations and takes place the larger context of a complex and tense relationship between the 'West' and the Arab and Muslim 'world,' which is highlighted in the previous section on motivations and Islamic terrorism. Identity-based theoretical frameworks including theories of social identity, social categorization theory, and psychodynamics are used to explain the reasons terrorism occurs.

Social identity is explained by Karina Korostelina as a "feeling of belonging to a social group, as a strong connection with social category, and as an important part of our mind that affects our social perceptions and behavior" This definition can be applied to the case of Osama bin Laden, who, according to this theory, had a highly salient perception of his social identity as a Muslim, a strong connection to the social category of the Muslim Ummah or 'community,' which affect his social perceptions and behaviors.

Bin Laden's ideology and interpretation of Islam led to the creation of al-Qaeda in response to perceived threats against the Muslim community by the Soviet Union, the U.S. in particular due to its troop presence in Saudi Arabia, and American support for Israel. The Islamist terrorist group al-Qaeda has a group identity, which includes "shared experiences, attitudes, beliefs, and interests of ingroup members," and is "described through the achievement of a collective aim for which this group has been created," which in this case is to achieve "a complete break from the foreign influences in Muslim countries, and the creation of a new Islamic caliphate."

Social categorization theory has been discussed as a three-stage process of identification, where "individuals define themselves as members of a social group, learn the stereotypes and norms of the group, and group categories influence the perception and understanding of all situations in a particular context" This definition can be applied to the U.S.-led war on terror, in which conflict features such as the phenomenon of Anti-Americanism and the phenomenon of non-Arab countries like Iran and Afghanistanlending support to Islamist-based terrorism by funding or harboring terrorist groups such as Hezbollah and al-Qaeda against Western nations, particularly Israel and theUnited States are, according to social categorization theory, influenced by a three-stage process of identification.

In this three-stage process of identification, the Arab and Muslim world(s) are the social group(s), in which their members learn stereotypes and norms which categorize their social group vis-à-vis the West. This social categorization process creates feelings of high-level in-group support and allegiance among Arabs and Muslims and the particular context within which members of the Arab and Muslim world(s) social group(s) understand all situations that involve the West. Social categorization theory as a framework for analysis indicates causal relationships between group identification processes and features of conflict situations.

THE VIEW THAT WESTERN FOREIGN POLICY IS A MOTIVATION FOR TERRORISM

Robert Pape has argued that at least terrorists utilizing suicide attacks – a particularly effective form of terrorist attack – are driven not by Islamism but by "a clear strategic objective: to compel modern democracies to withdraw military forces from the territory that the terrorists view as their homeland." However, Martin Kramer, who debated Pape on origins of suicide bombing, stated that the motivation for suicide attacks is not just strategic logic but also an interpretation of Islam to provide a moral logic. For example,Hezbollah initiated suicide bombings after a complex reworking of the concept of martyrdom. Kramer explains that the Israeli occupation of Lebanon raised the temperature necessary for this reinterpretation of Islam, but occupation alone would not have been sufficient for suicide terrorism. "The only way to apply a brake to suicide terrorism," Kramer argues, "is to undermine its moral logic, by encouraging Muslims to see its incompatibility with their own values."

Former CIA analyst Michael Scheuer argues that terrorist attacks (specifically al-Qaeda attacks on America) are *not* motivated by a religiously inspired hatred of American cultureor religion, but by the belief that U.S. foreign policy has oppressed, killed, or otherwise harmed Muslims in the Middle East, condensed in the phrase "They hate us for what we do, not who we are."

U.S. foreign policy actions Scheuer believes are fueling Islamic terror include: the U.S.-led intervention in Afghanistan and invasion of Iraq; Israel–United States relations, namely, financial, military, and political support for Israel.

U.S. support for "apostate" police states in Muslim nations such as Saudi Arabia, Egypt,Pakistan, Algeria, Morocco, and Kuwait; U.S. support for the creation of an independent East Timor from territory previously held by Muslim Indonesia; perceived U.S. approval or support of actions against Muslim insurgents in India, the Philippines, Chechnya, and Palestine; U.S. troops on Muslim 'holy ground' in Saudi Arabia; the Western world's religious discrimination against Muslim immigrants'; historical justification, such as the Crusades.

Maajid Nawaz, in a debate with Mehdi Hasan, countered Scheuer's contention: "a tiny minority, from within the non-Iraqi British Muslim communities, reacted with violence on 7 July 2005. To interpret this simply as a "nationalist struggle" to remove occupation ignores the blatantly obvious fact that, first, the terrorists were not Iraqis, they were British-Pakistanis (though British Iraqis have lived here for a long time); second, the vast majority of the Stop the War protesters were non-Muslims, yet only a handful from among a minority of Muslims reacted to the war with terrorism.

Even though occupation may have caused agitation among the 7 July bombers, these northern-born lads with thick Yorkshire accents confessed in their suicide tapes to considering themselves soldiers with a mission to kill our people (Britons) on behalf of their people (Iraqis). The prerequisite to such a disavowal of one's country of birth is a recalibration of identity; this is the undeniable role of ideological narratives."

The View that Islamic Terrorism Predates U.S. Action and is justified by Quranic Teachings

According to others, Islamic terrorism is linked to the practice of divinely sanctioned warfare against apostates. Many Muslim groups including the Council on American-Islamic Relations argue that references to violence in Muslim sources have been taken out of context. They argue that these Koranic ayahs are only for self-defense when non-believers endanger Muslim life. It should be noted that a number of well documented religiously motivated massacres by Muslims of largely Christian ethnic groups in the Near East occurred long before the United States became a presence on the world stage, such as the massacres conducted by Tamurlane in the 14th century, theMassacres of Bader Khan in the 1840s, the Hamidian massacres of the 1890s, the Armenian Genocide, Assyrian Genocide and Greek Genocide between 1915 and 1921, and the Simele massacre of 1933.

Societal Motivations

Scholar Scott Atran, research director and involved in a NATO group studying suicide terrorism, asserts that there is no single root cause of terrorism. The greatest predictors of suicide bombings, Atran concludes, is not religion but group dynamics: "small-group dynamics involving friends and family that form the diaspora cell of brotherhood andcamaraderie on which the rising tide of martyrdom actions is based".

Economical Motivations

The Muslim world has been afflicted with economic stagnation for many centuries. In 2011, U.S. President Barack Obama stated that apart from crude oil, the exports of the entire Greater Middle East with its 400 million population roughly equals that of Switzerland. It has also been estimated that the exports of Finland, a European country of only five million, exceeded those of the entire 260 million-strong Arab world, excluding oil revenue. This economic stagnation is argued by historian David Fromkin in his work A Peace to End All Peace to have commenced with the demise of the Ottoman Caliphate in 1924, with trade networks being disrupted and societies torn apart with the creation of new nation states; prior to this, the Middle East had a diverse and growing economy and more general prosperity.

Another cause of embarrassment and resentment is that for several decades, Muslim immigrants have been forced to emigrate to western countries in large numbers because fellow Muslim countries that are well-off economically and socially do not accept them. Out of the 57 Muslim majority countries, only two nations (Turkey and Malaysia) offer a formal path to becoming a naturalized citizen regardless of your religious beliefs, marital status or ethnic origin. Even the oil-rich Gulf states do not grant citizenship to Muslim immigrants, regardless of how long they have resided in those countries.

Profiles

Forensic psychiatrist and former foreign service officer Marc Sageman made an "intensive study of biographical data on 172 participants in the jihad," in his book *Understanding Terror Networks*. He concluded social networks, the "tight bonds of family and friendship", rather than emotional and behavioral disorders of "poverty, trauma, madness, [or] ignorance", inspired alienated young Muslims to join the jihad and kill.

Lawrence Wright described the characteristic of "displacement" of members of the most famous Islamic terrorist group, al-Qaeda: What the recruits tended to have in common – besides their urbanity, their cosmopolitan backgrounds, their education, their facility with languages, and their computer skills – was displacement.

Most who joined the jihad did so in a country other than the one in which they were reared. They were Algerians living inexpatriate enclaves in France, Moroccans in Spain, or Yemenis in Saudi Arabia. Despite their accomplishments, they had little standing in the host societies where they lived."

Scholar Olivier Roy describes the background of the hundreds of *global* (as opposed to local) terrorists who were incarcerated or killed and for whom authorities have records, as being surprising for their Westernized background; for the lack of Palestinians,

Iraqis, Afghans "coming to avenge what is going on in their country"; their lack of religiosity before being "born again" in a foreign country; the high percentage of converts to Islam among them; their "de-territorialized backgrounds" – "For instance, they may be born in a country, then educated in another country, then go to fight in a third country and take refuge in a fourth country"; their nontraditional belief that jihad is permanent, global, and "not linked with a specific territory."

This profile differs from that found among recent local Islamist suicide bombers in Afghanistan, according to a 2007 study of 110 suicide bombers by Afghan pathologist Dr. Yusef Yadgari. Yadgari found that 80% of the attackers studied had some kind of physical or mental disability. The bombers were also "not celebrated like their counterparts in other Arab nations. Afghan bombers are not featured on posters or in videos as martyrs." Daniel Byman, a Middle East expert at the Brookings Institute, and Christine Fair, an assistant professor in peace and security studies at Georgetown University say that many of the Islamic terrorists are foolish and untrained, perhaps even untrainable.

Ideology

One ideology that plays a role in Islamic terrorism is the principle of Jihad, which broadly means strive. Militants generally use jihad to mean defensive or retaliatory warfare against actors that have allegedly harmed Muslims.

Transnational Islamist ideology, specifically of the militant Islamists, assert that Western policies and society are actively anti-Islamic, or as it is sometimes described, waging a "war against Islam". Islamists often identify what they see as a historical struggle between Christianity and Islam, dating back as far as the Crusades, among other historical conflicts between practitioners of the two respective religions. Osama bin Laden, for example, almost invariably described his enemy as aggressive and his call for action against them as defensive. Defensive jihad differs from offensive jihad in being "fard al-ayn," or a personal obligation of all Muslims, rather than "fard al-kifaya", a communal obligation, that is, some Muslims may perform it but it is not required from others. Hence, framing a fight as defensive has the advantage of both appearing to be a victim rather than an aggressor, and of giving the struggle the very highest religious priority for all good Muslims.

Many of the violent terrorist groups use the name of jihad to fight against certain Western nations and Israel. An example is bin Laden's al-Qaeda, which is also known as "International Islamic Front for Jihad Against the Jews and Crusaders". Most militant Islamists oppose Israel's policies, and often its existence.

According to U.S. Army Colonel Dale C. Eikmeier, "ideology", rather than any individual or group, is the "center of gravity" of al-Qaeda and related groups, and that ideology is a "collection of violent Islamic thought called Qutbism." He summarizes the tenets of Qutbism as being:

- A belief that Muslims have deviated from true Islam and must return to "pure Islam" as originally practiced during the time of theProphet.
- The path to "pure Islam" is only through a literal and strict interpretation of the Qur'an and Hadith, along with implementation of the Prophet's commands.
- Muslims should interpret the original sources individually without being bound to follow the interpretations of Islamic scholars.
- That any interpretation of the Quran from a historical, contextual perspective is a corruption, and that the majority of Islamic history and the classical jurisprudential tradition is mere sophistry.

The historic rivalry between Hindus and Muslims in the Indian subcontinent has also often been the primary motive behind some of the most deadly terrorist attacks in India. According to a U.S. State Department report, India topped the list of countries most affected by Islamic terrorism.

In addition, Islamist militants, scholars, and leaders opposed Western society for what they see as immoral secularism. Islamists have claimed that such unrestricted free speech has led to the proliferation of pornography, immorality, secularism, homosexuality,feminism, and many other ideas that Islamists often oppose. Although bin Laden almost always emphasized the alleged oppression of Muslims by America and Jews when talking about them in his messages, in his "Letter to America" he answered the question, "What are we calling you to, and what do we want from you?," with We call you to be a people of manners, principles, honour, and purity; to reject the immoral acts of fornication, homosexuality, intoxicants, gambling's, and trading with interest (...) You separate religion from your policies, (...) You are the nation that permits Usury, which has been forbidden by all the religions (...) You are a nation that permits the production, trading and usage of intoxicants (...) You are a nation that permits acts of immorality (...) You are a nation that permits gambling in its all forms. (...) You use women to serve passengers, visitors, and strangers to increase your profit margins. You then rant that you support the liberation of women.

Given their perceived piety, *The Times* noted the irony when a major investigation by their reporters uncovered a link between Islamic Jihadis and child pornography; a discovery that, according to the London paper, "is expected to improve understanding of the mindsets of both types of criminals and has been hailed as a potentially vital intelligence tool to undermine future terrorist plots.". Similarly, Reuters reported that pornography was found among the materials seized from Osama bin Laden's Abbottabad compound that was raided by U.S. Navy SEALs.

In 2006 Britain's then head of MI5 Eliza Manningham-Buller said of Al-Qaeda that it "has developed an ideology which claims that Islam is under attack, and needs to be defended". "This" she said "is a powerful narrative that weaves together conflicts from across the globe, presenting the West's response to varied and complex issues, from long-standing disputes such as Israel/Palestine and Kashmir to more recent events as evidence of an across-the-board determination to undermine and humiliate Islam worldwide." She said that the video wills of British suicide bombers made it clear that they were motivated by perceived worldwide and long-standing injustices against Muslims; an extreme and minority interpretation of Islam promoted by some preachers and people of influence; their interpretation as anti-Muslim of UK foreign policy, in particular the UK's involvement in Iraq and Afghanistan." She also cautioned how difficult it was to gain a proper perspective, saying that although there are more important dangers we face daily without feeling so threatened by them such as climate change and road deaths and though terrorist deaths were few the intelligence services had prevented some potentially large threats and that vigilance was needed.

Interpretations of the Qur'an and Hadith

The role played by the Qur'an, Islam's sacred text, in opposing or in encouraging attacks on civilians is disputed.

The Princeton University Middle Eastern scholar Bernard Lewis, states that Islamic jurisprudence does not allow terrorism. In 2001, Professor Lewis noted:

At no time did the (Muslim) jurist approve of terrorism. Nor indeed is there any evidence of the use of terrorism (in Islamic tradition). Muslims are commanded not to kill women, children, or the aged, not to torture or otherwise ill-treat prisoners, The rules and regulations concerning prisoners of war in Islam to give fair warning of the opening of hostilities, and to honor agreements. Similarly, the laws of Jihad categorically preclude wanton and indiscriminate slaughter. The warriors in the holy war are urged not to harm non-combatants, women and children, "unless they attack you first." A point on which they insist is the need for a clear declaration of war before beginning hostilities, and for proper warning before resuming hostilities after a truce. What the classical jurists of Islam never remotely considered is the kind of unprovoked, unannounced mass slaughter of uninvolved civil populations that we saw in New York two weeks ago. For this there is no precedent and no authority in Islam.

But Bernard Lewis says Jihad is an unlimited offensive to bring the whole world under Islamic law; Christian crusades a defensive, limited response to, and imitation of, jihad.

Even the Christian crusade, often compared with the Muslim jihad, was itself a delayed and limited response to the jihad and in part also an imitation. But unlike the jihad it was concerned primarily with the defense or reconquest of threatened or lost Christian territory...The Muslim jihad, in contrast, was perceived [by Muslims] as unlimited, as a religious obligation that would continue until all the world had either adopted the Muslim faith or submitted to Muslim rule.... The object of jihad is to bring the whole world under Islamic law.

Bernard Lewis says Islam imposes, without limit of time or space, the duty to subjugate non-Muslims.

"...it is the duty of those who have accepted them [Allah's word and message] to strive unceasingly to convert or at least to subjugate those who have not. This obligation is without limit of time or space. It must continue until the whole world has either accepted the Islamic faith or submitted to the power of the Islamic state."

Michael Sells and Jane I. Smith (a Professor of Islamic Studies) write that barring some extremists like al-Qaeda, most Muslims do not interpret Qura'nic verses as promoting warfare; and that the phenomenon of radical interpretation of scripture by extremist groups is not unique to Islam.

According to Sells, "[Most Muslims] no more expect to apply [the verses at issue] to their contemporary non-Muslim friends and neighbors than most Christians and Jews consider themselves commanded by God, like the BiblicalJoshua, to exterminate the infidels."

According to Robert Spencer, Muhammad said in one Hadith:

> *"Allah's Apostle said, "I have been sent with the shortest expressions bearing the widest meanings, and I have been made victorious with terror (cast in the hearts of the enemy), and while I was sleeping, the keys of the treasures of the world were brought to me and put in my hand." Abu Huraira added: Allah's Apostle has left the world and now you, people, are bringing out those treasures (i.e. the Prophet did not benefit by them). Narrated in Abu Huraira. — Sahih al-Bukhari, 4:52:220, see also Sahih Muslim, 4:1062,Sahih Muslim, 4:1063,Sahih Muslim, 4:1066,Sahih Muslim, 4:1067 and Sahih al-Bukhari, 5:59:512*

Furthermore Muhammad said in another Hadith:

The Prophet said, "Who is ready to kill Ka'b ibn al-Ashraf who has really hurt Allah and His Apostle?" Muhammad bin Maslama said, "O Allah's Apostle! Do you like me to kill him?" He replied in the affirmative. So, Muhammad bin Maslama went to him (i.e. Ka'b) and said, "This person (i.e. the Prophet) has put us to task and asked us for charity." Ka'b replied, "By Allah, you will get tired of him." Muhammad said to him, "We have followed him, so we dislike to leave him till we see the end of his affair." Muhammad bin Maslama went on talking to him in this way till he got the chance to kill him. Narrated Jabir bin 'Abdullah — Sahih al-Bukhari, 4:52:270, see also Sahih al-Bukhari, 5:59:369,Sahih Muslim, 19:4436

And another Hadith:

The Prophet passed by me at a place called Al-Abwa or Waddan, and was asked whether it was permissible to attack the pagan warriors at night with the probability of exposing their women and children to danger. The Prophet replied, "They (i.e. women and children) are from them (i.e. pagans)." I also heard the Prophet saying, "The institution of Hima is invalid except for Allah and His Apostle. Narrated As-Sab bin Jaththama — Sahih al-Bukhari, 4:52:256, see also Sahih Muslim, 19:4321 Sunan Abu Dawood, 38:4390

Militant Islamic fundamentalist organisations portray their struggle in simply uncompromising terms. According to Antar Zouabri, a leader of a 1990s movement to establish an Islamic republic in Algeria, there can never be either dialogue or truce in his organisation's struggle against the illegitimate, secular government. The word of God, he argued, is immutable: God does not negotiate or engage in discussion.

THE IDEOLOGICAL FOUNDATION OF TERRORISM

Before the war against terrorism can come to any definitive conclusion, its underlying philosophy must first be identified, along with the means to be employed. This book, therefore, deals with terrorism's basic starting point, as well as the disasters to which it leads. Its starting point is the assumption that violence is a virtue in itself and a powerful means to solve social or political problems. While killing the innocents, damaging public order, and disrupting peace, any terrorist acts under the influence of ideas that have been imposed on him, coaxing him to believe that he's engaged in a justified struggle.

Terrorism can be healed only when such people understand the mistaken illogic of any ideology that inspires terrorism and incites to violence—and when they realize that going along with it can never get them anywhere. Until those ideologies' errors and contradictions are revealed, all measures taken against terrorism can be short-term only. Soon terrorism will emerge again, in different places and under different circumstances, behind a different mask.

We can put an end to terrorism only by destroying its ideological infrastructure. Modern terrorism's ideological foundations in fact go back to Social Darwinism and the materialist tendencies derived from it. People exposed to this indoctrination believe that life is a field of struggle, and that only the strong survive. The weak are condemned to be eliminated. Man and, in fact, the entire universe, are both products of chance. Therefore, no one is responsible for his actions to anyone else. These and similar ideas inevitably coax people into leading an animalistic form of life, where ruthlessness, aggression and violence are regarded as acceptable or even virtuous.

Anyone who resorts to terrorism, maintaining that violence is the only way to achieve his aims, is actually under the influence of Social Darwinism and materialist thought, no matter what his religion or race, or what group he belongs to. Modern terrorist groups that claim to act in the name of religion are also under Darwinism's influence and materialism, even though they claim to carry out their terroristic acts in the name of religion. This is because for anyone who lives by the morality of religion revealed by God, it's impossible to approve of violence of any kind, much less achieve a "higher" aim by murdering others. Those who resort to such methods are therefore pursuing the exact opposite of the moral values upheld by religion, carrying out their actions under the influence of materialist ideologies.

In *Islam Denounces Terrorism,* it was made clear that Islam fiercely rejects all forms of terrorism, no matter whom it may be directed against. In the light of verses from the Qur'an, it was explained how religion's morality calls people to peace, tolerance, and convenience. Also stressed was the dishonesty of condemning only those acts of terrorism directed against one's own side: Such an attitude only weakens the fight against terrorism; and anyone living according to Islamic morality needs to fight terror in all its all forms. The foundation of that intellectual struggle is based on revealing the true morality of religion.

Today's politicians, political commentators and academics agree that by itself, military force isn't enough to root out terrorism. This book concentrates on the only way it can be eradicated: by means of peace, tolerance, and love. All the divinely-inspired religions that God sent down by means of His messengers are helpful guides. This book offers examples from the Qur'an as well as from the Bible (even though the latter has been partially distorted) to show how each of the three divine religions forbids the use of unjust violence. It also gives examples to show that the only way to fight terrorism is to heal the root causes through the love, affection, compassion, humility, forgiveness, tolerance and concepts of justice that religion's morality instils in people—whom, following the verse from the Qur'an (10:25): "God calls to the Abode of Peace... " Such fortunates will do their utmost to build a world full of peace and love.

THE BLOODY TOLL OF TERROR

Terrorism is one of the gravest menaces facing our 21st-century world because it sees acts of violence as the only way to achieve political aims. The particular aim or problem depends on the terrorist's individual worldview. In a terrorist's eyes, political dilemmas and conflicts caused by ethnic and cultural differences can be resolved by violence alone. No group can get what it wants, except by "blood and iron". The terrorist believes that his objectives—enforcing his demands, spreading his organization's propaganda—can be attained only by damaging the fabric of society; when unease, fear, and conflict come to dominate daily life.

Some groups aim to take advantage of the climate of chaos that their actions bring about. They think that it will be easier to achieve their aims where social stability has collapsed, individuals are wracked with fear and uncertainty. From the destruction, they claim, will rise what they call "righteousness and justice." But expecting that acts of terrorism can establish righteousness and justice, or that problems can be resolved by violence, is a terrible mistake. Violence is counter-productive: All they that live by the sword shall perish by the sword.

In the Qur'an (13:25), God describes such people as "those [who] cause corruption in the earth." So far, they have managed only to increase the number of deaths among the innocent—and among their own supporters as well. Every year, terrorist attacks cause thousands to live in fear and anxiety and suffer economic harm, not to mention those who are wounded or killed. Terrorism threatens all of mankind, its toll so very terrible that fighting has become urgently essential.

TERRORISM IS CLOSE TO HOME!

There are an estimated 500 terrorist groups in the world. These include international cartels controlling trade in drugs, arms and prostitution, as well as underground organizations, marginal movements, various radical ideological groups, and deviant cults that stage actions allegedly in the name of religion. Many terrorist organizations do operate within their own countries' borders, but a number target what they have decided as "enemy" countries, through attacks on prominent sites and individuals that, they calculate, will elicit a huge public reaction. From the reaction, they seek to achieve fame, in fact notoriety, which they hope that will add to their power.

Though terrorism has existed since the earliest times, through esoteric organizations like the Sicarii or Assassins, and flourished in the modern times through revolutionary cadres like the sans-cullottes of the French Revolution or the Russian Nihilism of the 19th century, its threat really came to the fore in the 20th century, which saw an explosion in acts of terror and in the number of terrorists who committed them. Weapons of mass destruction and the rapid advance of technology made terrorist attacks much easier and vastly increased their destructiveness.

By the 1960s, people began to wonder seriously what might happen, if a terrorist group managed to acquire some kind of nuclear weapon that could result in the deaths of tens of thousands. A biological or chemical attack could wipe entire populations off the map. No such attack happened, fortunately. But by the 1990s, the chances of such attacks increased. These concerns only heightened with the collapse of the Soviet Union and the weakening of control over its nuclear arsenal. The spread of the Internet and the facilitation of all forms of information increased worries still further.1 Fear of terrorism became the subject of hundreds of films and books. Reports were written about the possible consequences; research was carried out. Now, all too obviously, terrorists could go beyond familiar, limited actions like bombings, armed robberies, skyjackings and kidnappings, to attack entire communities. Such attacks could be carried out by remote control or computer, with no direct human intervention.

A number of recent fears in the US involving biological weapons like of the anthrax bacteria revealed the scale of the threat posed by bio-terrorism and biological weapons. With the help of an experienced chemist in a simple laboratory, terrorists can now threaten the lives of thousands. One of the first examples of this occurred in 1984, when 750 people were poisoned in four restaurants in a small town in Oregon.2 Later, it was revealed that a Hindu-inspired New Age cult under the leadership of Baghwan Shree Rajneesh was responsible. Disciples had grown salmonella bacteria on their farms and placed them in salad bars in area restaurants. In 1995, the Aum Shinrikyo ("Higher Truth") cult released the poison gas sarin in the Tokyo underground subway system, leading to the deaths of 12 people and another 5,500 injured. Subsequent inquiries revealed that the cult had tried to construct biological weapons in its own laboratories—revealing just how large a threat terrorism poses to the public.

In the 21st century, computer technology is expected to play an important role in terrorist attacks. Meanwhile, more "conventional" ways of terrorism, like bombings, arson attacks, skyjackings and kidnappings are still going on all over the world, from Europe to America, from Asia to Africa. Since 1962, for example, members of the ETA (Euskadi Ta Askatasuna) terrorist organization, fighting for the Basque region's independence, has carried out many terrorist attacks in Spain, resulting in the deaths of more than 800.4 For years, the Irish Republican Army has seized world headlines with its bloody attacks to gain independence for Northern Ireland. The central aim of the IRA is to end British control of Northern Ireland and to achieve the reunification of the island of Ireland. Generally it has operated in Northern Ireland and London, but has also been involved in bombings in various European countries such as Germany. Since 1969, the IRA's terrorist attacks , and Britain's methods of "counter-terrorism", have caused the deaths of more than 3,200 on both sides of the conflict.5 Millions of dollars' worth of damage has been caused by IRA bombings of airports and underground stations, again aimed at civilians. During a European Football Championship match on June 15, 1996, an IRA car bombing in a Manchester shopping center resulted in some 200 injuries.

Currently, no country can feel safe from this kind of threat. The few examples just cited show just how deeply terrorism has come to influence peoples' lives. No longer the problem of just a few specific nations, it's a threat that faces all mankind. Because no one can tell when, where or how terrorists will strike, the fight against them can no longer be considered the duty of a handful of countries or organizations. Terrorism, threatening the entire world, can be resolved only if well-intentioned people support each other in search of peace, friendship and brotherhood.

TERRORISM'S DARK FACE

Terrorism is currently inflicting suffering and physical damage all over the world, not only in the United States, but in the African countries of Uganda, Angola and Nigeria; in the European nations of Great Britain, France and Spain; in Asian countries like Japan, and throughout the Middle East and Latin America. At any moment, civilians can find themselves facing a terrorist attack, whether sitting at home or at a movie theater, in a shopping center, riding a bus, or at their workplace. Naturally, terrorism's ability to enter peoples' homes has led to considerable anxiety and alarm. People are hesitant to enter crowded areas or use public transport; their daily lives are becoming intolerable. But that is exactly what terrorism wants to see: whole communities living in fear and alarm.

The evidence of terrible attacks throughout in the world certainly confirms that concern. In 1996, there were 296 incidents with 314 people killed and 2,912 injured. In 1997, terrorism's scope began to expand: Out of 439 attacks, 398 were aimed at workplaces or non-official premises, leading to the loss of 139 civilian lives, 39 of them civil servants or military personnel.

According to the U.S. State Department, the number of terrorist attacks in 2000 saw an eight percent rise over 1999, with 423 deaths and 791 injured. Between 1981 and 2000, the total number of dead resulting from terrorist attacks was 9,184. Nor do these figures include all the people who died in all terrorist attacks across the globe. The report considered only attacks by international terrorist organizations, not those inflicted by local terrorist groups. In Turkey alone there were 21,866 terrorist attacks between August 15, 1984 and October 31, 2001, costing the lives of 5,605 security personnel and 4,646 civilians. A further 16,562 security forces and 5,091 civilians were injured.

Terrorist actions' physical damage and economic harm add yet another sobering dimension to the picture. The chaos and anarchy provoked by such incidents prevent investment in the affected regions. Attacks aimed at the economic infrastructure doesn't just hold back development. Existing resources are also destroyed, creating economic difficulties that impede social life across a wide spectrum of areas, particularly education. Military costs of the struggle against terrorism impose yet another burden. This diversion of resources that should be spent on raising standards of living affects not just the nation in question, but the entire global economy.

This summary reveals the grim picture that terrorism represents—bringing destruction all over the world and causing untold harm to human lives.

ATHEIST IDEOLOGIES AND THE RISE OF TERRORISM

If a sick person is to be treated properly, an accurate diagnosis is essential. Whatever treatment follows that diagnosis must be followed meticulously and decisively, until the sickness is finally expelled from the body. If not, the illness will inevitably recur. The same applies to one of the most serious ills affecting society. One of the chief reasons why we can't find effective solutions to this century's social problems is that their causes aren't properly identified. When dealing with any social problem, the first thing to do is establish what causes give rise to it. Otherwise, whatever measures are taken can only be temporary.

The roots of terrorism are often sought in concrete matters; and thus the fight against it, aimed at these superficial targets, cannot provide lasting results. In order to free the world from terrorism, the principal factors behind it must be identified and eliminated.

THE TANGLED WEB OF TERRORISTS' LOGIC

It's not possible to defeat terrorism by security measures. By itself, military force is only likely to meet with increased violence, producing a vicious circle in which bloodshed continues to be answered with more bloodshed. When embarking on the fight against terrorists, we need to understand—and then combat—their way of thinking, the way they view life and other human beings, and how they justify their use of violence.

A terrorist believes that he can succeed only by using violence. He wants people around to fear him, and cloaks himself in pitilessness, ruthlessness and aggression to bring that fear about. Anyone opposing his ideas is an enemy, whom he regards as an object that needs to be eliminated. In his article, "Terrorists View us as Targets, not as Humans," psychotherapist and *Journal Sentinel* writer Philip Chard examines the terrorist mindset and how they justify violent attacks aimed at defenseless people:

> *"Researchers have glimpsed aspects of [the terrorists'] psyches. Most prominent among these is their capacity to view their victims as things, as objects, as statistics that, they hope, will show up on a casualty list.*

"They don't want to experience their victims as human beings, as they would a friend or loved one. Rather, they strive to view them as pawns on a political chessboard. Consequently, from their own vantage point, terrorists don't perceive themselves as killing 'people.' In order to slaughter with ease and callous indifference, they mentally dehumanize us into 'targets' ... Their 'cause,' whatever it may be, is sufficiently sacred, noble or desperate that it justifies the carnage they instigate ... For most terrorists, their chief interest resides in effects, not persons ... They are after ... the impact of the massacre, not the experience of the massacre itself. Terrorists want to murder hope, or a way of life, or the spirit of a group of people or an entire nation. They destroy human beings because they believe doing so is the fastest and most direct route to that goal."

Philip Chard draws our attention to a most important matter: that terrorists feel not the slightest pang of remorse at the death of others. On the contrary, the more they can kill, the more successful they consider themselves to be, and rejoice in that fact. Such minds can quite happily shoot innocent people and bomb small children. For them, shedding blood becomes a source of pleasure. They cease to be human and turn into savage monsters. If one of them does evidence the slightest remorse, he is immediately branded a traitor by his more radical comrades. Being more radical and more bloody is considered to be more devout in the cause, so the zeal to kill increases constantly. Since any dispute can easily be defined as treacher, terrorists invariably use guns against each other, and carry out attacks on other splinter groups within their own ranks.

This passionate attachment to violence goes deeper beyond political ideologies and in fact stems from an underlying misconception about human nature. The terrorist mindset finds its inspiration from the materialist philosophy and Darwinist thought. Darwinism regards human beings as animals and maintains that living things evolve through a struggle for survival in nature. Eliminating the weak, so that the strong can emerge victorious, forms the essence of any terrorist's twisted thinking.

5

Jihad Against the 'Enemies of Islam'

The subject of armed jihad runs right through the writings and pronouncements of Markaz spokesmen and is, in fact, the most prominent theme in the Markaz's discourse. Indeed, its understanding of Islam maybe seen as determined almost wholly by this preoccupation, so much so that its reading of Islam seems to be a product of its own political project.

The contours of its ideological framework are constructed in such a way that the theme of armed jihad appears as its central, over-riding concern. Not surprisingly, therefore, it constructs a discursive framework that, like Gilani's and the JIJK's, completely denies the legitimacy of the Kashmiri nationalist project, but at the same time goes considerably beyond the limited aims of the JIJK's jihad as Gilani conceives them in his writings.

There has been much discussion on the nature and forms of jihad in writings about Islam. Liberals have tended to explain it in terms of self-defence, while others have taken recourse to certain Sufi positions, where the foremost jihad (jihad-i akbar) is said to the struggle against the nafs or one's 'baser self' or ego. Yet others have suggested that jihad in the path of God (jihad fi sabil illah) can take many forms, and that armed struggle is just one of these. However, in the writings and speeches of Markaz spokesmen jihad appears unabashedly as qital or violent conflict waged against unbelievers. Indeed, it is projected as the one of the most central tenets of Islam, although it has traditionally not been included as one of the 'five pillars' of the faith. Thus, it is claimed that 'There is so much emphasis on this subject that some commentators and scholars of the Qur'an have remarked that the topic of the Qur'an is jihad', and that 'There is consensus of opinion among researchers of the Qur'an that no other action has been explained in such great detail as jihad'.

In order to properly understand the role of jihad for the Markaz's political project, it is necessary to situate it within the broader context of the Markaz's own understanding of Islam. Like other Islamist groups, the Markaz sees Islam as a perfect, all-embracing system and way of life. Islam is said to govern all aspects of personal as well as social life, in the form of the shari'ah. For the establishing of an Islamic system, an Islamic state is necessary, which would impose the shar'iah as the law of the land. This is seen as 'the solution to all our problems'. If such a state were to be set up and all Muslims were to live strictly according to 'the laws that Allah has laid down', then, it is believed, 'they would be able to control the whole world and exercise their supremacy'. Since Islam is seen as the very antithesis of nationalism, it demands the establishment of one universal Islamic state, ruled by a single khalifa. Thus, the present division of the Muslims into many nation-states must be overcome. Since 'the ummah is one', it follows from this that 'the system of khilafah does not recognize the physical borders or the independence of one Muslim country from another'. Hence, 'the state is one, the army is one, the flag is one, the budget is one, etc.'.

Islam is seen as a universal ideology meant for all humankind, and hence its message, and, in other words, the boundaries of the Islamic state, must be extended till the entire world comes under its domination. In order for the Islamic call to reach all peoples, it is the duty of the Islamic state to 'carry it to new lands'. This, it is acknowledged, 'will lead to a conflict with other states and ideologies', which can be resolved either peacefully, through diplomatic means, or by force. The Islamic state must first try the former option, but if that fails it is incumbent on it to take recourse to force and wage a jihad. No one can be forced to accept Islam, however, and jihad is to be waged only to bring 'recalcitrant' states under Islamic control by incorporating them within the ever-expanding boundaries of the Islamic state so that the new territories can be 'provided with the security that comes from the application of Islam', in other words, to be ruled by the shari'ah. The people of the conquered lands, if they choose not to convert to Islam, may continue to practise their own religion. In this way, jihad is seen as 'the method adopted by Islam to protect its lands and save humanity from slavery to man-made regimes'. It is, in short, 'the foreign policy of the Islamic State'.

The global jihadist programme of the Markaz presents itself in a liberationist garb, basing itself on widespread feelings of discontent and suffering of sections of Muslims who see themselves as being persecuted by Western-oriented elites in their own countries, as well as by the West more generally. The greatest problem of the Muslims, says Hafeez Muhammad Sa'eed, head of the Markaz, is their 'subjugation to the West'.

Thus, the Markaz is reported to have gone so far as to call for a jihad against the USA. Jihad is contrasted with other forms of war that are pursued for purely worldly concerns, and is described as 'the act of supreme sacrifice to preserve human rights bestowed by Allah'. It is portrayed as a struggle 'to help the oppressed against the atrocities committed by the aggressors', and is compared with 'a surgeon using a blade during an operation'. Jihad is thus a means for challenging oppression and of establishing the rule of Islam.

Eight specific objectives are laid out for this grand jihadist enterprise. These objectives, in the words of an official Markaz statement, are:

- To end persecution and tumult.
- To enforce the Islamic world order.
- To force the disbelievers to pay jizya.
- To protect and shield the weak and the oppressed from oppression.
- To avenge the millions of Muslims who were and are being mercilessly slaughtered in various parts of the world.

- To punish those who have broken covenants made with the Muslims.
- To restore Muslims' possession of territories now occupied by disbelievers, such as Spain, India, Ba'it ul-Muqaddas (Jerusalem), Turkistan (Xinjiang).
- To defend and protect the Muslims continuously facing offensives from the disbelievers all over the world

Jihad is seen as the secret of Muslim power in the past when much of the known world was under Muslim rule, and it is argued that when Muslims 'abandoned jihad and other injunctions they began to degenerate'. In Markaz discourse, jihad is seen as a religious duty binding on all Muslims today. Thus, it is claimed that the prevailing global situation warrants all Muslims to be involved in some way of the other in jihad against non-Muslims. As an official Markaz publication puts its, 'Struggle and fighting against the disbelievers is a comprehensive process, very vast in its nature and scope, and it cannot be carried out successfully and duly unless all the classes of the Muslim community [...] participate in it'. In this grand war there are different roles for different people to play. Those who are ordered by the khalifa to fight must do so, while others may be required to assist the mujahidin by supplying them food, arms and other supplies, providing medical assistance, looking after their families in their absence or even by exhorting others to participate in the war. Thus, every Muslim, man or woman, must be mobilized to assist in the struggle in some form or the other, and if any Muslim has 'never intended to fight against the disbelievers', his or her faith 'is not without traces of hypocrisy'. Those believers who have the capacity to participate or assist in the jihad but do not do so are said to 'be living a sinful life'.

PAKISTANI JIHADISTS AND THE KASHMIR JIHAD

The Islamic Revolution in Iran in 1979, followed by the jihad in Afghanistan (1979-89) against the Soviet occupation soon turned Pakistan into what one commentator termed as 'the original staging ground of Jihad as an international movement'. Large sums of money and huge quantities of arms now began pouring into

Pakistan from various sources, particularly from the USA and Saudi Arabia, apprehensive as both of them were of Soviet expansionism and the Iranian-style anti-monarchical and anti-Western Islamic radicalism in the region. From the early 1980s, Pakistan emerged as the major launching pad for numerous militant Islamist groups fighting in Afghanistan, with large numbers of activists flocking there not only from Afghanistan, but also from the Arab world and from Muslim communities in the West, fired by an irrepressible zeal for the cause of the jihad against the godless Soviets. Several Pakistani Islamic parties, particularly the Jama'at-i Islami, the Jami'at-i 'Ulama-i-Islam and the Jami'at-i 'Ulama-i-Pakistan were also drawn into the jihad, and set up or sponsored their own militant wings. Numerous Islamic seminaries (madrasas) sprang up all over the country, lavishly patronized by the Pakistani military dictator Zia ul-Haq and the Saudis, almost all based on sectarian affiliation, to train their students for the jihad. The consequent spread of what has been called the 'gun-culture' in Pakistan was a major consequence of all these factors. Thus, with arms and funds easily available, Pakistan was rapidly faced with widespread internal conflict, which took several forms—ethnic, between Mohajirs and Pathans in Karachi; and sectarian, between Sunnis and minority Shi'as and, among Sunnis themselves, between Deobandis and Barelwis.

Besides the Soviet presence at Pakistan's very doorstep, several internal factors were responsible for Zia's patronage of radical jihadist outfits. Having captured power through a military coup in 1977, and lacking legitimacy for his rule, he sought to win support for his regime through appeals to Islam, introducing cosmetic changes in the law, such as Islamic punishments, in the name of Islamization, for which he won the warm support of Islamist groups such as the Jama'at-i Islami. Linked to the Islamization project that Zia and Pakistani rulers after him sought to pursue at home was Pakistan's Kashmir policy. To begin with, Pakistan is believed to have extended armed support to the JKLF, arranging for training some of its fighters in the wake of the beginning of the armed uprising in Kashmir in 1989. Soon, however, it was clear to the Pakistani establishment that the JKLF, with its agenda of a free, democratic Kashmir, would not only not toe its line but also pose a threat to its own strategic interests. Hence, from the early 1990s began a policy of deliberate marginalization of the Kashmiri nationalists by the Pakistani establishment, alongside with the cultivation of Pakistani Islamists, who had emerged in the years of the Afghan war, to enter the Kashmir jihad, coupled with lavish patronage extended to Kashmiri Islamist groups such as the JIJK and the HM.

As a result of this change in Pakistan's Kashmir policy from the early 1990s onwards, particularly since the mujahidin victory in Afghanistan in 1992, numerous jihadist outfits in Pakistan began turning their attention towards Kashmir. By the late 1990s, these Pakistani jihadists were playing a key role in the fighting in Kashmir, eclipsing even local Kashmiri groups. Thus, a report brought out by the Indian army in 2000 highlighted the fact that almost all the militant groups active in Kashmir were pro-Pakistan or Pakistan-based, and that the JKLF, the only non-Islamist group included in its list, was 'presently on a low profile'. It estimated that there were some 2750 pro-Pakistan Islamist militants active in Kashmir, while it put the number of JKLF militants at only 60. The groups to whom these Islamists belonged groups were actively assisted by the Pakistani establishment, in particular by its ISI.

With increasing Western criticism of the Pakistani state's role in sponsoring what some have termed as 'Islamic terrorism', an increasing 'privitization of jihad' has occurred. Thus, Pakistan-based organizations that claim to be autonomous of the Pakistani establishment, but are, of course, still dependent on it for patronage, have taken up the task of spearheading the jihad. What is particularly striking about most of these groups is the relatively small Kashmiri presence in both the leadership as well as cadre levels, with almost all their leaders being Pakistani and most of their fighters being Pakistani nationals as well as some Afghans, Arabs and others. Apparently, it is felt that Pakistani strategic interests can be secured only if the leadership and even the rank-and-file of the jihadists remain in Pakistani hands. It has also been argued that the failure or the unwillingness of Kashmiri militant groups to engineer large-scale killings of non-Muslims in Jammu and Kashmir so as to reduce the Hindu population has been an important factor in the promotion of Pakistani-based groups, who have little such compunctions, to take over the armed struggle.

Jihadist Discourse: The Markaz Da'wat ul-Irshad and the Lashkar-i Tayyeba

If the JIJK seeks to seriously question the legitimacy of the discursive framework of the Kashmiri nationalists by seeking to present the Kashmiri armed struggle as a jihad between Islam and disbelief, a further radicalization of the jihadist discourse is clearly evident in the writings and statements of the several Pakistan-based Islamist organizations actively involved in fighting in Kashmir. The most prominent of these groups are the Harkat ul-Ansar, also known as the Harkat-ul Jihad-i Islami, al-Badr, Jami'at ul-Mujahidin, al-Jihad and, probably the most influential of them all, the Lashkar-i Tayyeba ('The Army of the Pure'). All these groups share a common Islamist ideology and advocate the merger of Kashmir with Pakistan.

The Pakistan-based Islamist groups actively involved in the Kashmir conflict are thus today central players in the Kashmiri armed struggle. One of the consequences of their emergence and growing influence has been the further radicalization of the terms of discourse within which the JIJK has sought to portray the Kashmiri armed struggle, arguing against the claims of the Kashmiri nationalists and further developing certain themes that are only vaguely touched upon in Gilani's writings. The jihad is no longer limited to liberating Kashmir from India, but goes far beyond, as we shall see. This is strikingly illustrated in the publications and statements of the Lashkar-i Tayyeba, the 'new masters of Kashmir', and said to be 'the largest jihadi organization in Pakistan'.

The Lashkar is the military wing of an organization called the Markaz Da'wat ul- Irshad ('The Centre for Preaching and Guidance'), set up in 1986 by two Pakistani university professors, Hafiz Muhammad Sa'eed and Zafar Iqbal. Its headquarters are located in a sprawling 160-acre campus at Muridke, a small town in the Gujranwala district of Pakistani Punjab, some thirty kilometres from Lahore. The Markaz is affiliated to the Ahl-i Hadith school, known for its fierce opposition to Sufism and to the established schools of Islamic jurisprudence, insisting that Muslims must go back to the original sources of inspiration—the Qur'an and the Hadith.

It seeks to refashion the worldwide Muslim community in the mould of the Companions of the Prophet. It sees itself as the inheritor of the legacy of the first major jihadist movement in modern times in India, the movement launched by Sayyed Ahmad Barelwi and his band of followers, who, in the early nineteenth century, attempted to set up an Islamic state in the Pathan borderlands and launched an abortive jihad against the Sikhs. The Markaz is believed to be closely linked to the Pakistani establishment as well as to the Jama'at-i Islami of Pakistan.

The Markaz, like many other Pakistani Islamist outfits, was originally designed to serve as a training base for Pakistani militants involved in the Afghan jihad against the Soviets. In 1987, a year after its founding, it set up a training centre inside Afghanistan itself, at Jaji in the Patkia province, and then, shortly after, another in the Kunnar province. It claims that the warriors produced at these centres 'performed outstanding operations' against the Russians. In Afghanistan it carried out its jihad in league with an Afghan outfit, the Jama'at al-Da'wat il al-Qur'an. As the Markaz's activities rapidly grew, it was decided to divide its work into two separate but related sections: the educational and the jihadist. Thus, in 1993, the Markaz established its separate 'jihadic and warfare' wing, the Lashkar. The Lashkar later established four training centres in Pakistan and Afghanistan, where, 'thousands of mujahidin from all over the world are being trained'. Markaz authorities claim that militants produced at these centres have played a leading role in the armed struggles in Afghanistan, Bosnia, Chechenya, Kosovo, the southern Philippines, Kashmir and 'in other areas where Muslims are fighting for freedom'. According to one report, in recent years the spread of the Markaz in Pakistan has 'been phenomenal', and today it has some five hundred offices all over the country, most of them in Punjab, which operate as recruitment centres for would-be mujahidin.

At its Muridke headquarters, the Markaz runs an Islamic school and university, most of whose students are local Pakistanis, with some from Pakistan-administered Kashmir, a few Kashmiris from the Indian-ruled part of the state, and several Afghans and Arabs. Besides, the Markaz has established a network of over seventy schools, mainly in Punjab, where Islamic and modern education are imparted. Young boys of the age of eight are taken in and are given a twelve-year training. A strict military atmosphere is enforced, students must wear military uniforms, abide by military discipline and 'properly assimilate the commandments of their theologians and military instructors that their future profession—as mujahidin—will be in great demand in the Muslim world on the threshold of the new millennium'. At its four training centres, would-be mujahidin are given rigorous military training. This is of two kinds. Firstly, a short twenty-one day course, the daura-i 'ama ('general course'). Secondly, a three month intensive course, the daura-i khasa ('special course'), geared to guerrilla warfare, in which trainees learn how to handle small arms as well as survival and ambush techniques. These courses, it is claimed, 'change the course of life' of the trainees completely', and a sign of this is said to be that they 'no longer shave' and 'wear their shalwars above their ankles, as enjoined by the Prophet Muhammad'.

As in the case of the other Pakistan-based militant groups active in Kashmir today, the Markaz's direct participation in the Kashmir conflict dates to the end of the Afghan war in 1992, in which an estimated 1600 of its militants are said to have participated. After the Soviet withdrawal from Afghanistan, it shifted its attention to Kashmir to 'help the oppressed and innocent Kashmiris who were undergoing Indian aggression for the past fifty years'. In this, they were assisted by the Jama'at-i Islami of Pakistan and the Pakistani intelligence agency, the ISI, key players in the Afghan jihad. The Lashkar is said to have first entered Kashmir in 1990, and then to have 'upgraded' its jihad there in 1993, when its militants attacked an Indian army base in Poonch. In 1994 it began sending large numbers of its fighters into Kashmir, most of them non-Kashmiris. From 1995 it claims that its fighters have been 'engaged properly and striving hard' against the Indian forces. 1996 witnessed a major shift in the Lashkar's Kashmir strategy, with greater attention being paid to the border districts of Jammu, particularly Rajouri and Poonch, as well as Doda. Reports suggest that some of the mass killings of Hindu villagers in these areas have been the work of the Lashkar, with the aim of causing an exodus of the Hindu population of these areas so as to make their task easier. By 1998, it was estimated that the Lashkar had some 350 mujahidin present in Indian-controlled Kashmir. Its fighters are considered by the Indian armed forces to be the best trained among all the militant groups in the region.

In mid-1999 India and Pakistan almost came to war after Pakistan-based militants, believed to be backed by the Pakistani army, occupied certain strategic heights in the Kargil sector in the Ladakh province in the remote northern part of Indian-controlled Kashmir. The four principal militant groups taking part in this operation, all Islamist and manned almost entirely by non-Kashmiris, were the Harkat ul-Mujahidin, the Tahrik-i Jihad, al-Badr and the Lashkar. These groups together formed a joint military command to co-ordinate their military operations against the Indian army. The Lashkar contingent consisted, among others, of several students from its college at Muridke, led by one 'Abdur Rahman 'Abid, a graduate of Medina University. They were joined by some two hundred militants from the Nuristan province of Afghanistan, the first time that such a large number of Afghan fighters had entered Kashmir in recent years.

The Pakistani attempt to enter Kashmir through Kargil failed, however, and under pressure from the West, the country's then Prime Minister, Nawaz Sharif, appealed to the militants to withdraw from the heights that they had captured. The militants, on their part, were reluctant to obey, and they saw Sharif's capitulation to the USA as a betrayal of their jihad. Instead of toeing Sharif's line, they announced what they called 'the second stage' of the Kashmir jihad—taking the battle against the Indian army right inside the Kashmir valley itself, in order, as Zaki ur-Rahman Lakhvi, the amir of the Lashkar, put it, 'to avenge' the atrocities of the Indian army. According to the amir of the Markaz,

Hafiz Muhammad Sa'eed, in this second phase 'the jihad would spread all across Kashmir. It would spread to every peak, every forest and every path'. As part of this new strategy, the Lashkar came up with a new means of attack—suicide bombers, which it named as Ibn Taimiya Fida'i Missions, in memory of the medieval Arab Islamic scholar who crusaded against what he saw as un-Islamic practices, and to whom the Ahl-i Hadith as well as the Lashkar owe much of their inspiration. So far, the Lashkar has conducted scores of fida'i missions in Kashmir and beyond. In all, the Lashkar claimed that by early 2000, it had killed some 2100 Indian army personnel, including senior officers, and to have lost some 500 of its own men in its Kashmir operations.

In the wake of a Lashkar attack on the Indian army headquarters in Srinagar, the capital of Kashmir, in 1999, the head of the Markaz, Hafiz Muhammad Sa'eed declared before an audience of an estimated three hundred thousand people that his fighters could now 'strike anywhere in India', threatening to target even the Indian prime minister's office if India did not stop its aggression on the Kashmiri Muslims and vacate Kashmir.

The jihad, declared Hafiz, was not limited simply to freeing Kashmir from Indian control. Rather, he stressed, it was aimed at 'liberating' India itself. He revealed that the Lashkar was now planning to extend its activities beyond the borders of Kashmir, deep inside India. 'To set up a mujahidin network across India is our target', said Zaki ur-Rahman Lakhvi, chief of the Lashkar, addressing the same congregation. He claimed that his organization was 'preparing the Muslims of India against India' and that once they were ready, 'it would be the start of the disintegration of India'. Some 50,000 Pakistani youth are said to have responded to this appeal to join the grand anti-India crusade.

THE HISTORY OF KASHMIRI JIHAD

More than half a century after Partition, the vexed Kashmir issue continues to fester, threatening to plunge India and Pakistan into the throes of nuclear war. Meanwhile, an estimated 80,000 Kashmiris have lost their lives in the on-going civil war in the area, leaving thousands more raped, orphaned and permanently maimed for life. Religion plays a central role in defining the very way in which the Kashmir issue is seen, by the Kashmiris themselves, and by both India and Pakistan. As a Muslim majority state, albeit with a significant Hindu minority, Pakistan insists that the very logic of the 'two-nation' theory on which it is founded demands that Kashmir should be a part of it. India, on the other hand, claims that the Kashmiris had thrown in their lot with it in 1947, thus forcefully challenging the legitimacy of the theory of Hindus and Muslims being two separate and antagonistic nations. For many Kashmiri themselves, religion per se is not at the root of the problem, which is seen as essentially political, a quest for self-determination of their own political future. A considerable section of the Kashmiris themselves would seem to support the idea of an independent Kashmir. Indeed, the Kashmiri nationalists who launched the militant struggle in the region in the late 1980s aimed at setting up a sovereign, democratic state, with equal rights for all its citizens, irrespective of religion. From the early 1990s, however, owing particularly to growing Pakistani involvement, Islam emerged as a central issue defining the way in which the Kashmiri struggle came to be framed. For a new breed of Islamist militants, their struggle against India was seen as an Islamic jihad, fired by an irrepressible zeal against the 'enemies' of the faith. This so-called jihad is now being sought to be taken further into India, with attacks by Islamist suicide squads on temples, government buildings and other sensitive locations in various parts of the country.

Muslim militancy in Kashmir and Hindu militancy in India feed on each other, with Hindu chauvinist outfits portraying the conflict in Kashmir as a defence of the indivisible 'Hindu' motherland from marauding Islamic hordes. The events in Kashmir have led to a complete breakdown of inter-faith relations in the state of Jammu and Kashmir, with most of the Hindus of the Kashmir valley having fled their homes, and scores of Hindus and Muslims having lost their lives in internecine violence. Elsewhere in India, the Kashmir imbroglio has contributed to a general heightening of Hindu-Muslim strife and conflict, as well as a rapid deterioration of relations between India and Pakistan, setting off fears of a nuclear catastrophe in the region.

This article looks at how the terms of discourse of the Kashmiri struggle have been transformed over time, and how the secular, nationalist Kashmiri movement has been overtaken by radical Islamists pursuing a very different political project, as represented by the Jama'at-i Islami of Jammu and Kashmir and the Lashkar-i Tayyeba. It focuses, in particular, with the issue of how Islam has been understood by Islamists to legitimize their involvement in the current struggle in the region as a jihad, looking at what this means for relations between Kashmiri Muslims and the Kashmiri Hindus and for the ways in which the former are expected to relate to the Indian state. It seeks to grapple with the crucial question of the shifting identities of the Kashmiri Muslims, faced with the might of the Indian state, increasingly defined by an aggressively militant Hindu agenda, on the one hand, and with the increasing salience of Islamist organizations, on the other.

Roots of Revolt

The early Kashmiri independence movement, whose roots go back to the uprising against the Hindu Dogra regime in the 1930s, saw itself principally as a nationalist struggle. From the 1930s till 1947, the Kashmiri movement, under the charismatic Shaikh Muhammad 'Abdullah, aimed at challenging the autocratic rule of the Dogras, demanding proper representation for the Kashmiri Muslims in the administration of the state. In 1947, most of Kashmir came under Indian rule, and from then onwards, a sizeable section of the Muslims of Kashmir carried on, largely through peaceful agitation, a movement for the establishment of an independent state. As 'Abdullah's charisma's gradually declined, with the failure of his National Conference to meet the aspirations of the people and to preserve the autonomy of Kashmir, a new breed of Kashmiri nationalists emerged, disillusioned with what they saw as 'Abdullah's complicity with the Indian state. The leadership of the movement was provided by young Kashmiri Muslims who had received a modern education in the colleges that began to be set up in the region after 1947. Their principal demand was that India should fulfil its commitments to the United Nations and allow a plebiscite to be held in the territory to enable the people to decide their own political future. Challenging the legitimacy of Indian rule, these Kashmiri nationalists advocated an independent, secular democratic Jammu and Kashmir. The ideology informing their nationalist project was that of Kashmiriyat or 'Kashmiri identity', which they saw as a unique amalgam of traditions drawing upon local Muslim, Hindu and other sources. The Kashmiri nationalist project was spearheaded by several organizations and parties, the foremost being the JKLF, established in 1964. The JKLF demanded that the state of Jammu and Kashmir as it existed prior to 1947 be united as 'one fully independent and truly democratic State'. It advocated 'equal political, economic, religious and social rights' for all citizens in the proposed state, 'irrespective of race, religion, region, culture and sex'.

Parallel to the rise of the Kashmiri nationalists, Kashmir in the late 1930s also witnessed the emergence of an Islamist movement. The roots of the Islamist emergence can be traced to the reformist efforts of the Ahl-i Hadith ('People of the Prophetic Tradition'), established in Kashmir in 1925. The Ahl-i Hadith saw themselves as inheritors of the legacy of the Prophet and his Companions, crusading against popular Sufism, the dominant form of Islamic expression in Kashmir, branding it as un-Islamic. Given the deep-rootedness of the Sufi tradition in Kashmir, the Ahl-i Hadith singularly failed to develop a mass following. Rather, it remained, as it does even today, a largely elitist phenomenon, with its core support base among a limited section of the urban middle classes. Ahl-i Hadith-style reformism did, however, provide fertile ground for the emergence of other Islamist trends from the 1930s onwards. Islamism in Kashmir found its most vocal champion in the Jama'at-i Islami, established in 1941 by Sayyed Abul 'Ala Maududi, and organised as an independent organisation and political party in Kashmir in 1952.

The Jama'at-i Islami of Jammu Kashmir (JIJK) remained, at least at the political level, a marginal force in Kashmir till the 1980s, but with the launching of the armed struggle in 1989 it came to play a central role in Kashmiri politics. It forcefully sought to present the armed struggle as a jihad between Islam and disbelief (kufr), thereby challenging the Kashmiri nationalists' definition of the struggle as one between the Kashmiri nation and the Indian state. The Jama'at sees the struggle as a war between Muslims and the 'enemies' of the faith, and is bitterly critical of the notion of a separate Kashmiri national identity. Rather, it insists that the Kashmiris are simply a part of the worldwide Muslim ummah, not a nation by themselves, for, according to it, Islam and nationalism are incompatible with each other. Hence, it argues, the mission of the Kashmiri struggle is not to set up an independent state, which is what the nationalists' project is all about, but, rather, to make Kashmir a part of Muslim Pakistan.

The JIJK's efforts at restructuring the framework of discourse within which the Kashmiri struggle sought to express itself has, from the early 1990s, been given further impetus by the growing intervention in Kashmir of Islamist groups based in Pakistan. These groups tend to see the Kashmiri struggle not simply as a jihad between the Muslims of Kashmir and the Indian state, but in far wider terms: as a 'holy war' between the Muslims of the world, on the one hand, and the Hindus as an entire community, in league with other 'disbelieving' 'enemies of Islam', on the other. In this grand battle, all national and geographical barriers are completely demolished—all Muslims, wherever they may be, are seen as being responsible for contributing in some way or the other in this jihad. On the other hand, Hindus are seen as complicit in the oppression of the Kashmiri Muslims, and hence, considered as enemies. Interestingly, the Hindus are regarded as being hand in glove with other 'enemies' of the Muslim ummah—the Jews and the Christian West—against whom, too, a jihad needs to be waged.

The JIJK and the Kashmiri Jihad

The JIJK was established as an independent organization in 1952, although from the late 1930s a growing number of Kashmiri Muslims had come under the influence of the founder of the Jama'at, Maulana Maududi, principally through his powerful writings. The JIJK presented itself as committed to establishing an Islamic state in Kashmir based on the shari'ah, but using democratic means of peaceful persuasion for attaining its goals. This was stressed in its Constitution, adopted in 1953. Article 2 [b] of its

Constitution states that, The Jama'at shall not employ ways and means against ethics, truthfulness and honesty or which may contribute to strife on earth.

Article 2 [c] of its Constitution lays down that the Jama'at shall use democratic and constitutional methods, while working for the reform and righteous revolution. Till the late 1960s, the JIJK sought to cultivate a constituency for itself through publishing and distributing literature, establishing reading rooms and discussion groups, setting up a network of schools all over the state, and through public lectures. In 1969, for the first time, the JIJK decided to enter the electoral fray, by sponsoring a number of candidates for the local level (panchayati) elections which were held on a non-party basis. Apparently, it was felt that by remaining outside the sphere of electoral politics it was being rendered increasingly ineffective. It was thought, therefore, that elections were 'the best platform to popularize the message of the movement'. Later, the JIJK went on to participate in successive provincial as well as general elections as an independent political party. It failed, however, to win an impressive number of seats in any election, owing both to widespread rigging engineered by the Indian authorities as well as a definite lack of enthusiasm for the JIJK's agenda on the part of the electorate.

The last time that the JIJK participated in the electoral field was in the 1987 elections, as part of the eleven-party alliance, the Muslim Muttahida Mahaz (Muslim United Front or MUF), a group of several Kashmiri parties championing the right to political self-determination of the Kashmiri people. It was widely expected that the MUF would do well in the elections and might even be able to win a majority. However, these elections, like all the others previously held in Kashmir, were marked by massive rigging by the Indian authorities, as a result of which only four MUF candidates were officially declared elected. The election results met with an upsurge of rage and opposition, with mass demonstrations being held against the Indian state for subverting the democratic process. Then, in 1988, having tired of the democratic path of seeking to win the right to self-determination, an armed struggle for the liberation of Kashmir from Indian rule was launched. On 31 July 1989, two massive bomb blasts in the heart of Srinagar, the capital of the state, heralded the launching of the armed struggle. The JKLF claimed responsibility for the act.

The armed struggle launched by the JKLF for the independence of Kashmir found mass support among the Kashmiri Muslims, disillusioned as they were with Indian rule and with the subversion of democratic institutions in Kashmir. The MUF initially hesitated in joining the armed struggle, directing its four representatives within the state assembly, including Sayyed 'Ali Gilani, chief ideologue of the JIJK, to retain their seats so as to be able to air the grievances of the people. However, the rising tide of the JKLF-led struggle soon proved too much for the MUF high command to ignore, and in 1989, it instructed its members in the state assembly to resign and to join the struggle. The JIJK now decided to fully immerse itself in the militant movement, and in 1990 it set up its own militant wing, the Hizb ul-Mujahidin ('The Army of the Holy Warriors', HM).

Given the JKLF's immense popularity among the Kashmiri Muslims, and the mass support for its goal of an independent, democratic and secular Jammu and Kashmir, the JIJK and the HM had to struggle against great odds in putting forward their own agenda of making Kashmir part of Pakistan and establishing an Islamic state in the region. One of the major hurdles that the JIJK had to face in expanding its base beyond a narrow circle of middle class sympathizers was its perceived attitude towards popular Sufi traditions. The JIJK, rooted as it was in a fierce opposition to popular Sufism, was seen by many Kashmiris as opposed to the Sufi saints as such, whom they held in great respect, and despite its efforts to convince people that this was not the case, the JIJK was unable to dispel the notion. Since Sufism is still a dominant form of Islamic expression in Kashmir, this was seen by many as hostility towards Islam itself. Making the JIJK's project more difficult for itself was the fact that although most Kashmiri Muslims were certainly disillusioned with India, it is unlikely that a majority of them would have preferred to join Pakistan instead or to be ruled under a strict Islamist regime, as the JIJK and the HM advocated. To make matters even more difficult for the Islamists was the widespread abuses of human rights by the Indian armed forces, resulting in the killings of many Kashmiri Muslims, among whom were several known Islamist activists and sympathizers.

Despite the immense odds that the Islamists had to contend with, from both the Kashmiri nationalists as well as the Indian armed forces, they strove, through publications, mass meetings, public rallies and the work of their activists, to convince the Kashmiris that the solution to the crisis lay in the project that they were advocating, a counter to both Indian rule and demands for independent nationhood. In this manner, a shift was sought to be made in the terms within which the liberation struggle was being waged. Islam, not Kashmiriyat, and accession to Pakistan, not an independent Kashmir, were presented as the solutions to the Kashmir problem.

Such arguments now began to exercise a broader appeal, especially with the rise of militant anti-Muslim Hindu groups in India, and the subsequent large-scale killings of Muslims in the wake of the destruction of the Babri mosque in 1992. Indeed, the growing popularity of the Islamists in Kashmir and the consequent marginalization of the Kashmiri nationalists has much to do with the rapid spread of the radical Hindu Right in India.

The very real dangers that the rise of Hindutva posed to Muslim lives and identity in India, and to the Muslims of Kashmir as well, made the argument more convincing that the struggle being waged in Kashmir was one between kufr and Islam.

The Islamist reworking of the discursive framework in which the Kashmiri struggle has sought to express itself is well illustrated in the case of the writings of Sayyed 'Ali Shah Gilani.

Gilani has held many top positions in the JIJK, and was for long the chief political spokesman of the party, besides holding the post of chairman of the All-Parties' Hurriyat Conference, an alliance of thirty-four Kashmiri Muslim parties and organizations fighting for Kashmir's freedom from Indian control. He is one of the most senior present-day Kashmiri political leaders and also has the distinction of being the most prolific writer among them all.

Gilani's major writings all date to the 1990s, a period when the JIJK had already immersed itself in the armed struggle, in which Gilani himself played a key role, and for which he was forced to spend several years in various jails.

Not surprisingly, Gilani's writings focus almost solely on the issue of Kashmir's freedom from Indian control. He devotes little attention in his writings to Islamic law, theology and doctrines, for being an ideologue of the JIJK, he takes Maududi's voluminous writings on these subjects as authoritative. Gilani's concern is to place the Kashmiri struggle within the Islamist discursive framework. Thus, the struggle is depicted as a jihad, the goal of which is the merger of Kashmir with Pakistan and the establishing of an Islamic state in the region. As we shall see, however, Gilani's understanding of the struggle differs at some crucial points with the views of the Pakistan-based jihadist outfits, being considerably less radical and uncompromising, at least in some crucial aspects.

Three features are of particular importance in Gilani's description of what he calls the Kashmiri jihad. Firstly, the jihad is seen as directed against the Indian state and its agents, and not against Hindus or Indians as such. Secondly, the jihad has the limited goal of freeing Kashmir from Indian control. Thirdly, the mujihadin have no intention of intervening in Indian internal affairs after the liberation of Kashmir. Once the Kashmir issue is solved by freeing the territory from Indian control and merging it with Pakistan, India and Pakistan, Gilani writes, will be able to establish peaceful and cordial relations with each other, for the root cause of the tensions between the two countries is the dispute over the issue of Kashmir.

Gilani sees the armed struggle being waged in Kashmir not as a war of national liberation, but as a jihad between Islam, on the one hand, and the forces of kufr or disbelief, on the other. He argues that a combination of various developments—India's denial to the Kashmiris of their right to self-determination, its brutal suppression of the Kashmiri struggle which has resulted in the deaths of many thousand Kashmiris, and the rapid rise in India of anti-Muslim Hindu chauvinism—have necessitated the launching of a jihad against India.

He writes that the Indian state has, by its actions, 'proved its extreme hostility towards the religious and moral sensibilities [of the Muslims] and the tenets of Islam'. 'Wherever and whenever the laws of Islam are held out for insult and the religious rights [of the Muslims] are trampled upon', he declares, 'jihad becomes a binding obligation (farz) for all Muslims'.

Such a situation, he says, prevails in Kashmir, and hence the need for a jihad to be waged there. This jihad, he stresses, calls for the participation of all Muslims, not just Kashmiris alone. In a telephonic interview in 1992 with a Lahore-based journalist soon after his release from a long spell in prison, Gilani declared: It has now become incumbent, in the light of the teachings of the Holy Qur'an, upon all the people of Pakistan to participate in the [Kashmir] jihad. They should now stand up determinedly and assist their Kashmiri brethren in the practical jihad. This jihad is a religious duty binding not only on the people of Pakistan, but, in fact, on the entire Muslim ummah [...] The extreme oppression that the Kashmiri Muslims are having to face is an open challenge for the entire Muslim ummah. All Muslims must now move ahead, help the oppressed Muslims [of Kashmir] and stop the hands of the oppressors.

While declaring the armed struggle a jihad, Gilani makes it clear, however, that the armed struggle is directed against the Indian state and not against Hindus or Indian citizens per se.

He makes a clear distinction between the Indian state, on the one hand, and ordinary Indians and Hindus, on the other. Thus, in an appeal to the Kashmiri militants in April 1992 Gilani asserted that, 'The mujahidin have just two enemies: the Indian state and its agents. To waste the power of our youth on targets other than these two is like pouring salt on the wounds of our oppressed people'.

Gilani has, on numerous occasions, appealed for communal harmony between Hindus and Muslims in Kashmir. He stresses that Hindu-Muslim relations in the state have traditionally always been cordial, and that in the past the Valley has never known the wild bloodletting between Hindus and Muslims that has erupted periodically, and now on a menacingly increasing scale, in India. Defending the armed struggle from charges of being anti-Hindu, he asserts that the mass exodus of the Kashmiri Pandits in the early 1990s was actually instigated by the Indian authorities in order to project the Kashmiri struggle as an 'Islamic terrorist' movement, so as to discredit it in the eyes of the West.

Gilani has issued several appeals to the Kashmiri Pandits who have fled from their homes to return and join their Muslim brethren in the struggle. He has also warned the mujahidin that they should desist from any actions 'which will give their opponents a chance to brand them as terrorists'.

Gilani's opposition to the Indian state is limited insofar as his prime objective is to liberate Kashmir from Indian control. The jihad against India, in other words, is circumscribed by the limited objective of freeing Kashmir from Indian rule. Thus, he asserts that after Kashmir is freed from Indian occupation, the JIJK would 'like to see India as free, prosperous and peaceful'. Criticizing certain un-named Kashmiri militant groups for spreading anti-India hatred, he says:

Emotional slogans such as 'Crush India!' are neither realistic nor do they reflect the spirit of Islam. At root, Islam is based on invitation to prosperity, witness to the truth, salvation in the Hereafter, protection of the truth, the ending of every form of oppression and creating understanding between all children of Adam. This, indeed, is the message of the life of the Prophet Muhammad (may peace be upon him). Even when the people of Ta'if unleashed a wave of unlimited oppression on the Prophet of Islam (may peace be upon him), he did not pray to God that they should be destroyed but, rather, that He should guide them [to the right path]. This is why I believe our struggle should be geared only to gaining our rights [...] The slogan of Islam is not one of destruction but of invitation [to the Truth], prosperity, peace and truth.

The legitimacy of the category of the 'Kashmiri nation' that forms the subject of Kashmiri nationalist discourse is vehemently denied by Gilani, this being a logical outcome of his own Islamist position that sees Islam and nationalism as being in complete contradiction to each other.

Here, of course, Gilani seeks to question the very basis of the political agenda of the major rivals of the JIJK, the various Kashmiri nationalist groups such as the JKLF. Gilani argues that nationalism is a 'poisonous philosophy' which the 'enemies of Islam', foremost being 'various Western philosophies', have deliberately sought to infect Muslims with so as to divide and weaken them so that they can be kept under their control.

He insists that the Muslim world-wide ummah is one, monolithic ideological community, cemented together on the basis of 'common belief and faith', which sees no differences of colour, race, language, caste, tribe or family.

He asserts that 'whenever Muslims have ignored the principles of Islam, which sees no boundaries of region, they have lost their power and have become like any other community'. Territorial nationalism, he writes, has proved to be the bane of the Muslims, for it has divided them into different states and, thereby, has deflected them from the task of 'changing the conditions of the entire human race'.

Islam, says Gilani, makes a clear distinction between 'love for their country' (watan dosti), which it allows, and territorial nationalism or 'nation worship' (watan parasti), which it clearly forbids.

'Nation worship', based on the principle of 'my nation, right or wrong', Gilani writes, leads to group prejudice, a quality of the period of the pre-Islamic period of jahiliya, an age of utter darkness. He lays much of the blame for strife, war and bloodshed that characterizes the world today on territorial nationalism. 'Nationalism is the slogan of the jahiliya', he argues, because the nation has usurped from Islam the 'right to decide the criterion for what is right and what is wrong'.

Because of this, large states, such as India, prey on smaller, weaker states, causing endless suffering and misery, 'with millions of people being sacrificed at the altar of nationalism'—in the Kashmiri case, 'at the hands of the priests of Mother India'. However, he asserts, by denying the narrow boundaries that 'nation worship' has inscribed, Islam has 'destroyed into smithereens the idol of nationalism until the Day of Resurrection'.

All Muslims being considered as one nation, Muslims and Hindus in India, and Kashmir as well, are considered to be members of two different nations despite living in the same territory. This, Gilani says, is 'an undeniable truth' (na qabil-i tardid haqiqat).

He writes, conveniently glossing over the remarkable degree to which Muslims in India and Kashmir share a common culture with the Hindus, that not just in matters of faith, beliefs and customs do the two differ, but that they are also distinct and sharply set apart from each other in such matters as food, clothing and lifestyles. For Muslims to stay among Hindus or in an environment which is very different from their own is said to be as difficult as it is 'for a fish to stay alive in a desert'. Muslims, he says, cannot live harmoniously with a Hindu majority without their own religion and traditions coming under a grave threat, one major factor being Hinduism's capacity to absorb other religions and communities into its fold. Hence, for Islam to be preserved and promoted in Kashmir, he insists, it is necessary for Kashmir to be separated from India. Curiously enough, he is silent on the fate of the over 150 million Muslims living in the rest of India.

If all Muslims form one nation and nationalism is antithetical to Islam, then, Gilani implicitly argues, the Kashmiri nationalist project of groups such as the JKLF is itself 'un-Islamic'. From this it follows that the 'Islamic' solution to the Kashmir question is not the establishment of an independent Kashmiri nation-state but, rather, the incorporation of Kashmir into an already-existing existing Muslim state, Pakistan. This is seen as the first step towards the eventual unity of all Muslims. In a pamphlet titled Masla Ka Hal ('The Solution to the Problem'), issued in 1992, Gilani expressed this view thus:

> To advocate that one Muslim group (qaum) be kept apart from the rest would be against the very definition of a people (millat), whose communal identity is based only on one pure creed (kalima tayyiba), especially so when that group shares common ideological, cultural and communal relations with a neighbouring [Muslim] group as well as a common border [...] For such a group to maintain a separate political identity of its own is against the broader interests of the entire Muslim millat.

The JIJK has, in fact, been among the most vocal champions of the merger of Jammu and Kashmir with Pakistan. In a letter to Nawaz Sharif, the then Prime Minister of Pakistan, in June 1993, Gilani commented that in Kashmir the JIJK and the HM 'were the most reliable groups supporting the ideology of Pakistan', and declared that the final goal of the JIJK was Kashmir's accession to that country. In the Kashmir jihad, therefore, the Pakistanis state is seen as having a central role to play, in addition, of course, to the Pakistani people, who are asked to assist the jihad. Thus, in his letter Gilani appealed to the Pakistani Prime Minister for further assistance, but bitterly criticized Pakistan's alleged policy of 'taking everyone together', by which he meant Pakistani support for Kashmiri nationalist groups, in addition to the Islamists. Gilani complained that such a policy was not only 'un-Islamic'; it also is against the very interests of Pakistan itself. He labeled the nationalists as 'enemies of the jihad', and foes of Pakistan, and cautioned that assistance to such groups as advocate secular nationalism posed a grave threat 'to Pakistan's stability and existence'.

MILITANT ISLAM AND AL QAEDA

For years, in a number of South Asian nations, Islamic militancy is continuing to gain strength, thus finally leaving potential threat to regional as well as global security and peace. On the other hand, Jihad and terrorism is being preached in Madrassas, not only in Muslim nations but also in several non-Muslim countries. Jihadist notions are also planted in the minds of people through 'Dawah' promoted by Tablighi Jamaat. First of all, it is essential to understand the latest situation of Madrassa education in Muslim and non-Muslim countries.

Madrassas in Pakistan and Bangladesh

The madrassas in today's Pakistan and Bangladesh, as in India, represent the legacy of the spectacular resurgence of Islamic religious education in India during the late nineteenth century, beginning with the establishment of the Deoband Madrassa in 1867. In most of the madrassas there are no formal admission procedures and legitimacy to the respective madrassas. Major policy decisions regarding doctrinal preferences, curriculum, and selection of teachers and students remain the exclusive prerogative of the ulema. Unlike Pakistan, Bangladesh has two kinds of madrassas: Quomi madrassas—estimated at more than 57,000 at the secondary, intermediate, and higher levels with about 5,762,000 students and 400,000 teachers. The Quomi madrassas are private, receive no financial support from the government, and are supported by local and foreign donations, mostly from the Middle East.

According to the latest data [2007–08) available to the madrassa education board, there are 6,906 non-government Alia madrassas in Bangladesh with the largest number, 12,740, at the dakhil level. The total number of students at all levels in the Alia system is 3,786,500. The number of teachers in these madrassas is 312,898. Unlike the graduates of Quomi madrassas, whose degrees are not recognized by the government and who pursue their careers in religious establishments and private businesses, the majority of the graduates of Alia madrassas merge into the general stream of education by continuing their education in colleges and universities. It is no wonder that a recent survey found that 32 percent of Bangladesh university teachers in the humanities and social sciences were graduates of Alia madrassas.

There are also elementary level madrassas known as maktabs, or ibtedai madrassas, first formally approved by Bangladesh's the then President Ziaur Rahman in 1978. The Madrassa Education Board has approved 9,320 of all independent ibtedai madrassas, with 45,300 teachers and 689,865 students. But in reality there are more than 38,000 ibtedai madrassas with 130,000 teachers and close to four million students. This latter figure is supported by Bangladeshi Ministry of Education estimate made in 1992 which shows the total number of ibtedai madrassa at 17,279. More than 50 percent of students in Quomi madrassas and more than 70 percent of students in Alia madrassas come from an ibtedai background. In Pakistan, the number of secondary and higher madrassas 12,000; Senior and graduate level madrassas 7,446; Deobandi madrassas 5,120; Barelvi madrassas 3,765; Ahl-i-Hadith madrassas 400; Shia madrassas 280; Number of all students

Pakistani students in madrassas 15,765 and Afghan students 61,876. There are a few thousand madrassas in Pakistan which are not registered with the government. And, while in 1947, there was only 137 Madrassas in Pakistan, in 2001, the figure went upto 4,345.

There are approximately eighteen million students in various Madrassas in Pakistan, Bangladesh and India. Majority of these students come from poor families. In Pakistan, the majority of madrassa students belong to the rural areas of the North West Frontier Province [NWFP], Pakistani part of Kashmir, and Punjab. They are mostly drawn from the low strata of society. In a survey conducted in 1976, more than 80 percent of the madrassa students in Peshawar, Multan, and Gujranwala were found to be sons of small or landless peasants, rural artisans, or clergies of the village mosques. They remaining 20 percent came from families of small shopkeepers and rural laborers. A survey, conducted in 2000, found that 55 percent of madrassa students came from peasant families and petty traders. The interesting thing to note is that the number of students whose fathers were employed in lower level private sector jobs rose from 5 percent in 1976 to 35 percent in 2000. Only 3 percent of students in the 2000 survey said their fathers were imams [clergies] of the mosques. The majority of students come from large but low-income families. The 2000 survey found that 63 percent of madrassa students had five or more siblings, and 28 percent of them had seven or more brothers and sisters. In the case of Bangladesh, an overwhelming majority of Quomi madrassa students [82 percent] come from poor families of rural areas and small towns. Sylhet, Chittagong, Comilla, Noakhali and some northern districts have traditionally been the main base of recruitment for the Quomi madrassas.

Madrassas are Breeding Ground of Jihadists

Several reports on internationa media including CNN, BBC etc, as well as Jessica Stern's article in Foreign Affairs and Jeffrey Goldberg's article in the New York Times Magazine, besides several dozen columns of Thomas Friedman, have suggested that the madrassas in Pakistan have become a hotbed of Islamic extremism and the breeding ground of terrorism. They have been variously described as dens of terror, Jihad universities, Jihad factories, and, as the then Indian Prime Minister Atal Behari Vajpayee described them, factories of terror.

There is no doubt that Madrassas have become actibely linked to terrorism and terrorist training camps. Many journalists and commentators have suggested that these madrassas teach Jihadist literature in their course of studies and that their entire curriculum is intended to produce holy warriors. It has also been suggested by many Western scholars that there is an inherent relationship between what is taught in the madrassas on the one hand and religious extremism, Talibanism, militancy, anti-Americanism, anti-Semitism and terrorism, on the other. Madrassa students, through their reading of religious texts, become soldiers of Allah [God] and engage in militant activities against those they consider enemies of Islam [Clergies and teachers in Madrassas teach the students to hate Jews and Christians and term them as enemies of Islam, thus giving provocations of Jihad, alluring heaven and 72-virgins, if anyone would become martyr.

Understandably the US Congress keeps itself informed of the madrasa education in South Asia. A report by the Congressional Research Service [International Terrorism in South Asia] states that among the approximately ten thousand madrasas in Pakistan some that have been implicated in teaching militant anti-western, anti-American and anti-Hindu values. Many of these madrasas are financed and operated by Pakistani Islamist political parties and foreign entities. Foremost US analyst on South Asia Stephen Cohen states that the largest Islamic sects with the greatest control over religious schools are the Deobandis, who are among the most militant in their demand for Pakistan to become truly Islamic. Incidentally Deobandi groups were in the forefront of declaring Ahmadiyyas as non-Muslim in Pakistan. In Bangladesh, anti-Ahmadiyya activities started under the patronization of some Islamist clergies as well as some Islamist leaders thus finally causing series of attacks on Ahmadiyya mosques in various parts of the country under the leadership of Mufti Noor Hussain Noorani and Moulana Momtaji.

Radical Islam and Madrassa

The Iranian Revolution and the Soviet occupation of Afghanistan, both in 1979, inspired a profound shift in the Muslim world—and in the madrasas. Iran's mullahs had managed to overthrow the Shah and take power, undermining the idea that religious education was useless in worldly matters. Although Iranians belong to the minority Shiite sect of Islam, and their madrasas have always had a more political character than Sunni seminaries, the image of men in turbans and robes running a country provided a powerful demonstration effect and politicized madrasas everywhere.

Ayatollah Khomeini's revolutionary regime promised to export its revolutionary Shiite ideas to other Muslim states. Khomeini invited teachers and students from madrasas in other countries to Tehran for conferences and parades, and he offered money and military training to radical Islamic movements. Iranians argued that the corrupt Arab monarchies must be overthrown just as Iranians had overthrown the Shah. Iran's Arab rivals decided to fight revolutionary Shiite fundamentalism with their own version of Sunni fundamentalism. Saudi Arabia and other gulf countries began to pour money into Sunni madrasas that rejected the Shiite theology of Iran, fund ulema who declared the Shiite Iranian model unacceptable to Sunnis, and call for a fight against Western decadence rather than Muslim rulers.

When Awatollah Khomeini captured power in Tehran, he stared funding anti-West and anti-Semitic groups under the umbrella of 'Al Quds Society' and Iranian embassies in various countries openly or secretly continued to fund such activities. Even in the official newsletter published by the Iranian embassies in a number of countries, extreme propaganda against United States, Israel, Jews and Christians are continuing in the name of re-capturing the Al Aqsa [Temple Mount] by the Muslims through Jihad. Leaders and ministers in Khomeini's regime even visited several Muslim and non-Muslim nations to deliver cash to the Islamist groups promoting Tehran's theology. Unites of Hezbollah were created in several Muslim nations and were assigned to recruit members mostly from the madrassas.

In the midst of this conflict, and the madrasa boom it spawned, the United States helped create an Islamic resistance to communism in Afghanistan, encouraging Saudi Arabia and other oil-rich states to fund the Afghan resistance and its supporters throughout the Muslim world. Pakistan's military ruler at the time, Gen. Mohammed Zia ul-Haq, decided to establish madrasas instead of modern schools in Afghan refugee camps, where 5 million displaced Afghans provided a natural supply of recruits for the resistance. The refugees needed schools; the resistance needed mujahideen. Madrasas would provide an education of sorts, but they would also serve as a center of indoctrination and motivation.

General Zia's model spread throughout the Muslim world. Maulana Samiul Haq, headmaster of the Haqqania Madrasa, is a firebrand orator who led anti-U.S. demonstrations soon after the beginning of the war in Afghanistan. When asked if he thought it appropriate to involve his 5 and 6-year-old charges in political demonstrations, Haq remarked, "No one is too young to do the right thing." Later, he added, "Young minds are not for thinking. We catch them for the madrasas when they are young, and by the time they are old enough to think, they know what to think." The 'success' of General Zia's experiment led to the creation of similar free schools in places as diverse as Morocco, Algeria, Indonesia, and the Philippines. Muslim immigrants in Europe and North America established madrasas alongside their mosques, ostensibly to teach religion to their children. Islam requires Muslims to set aside 2.5 percent of their annual savings as zakat [charity], and religious education is one area on which zakat can be spent. Madrasas do not need huge funds to run, though. Teachers' salaries are low, the schools need no funding for research, and books are handed down from one generation to the next.

Madrasas have proliferated with zakat and financial assistance from the gulf states. [Some classrooms at Haqqania Madrassa in Pakistan have a small inscription informing visitors that Saudi Arabia donated the building materials for the classroom]. Modern technology has also played a role, whether by creating international financing networks or new methods of spreading the message, such as through online madrasas. Pakistan had 244 madrasas in

1956. By the end of 2004, the number had risen to 10,000. As many as 1 million students study in madrasas in Pakistan, compared with primary-school enrollment of 1.9 million. Most Muslim countries allocate insignificant portions of their budgets for education, leaving large segments of their growing populations without schooling. Madrasas fill that gap, especially for the poor. The poorest countries, such as Pakistan, Bangladesh, Somalia, Yemen, and Indonesia, boast the largest madrasa enrollment.

ISLAMIST MILITANCY

Islamist militancy is showing new signs of life in Bangladesh despite crackdowns. According to a Christian Science Monitor [CSM] report, terrorist groups are showing a persistence and resilience that has left local authorities worried. However, the CSM says that militancy in Bangladesh is not on the scale or tone that exists in Pakistan or Afghanistan, but has shown a frightening persistence in recent years.

It says that in 2006, police and paramilitary forces systematically targeted and took down the top terrorist organization, Jamat'ul Mujahideen Bangladesh, or JMB. Seven of JMB's leaders were hung in 2007. One estimate suggested there were about 12,000 cadres actively operating in the country, mostly madrassa [Islamic seminary] teachers, students and clerics of mosques.

In April of this year, Bangladesh intelligence agencies declared that the Islamist terrorist groups are reorganizing with the aim of making a deadly comeback.

Bangladesh's teeming cities and rugged countryside have proven an unlikely safe haven for some of the jihadi world's most hardened operatives. In September 2009, police in Dhaka [capital city of Bangladesh] arrested an Afghan war veteran with ties to Lashkar-e-Taiba, the banned Pakistani terrorist organization held responsible for the Mumbai attacks in November 2008. The Christian Science Monitor reported in June that Bangladesh was becoming a hideout for South Asia's terrorists: Bangladeshi police in June uncovered a plot that used Bangladesh to funnel thousands of weapons to an Indian separatist group.

The police also arrested an operative working for notorious South Asian terrorist Daud Ibrahim, who is alleged to have ties to Al Qaeeda. The operative disclosed that 150 of Daud Ibrahim's operatives are stationed in Bangladesh.

Religious Extremism in Bangladesh

Definition of political parties has changed for some from the time of Edmund Burke as "an organized assembly of men, united for working together for national interest" to one that may not accept members from the minority community and is insistent on establishing Islamic rule or Khilafat. Indeed the head of the Hizb-Ut-Tehrir [HuT], Hizbut Towhid [HT], Khelafat Majlish [KM] as did few other Islamist parties publicly announced that "we always want to oust all governments in all Muslim countries in the world to establish Khilafat states". The world is already mired in the militant activities of al-Qaeda operatives, their latest victims being the carnage at Mumbai [India] and the Marriot Hotel in Islamabad [Pakistan]. In recent months, although Dhaka is governed by a political party having secularist ideology, notorious Islamist militancy group named Hizbut Towhid is allowed to openly publish and sell books and DVDs pronouncing Jews and Christians as 'enemies of Islam' and instigating the Muslims in waging 'holy war' against them. Hizbut Towhid denounces democracy and promotes Caliphate Rule in Bangladesh and other nations in the world. Leaders of this extremist group consider notorious terrorists like Osama Bin Laden as 'hero of Islam'. It was already reported in local and international media that Hizbut Towhid has expanded its activities in a number of Asian nations as well 'successfully' created its base in some Western countries.

After Afghanistan, Islamic fundamentalism went global with its appeal to a section of Muslim society based on moral, cultural and political grounds. The Islamists argue that western culture particularly the one practiced by western women is essentially degenerative and incompatible with Quranic literalism. They argue that the values propagated by the West threaten Islamic "purity" and hence their advance is to be thwarted at any cost. Political argument is by far the easiest to sell to the wayward Muslim population who despite declaration of piety could have nursed in the darkest corner of their heart a desire to commit the original sin. The Islamists argue that the reasons for economic backwardness, political repression and societal dysfunction were caused by Western, particularly American assistance given to the repressive regimes in the Muslim world. The situation in Bangladesh is no exception. Under the embrella of "Organization for welfare of the reptariate soldiers from Afghanistan and Palestine", militancy and anti-Semitic notions are planted in the minds of people. It was clearly proved that several terror patron nations, including Iran, is continuing to finance such activities. Later, a large number of people belonging to Organization for welfare of the reptariate soldiers from Afghanistan and Palestine, entered Harkat-Ul-Mujahedin Bangladesh, Harkatul Jihad [Huji] and other ferrocious Islamist militancy outfits. There are also evidences that a number of Islamist political parties in Bangladesh, as well as some 'secularist' forces have openly or secretly joined hands with such extremist Islamist groups either with ulterior political motive or for expanding their vote banks.

Democracy and Islam

An inconclusive debate remains about the incompatibility of democracy with monotheistic religions. Robert Dahl in his classic book 'Polyarchy' had set eight essential requirements for democracy: right to form and join organizations; freedom of expression; right to vote; eligibility for public office; right of political leaders to compete for support for vote; and institutions for making government policies dependant on vote and other expressions of preference. Other political scientists have added that democracy must also have a constitution that by itself is democratic in that it respects fundamental liberties and offers protection to minorities. Additionally democratically elected governments must rule within the confines of their constitutions, be bound by law and be accountable. From historical observations it has been found that religions place inherent obstacles in the way of democracy. Philosopher John Rawls found it particularly difficult in a pluralistic society in which citizens hold a variety of socially embedded, reasonable yet deeply opposed comprehensive doctrines to arrive at an overlapping consensus. In the case of Islam some western scholars have found that because of its Prophet's fusion of military and spiritual authority and because Quranic laws are deemed to be final the space for democratic debate for the formation of secular laws does not exist in Muslim societies. Some other scholars however have found that appropriation of political Islam by Islamic fundamentalists is untenable and millions of Muslims living outside the Arab world live in intermittent democracies and they may not become victims of so-called Islamic Free Election Trap in which fundamentalists use democratic means to get to power only to abolish democratic practices through legislation.

Democracy is a dynamic process and "a state's raison d'etre does not lie in the protection of equal individual rights but in the guarantee of an inclusive process of opinion and will formation in which free and equal citizens reach an under standing on which goals and norms lie in the equal interest of all". Clearly then an ethical question would arise as perceived by Italian political scientist Luigi Bonante while discussing the difference between the individual and the state. He argues that while the state has sufficient tools to defend its rights and reject its duties; for the individual as recipient it is much harder to elude his duties than to achieve his freedom.

This kind of asymmetry of power during the BNP-Jamaat [2001-2006] rule in Bangladesh provides strong argument for the protection of human rights. The Orwellian tyranny of the majority was further compounded by increasing activism of Islamists who wish to recreate a truly Islamic society not simply by imposing the Sharia but by establishing an Islamic state where religious edicts will be integrated into all aspects of society.

6

ISI and Fomenting of Global Terror

In the post 9/11 decade, ISI's involvement in fomenting terror modules in different parts of the world, using proxy outfits like the LeT or the HUJI has been exposed, be it through the arrest of Virgil Brigitte in Australia (2003) or the failed terror plots in the UK and the US in more recent times.

This global terrorist networks with linkages to ISI us shown in the diagram that follows. Outfits inside Pakistan which have had links with or were spawned by the ISI include the LeT, the Jaish e Mohd (JeM), Lashkar e Jhangvi (LeJ – more into sectarian terrorism), Harkat ul Mujahideen (HuM) which morphed into HUJI, and the Dawood underworld mafia. On the periphery ring are outfits with presence in countries like Bangladesh-the Ahle Hadis al Bangladesh (AHAB), HUJI-BD, Jamiyatul Mujahideen Bangladesh (JMB) and Jagrata Muslim Janata Bangladesh (JMJB). In recent years though, security agencies of the new government in Bangladesh havedone much to dismantle these outfits. Nevertheless, linkages persist between ISI and Pakistan based religious or ideologically motivated terrorism outfits like LeT, Jaish and HUJI in countries like Afghanistan. Modules have also been found in Europe or USA.

Decision makers in army/views and orientation of senior officers in Army/ISI on matters of geo-strategic import.

A career or a posting in the ISI has now emerged as a desirable option, with young officers of the rank of captain, major or colonel enjoying far greater power, perks and privileges in the ISI than many of their peers in more routine army field assignments. At any given time, the decision makers in the ISI are the army chief and the DG, ISI.

At the second rung of ISI are major generals, one or the other of them could be personally close to the COAS, in which case they may be able influence policy decisions but this may be the exception than the rule. As in the army itself, a collegiate or consensus decision making pattern is usually the norm and prevails in decision making and operational initiatives undertaken by ISI.

Army/ISI & Politicization

With regard to military-civilian interaction, all ISI officers believe in the primacy of the army and its status as the vanguard institution of state. There is a general contempt for all manner of politicians and political parties. This is compounded by the fact that there are no politicians of individually high popularity or charismain Pakistan at present.

Though the lustre attaching to ISI was somewhat tarnished by the US sealsmission to take out Osama bin Laden in Abbotabad in Ma,2011, as well asthe opprobrium following the Saleem Shehzad murder post the attack on theMehran Naval Base.

But by and large, all army officers, especially those in ISI,even at middle or relatively junior levels believe that the army's dominant rolein taking vital foreign policy decisions has only been good for the country andcannot be questioned.

They would not readily countenance any erosion in thisdominance, unless the army chief himself and the collegiate leadership group of Corps Commanders acquiesce in such a role re-definition. This is not likely to happen in the foreseeable future.

TERRORISM AND THE PAKISTANI INTELLIGENCE AGENCY

Pakistan's intelligence agency, the Inter-Services Intelligence (ISI), has long faced accusations of meddling in the affairs of its neighbors. A range of officials inside and outside Pakistan have stepped up suggestions of links between the ISI and terrorist groups in recent years. In autumn 2006, a leaked report by a British Defense Ministry think tank charged, "Indirectly Pakistan (through the ISI) has been supporting terrorism and extremism—whether in London on 7/7, or in Afghanistan, or Iraq."

In India, Mumbai's police chief has claimed to have proof that the ISI planned the July 2006 bombing of the Indian city's commuter rail system, which was carried out by the Kashmir-based militant group Lashkar-e-Taiba.

After massive bombings marred former Prime Minister Benazir Bhutto's October 2007 return to Pakistan, some of her supporters blamed the ISI; Bhutto herself called for the sacking of the country's intelligence chief.

In a September 2006 BBC interview, President Pervez Musharraf underscored the importance of his nation's role: "Remember my words: if the ISI is not with you and Pakistan is not with you, you will lose in Afghanistan." In a later appearance on NBC's "Meet the Press," Musharraf acknowledged some retired ISI operatives could be abetting the Taliban insurgency in Afghanistan. But Pakistan's government denies allegations of supporting terrorism, citing as evidence its cooperation in the "war on terror," in which it has taken significant losses, politically and on the battlefield.

Does ISI Support Terrorists?

"The ISI probably would not define what they've done in the past as 'terrorism,'" says William Milam, former U.S. ambassador to Pakistan. Nevertheless, experts say the ISI has supported a number of militant groups in the disputed Kashmir region between Pakistan and India, some of which are on the State Department's Foreign Terrorist Organizations list. Though the level of assistance to these groups has varied, Kathy Gannon, who covered the region for decades for the Associated Press, says previous support consisted of money, weapons, and training.

Though Pakistani officials deny any current support for the Taliban—which the State Department does not deem a terrorist group—the ISI certainly has supported Afghan insurgents in the past. ISI's first major involvement in Afghanistan came after the

Soviet invasion in 1979, when it partnered with the CIA to provide weapons, money, intelligence, and training to the mujahadeen fighting the Red Army. At the time, some voices within the United States questioned the degree to which Pakistani intelligence favoured extremist and anti-American fighters. Following the Soviet withdrawal, the ISI continued its involvement in Afghanistan, first supporting resistance fighters opposed to Moscow's puppet government, and later the Taliban.

Pakistan stands accused of allowing that support to continue. Afghan President Hamid Karzai has repeatedly said Pakistan trains militants and sends them across the border. In May 2006, the British chief of staff for southern Afghanistan told the Guardian, "The thinking piece of the Taliban is out of Quetta in Pakistan. It's the major headquarters." Speaking at the Council on Foreign Relations in September, President Musharraf responded to such accusations, saying, "It is the most ridiculous thought that the Taliban headquarters can be in Quetta." Nevertheless, experts generally suspect Pakistan still provides some support to the Taliban, though probably not to the extent it did in the past. "If they're giving them support," Gannon says, "it's access back and forth [to Afghanistan] and the ability to find safe haven."

How much Control does Pakistan's political Leadership have over the ISI?

Experts say Musharraf exercises firm control over his intelligence agency. "I do not accept the thesis that the ISI is a rogue organization," Milam says. "It's a disciplined army unit that does what it's told, though it may push the envelope sometimes." With a reported staff of 10,000, ISI is hardly monolithic: "Like in any secret service, there are rogue elements," says Frederic Grare, a South Asia expert and visiting scholar at the Carnegie Endowment. He points out that many of the ISI's agents have ethnic and cultural ties to Afghan insurgents, and naturally sympathize with them.

President Musharraf's admission that retired ISI agents may be helping Taliban fighters suggests his government knows of at least some unsanctioned Pakistani support for the Afghan insurgency. Experts note Musharraf's acknowledgement also gives him plausible deniability of any sanctioned assistance Pakistan may also be providing. Marvin G. Weinbaum, an expert on Afghanistan and Pakistan at the Middle East Institute, says Pakistan has sent "retired" ISI agents on missions the government could not officially endorse. Some observers believe Pakistan's duplicity is deliberate: "Musharraf's been playing with us since day one," Grare says.

What has Pakistan done to Combat Terrorism?

Pakistan has arrested scores of al-Qaeda affiliates, including Khalid Sheikh Mohammed, the alleged mastermind of the 9/11 attacks. The ISI and the Pakistani military have worked effectively with the United States to pursue the remnants of al-Qaeda. Pakistan also stationed 80,000 troops in the troubled province of Waziristan near the Afghan border. Hundreds of Pakistani soldiers died there in resulting clashes with militants, which Musharraf told a recent CFR meeting "broke the al-Qaeda network's back in Pakistan." Though Pakistan has effectively battled al-Qaeda, Weinbaum says it has largely ignored Taliban fighters on its soil. "There are extremist groups that are beyond the pale with which the ISI has no influence at all," he says. "Those are the ones they go after."

What is Pakistan's Interest in aiding the Taliban?

Pakistan does not enjoy good relations with the current leadership of Afghanistan, partly because of rhetorical clashes with Afghan President Hamid Karzai, and partly because Karzai has made strong ties to India. Some experts say Pakistan wants to see a stable, friendlier government emerge in Afghanistan. Though the raging insurgency certainly doesn't serve this goal, increased Taliban influence, especially in the government, might. Supporting the Taliban also allows Pakistan to hedge its bets should the NATO coalition pull out of Afghanistan. Not everyone agrees with this analysis. According to Weinbaum, Pakistan has two policies. One is an official policy of promoting stability in Afghanistan; the other is an unofficial policy of supporting jihadis in order to appease political forces within Pakistan. "The second [policy] undermines the first one," he says.

Pakistan's interest in aiding Kashmiri Militants

Throughout its existence, Pakistan has viewed India as its enemy. Though Islamabad has a real interest in fostering better relations with New Delhi, little love is lost between the nations. Some experts say the Kashmiri militants keep pressure on the Indian government, though others point out the militants' actions have sparked tense showdowns between the two nuclear-armed states in the past. While Pakistan has a formidable military presence near the Indian border, Gannon says the militant groups there serve as "their second line of defense and offence."

British and Indian Charges against Pakistan

Experts are skeptical. Indian officials claim to have evidence that the ISI planned the July bombing of the Mumbai commuter trains, but the charges seem unlikely to some observers of the long, difficult India-Pakistan relationship. The two nations have a history of finger-pointing, and while some of the allegations hold water, there is a tendency to exaggerate. Furthermore, endorsing an attack on India would undermine Musharraf's own policy. "Pakistan is genuinely trying to open up relations with India," Gannon says.

In Weinbaum's view, the British report—which London insists is not a statement of policy—makes "too broad a statement." Though Pakistan does offer safe haven to Kashmiri groups, and perhaps some Taliban fighters, the suggestion that the ISI is responsible for the 7/7 bombings of London's mass transit system is "a real stretch," Gannon says.

Pakistan's Relationship with the Tribal Leaders in its Northwestern Provinces

Despite President Musharraf's claims of success in Pakistan's three-year military incursion into Waziristan, the region remains problematic. Local tribesmen are the traditional power brokers, and over the last two decades, they have earned large sums of money offering safe haven to Taliban and foreign fighters. At the outset of the U.S.-led war in Afghanistan, many militants fled across the border into Waziristan, putting pressure on the Pakistani government to address the situation. ISI officials met resistance when they asked local leaders to hand over foreign militants. Pakistan deployed troops to the area, though reports suggest that they took as many casualties as their adversaries. Unable to make military progress, Pakistani officials negotiated a peace deal with the local tribesmen, which was seen by many as a capitualtion to tribal influence in the area.

ISI AND ITS CHICANERY IN EXPORTING TERRORISM

Spying is the second oldest profession and nowhere else has it flourished more in a short span of time, that too, with professional élan, than in Pakistan. Known by an innocuous sounding Inter Services Intelligence, abbreviated ISI, it is a wellspring of power and one of the most virile intelligence agencies in the Third World. Its forte lies in intrigue, hatching conspiracies, brokering terrorism and paddling misinformation.

In recent months, the ISI has been in the limelight, its skulduggery having received a new thrust; - and notoriety, fresh showing. A report has been submitted to the House of Representatives by a US task force on terrorism and unconventional warfare. The report, titled, *"The New Islamic International"* is significant in revealing the exploits of the ISI. That the original document is dated 1 Feb, 1993 and that it has some inaccuracies, does not make the findings any less weighty.

A chilling account" of the role of the ISI's involvement with Sikh militants, bombing of *Kanishka* and American, indifference, even complicity, has been chronicled in a TV documentary of the "Fifth Estate" of the Canadian Broadcasting Corporation (CBC). The documentary deplores the stark incertitude of the US administration, although it had all the evidence at its command. What is worse, by overplaying India's human rights record, Washington has rewarded and encouraged ISI in its evil pursuits. Another TV feature produced by CNN, traces the ISI connection to Afghan *Mujahideen* and their involvement with the bomb explosion at the World Trade Centre. The two documentaries together, and the Canadian one by itself constitute the most damning indictment of the ISI Involvement in terrorism in India.

There is no let-up in ISI's activities in Kashmir, which include recruitment, training, arming and induction of terrorist bands, besides guidance in planning and conduct of operations. ISI has a strong connection with Sheikh Mubarak Shah Jiiani and his fundamentalist outfit AI Fuqra. The group was responsible for "a decade long string of assassinations and bombings in the name of Islamic purity."' Lately, the ISI has ventured in the heartland through promotion of narco- terrorism chauvinism. That the organisation has a collaborator in the Nepalese Parliament, is sinister enough, but far more portentous is the patron-age bestowed by the Bangladesh Government to the organisation for promoting insurgency in the North East. Recently, a diabolic plot has been unravelled, which suggests that ISI, with a view to destabilising the country and creating mayhem, had planned to repeat the Bombay blasts and ignite communal riots all over India to coincide with the Republic Day celebrations. With the arrest of four Pakistanis, one Bangladeshi and one Indian in the capital by the Delhi police, a major breakthrough in exposing diabolic designs of the ISI has been achieved. "Though intelligence agencies are still trying to fully comprehend the ramifications of the latest ring unearthed by them, the case is perhaps the most brazen attempt of Pakistan-trained nationals being sent to create terror countrywide; the low intensity proxy war transcending to practically open hostilities."

Mission, Budget and Organisation

The ISI was founded in 1948 by a British army officer, Maj Gen R Cawthome, then Deputy Chief of Staff in Pakistan Army. He conceived it as part of the military establishment, intended to combine and co-ordinate intelligence set-ups of the Services. Over the years, it gathered influence and when Zia seized power, it acquired real muscle. Today, the ISI has achieved the dubious distinction of being the most dreaded outfit, within; and a master-hand in dispensing terrorism, without.

ISI charter incorporates gathering of external and internal intelligence; co-ordination of intelligence functions of the three Services; surveillance over its cadre, foreigners, media men, politically conscious segments of Pak society, diplomats of other countries accredited to Pakistan and Pak diplomats serving outside the country; interception and monitoring of communications; and conduct of covert offensive operations.

Unlike intelligence agencies of other countries, the top and middle rung officers of the ISI are exclusively drawn from the military establishment. Its chief is designated as director general and appointed from amongst the serving lieutenant generals; although there has been one exception when a retired officer was assigned to the post. During Yahya Khan's rule, the DG also headed the newly created National Security Council and that added to his stature and influence. Under the DG there are three deputy director generals (DDGs), one each from the army, the navy and the air force. The ISI mans a Military Liaison Section (MLS) in the Ministry of Interior. ISI is a major beneficiary of Pakistan's national budget, with a large unaccountable chunk coming from the defence outlay. In Pakistan, no one knows, not even the Prime Minister, as to how much ISI costs to run or precisely how many people it employs. But today, the ISI enjoys total support of the Prime Minister.

The fact that, both, she and her father had suffered at the hands of ISI has been forgotten and treated as a closed chapter. She has learnt the bitter lesson from her previous tenure as the Prime Minister, when she confronted the organisation and tried to clip its wings. In the battle of wits, the ISI won and retained its clout; she lost and was sent packing. ISI continues to call the shots, the inspired views of its devaluation notwithstanding.

During the late 80s the most powerful component of the organisation was Joint Intelligence Bureau (JIB), which handled political intelligence. In her earlier incarnation as the PM, Benazir ordered transfer of the functions of JIB to the Interior Ministry, but the rumour has it that the sensitive files and dossiers were, instead, moved to the GHQ. Later, they found their way back to the very drawers and cabinets from which they were taken out. And now the ISI has become a law unto itself.

An equally powerful component of the ISI is the Joint Counter Intelligence Bureau (JCIB), it continues to wear authority and influence on its sleeves.

It has a director for field surveillance, who keeps a watch on Pak diplomats accredited to other countries. The bureau conducts intelligence operations in Asia and the Middle East. Its special spheres of interest are. the countries of South Asia, a common knowledge; and China, a fact not so well known. ISI's operations in China were started in collaboration with the CIA and perhaps continue to be so; this activity is passionately disguised and denied for obvious reasons. Lately, Afghanistan and Muslim republics of the former Soviet Union too, are being handled by JCIB and these countries have become a favourite haunt of ISI agents." The wing also keeps IS Directorate under surveillance through a section referred to as ISSS and prepares reports for the chief executive; for the latter purpose, there is a director attached to the PM's Secretariat.

Joint Intelligence Miscellaneous (JIM) deals with espionage in foreign countries and offensive intelligence operations. J&K affairs, including infiltration, exfilteration, propaganda and shady operations, is the mission assigned to JIN (an abbreviation standing for Joint Intelligence : North) under DDG External II, a post generally held by a major general. While the IN is staffed by military technocrats, who could be described in modern parlance as system analysts, the cloak and dagger stuff is the preserve of operational cells and forces, dedicated to the mission. Those exclusively set up for J&K have been periodically wound up and then re-created with the aim of causing confusion. During Zia's time, a special cell was established for Afghanistan which had under it deputy directors responsible for political affairs, training, arms distribution and refugees. This was disbanded after the Jallalabad fiasco. Although no precise information is available, it is believed that a similar cell was created for imparting training and distribution of arms to the Sikh extremists and it continues to be active.

Another field in which the ISI has been highly successful, is gathering of signal Intelligence. This mission is assigned to JSIB (Joint Signal Intelligence Bureau) which has DDs (Deputy Directors) Wireless, Monitoring and Photos on its establishment. The organisation runs a chain of intercept stations along the entire

Indo-Pak border, besides providing communication support to the militants operating in the Valley. In the spring of 1992, it was estimated that there were about 200 clandestine radio stations operating on the Indian soil.

JIX is the largest wing, which serves as the secretariat. It co-ordinates the functions of other wings and field organisations, prepares intelligence estimates and threat perceptions, besides giving administrative support to the organisation.

Zia's Contribution to ISI's Growth

It is tragic that in the middle ages, most Islamic politics degenerated and settled down as personal despotism, the egalitarian spirit and appeal of the religion notwithstanding. Aggressive Islamization in Pakistan, true to historical legacy, has proceeded in tandem with Zia's totalitarian statecraft. Zia found in the ISI a useful instrument to synthesise the two with a view to eliminating internal opposition and promoting fanaticism, which *inter alia* included such insidious ploys as exporting terrorism and conducting raids in the name of *jihad*. He cleverly manipulated the diverse, yet coterminous aphorism of Khomeini's Islamic revolution and American foreign policy objectives in support of policy of subversion in Afghanistan and when that showed promise, made a grand design to destabilise India.

A strong component of American foreign policy interest at the fag end of the Cold War was to ostracise communist influence in Afghanistan and teach the former Soviet Union a lesson for its interventionist policies.

"In pursuance of this objective CIA forged a close relationship with the ISI, through which three billion dollars worth of arms were channelled to the Afghan *Mujahideen*. Hekmatyar was adopted as the intelligence agencies favourite surrogate to prosecute America's Proxy war against the Soviet Union." Zia utilised the opportunity not only to rehabilitate his tarnished international image by becoming a front-line warrior against the communist menace but also to settle scores with India.

During Zia's reign, the ISI fuelled the separatist movements in Punjab and Kashmir. In domestic affairs, it acquired a special status and immense power. Experience in Afghanistan, where in collusion with the CIA, It conducted one of the biggest covert operations in the world since the end of the Vietnam war gave its teeth a sharper bite. It luxuriated in joint collaboration with CIA and was privy to arcane ways, learning the latest tricks of the trade. In Afghanistan, it played one group of the *Mujahideen* against the other and then presided over the assemblage to compose differences and broker accords. It did not spare its mentors, the CIA. Without their knowledge and concurrence, it helped itself to dollars and siphoned off arms meant for *Mujahideen* to Iran, an arch enemy of the US. When the beans were spilled and the US decided to send a fact-finding and stock-taking board, it fudged records, put Ojhri camp to the torch and destroyed the incriminating evidence.

Internal Involvements

In his book, *If I am Assassinated,* Bhutto charged that the ISI was actively used to spy on him, whereas it had failed miserably when it came to gathering hard intelligence in both, 1965 and 1971 operations. He writes, "How did Ayub Khan and Yahya Khan use the intelligence agencies? Yahya Khan used to the hilt the intelligence agencies for political purposes to divide the politicians and influence the elections of 1979." In the same vein, he repeats, "Ayub Khan also used the intelligence agencies for political purposes to the hilt... He tried to prevent my party from getting off the ground." Narrating the episode when Ayub Khan sought an explanation about the inability of the ISI to locate the Indian Armoured Division, he quotes DG, ISI Brig Riaz Hussain of having replied, "Sir, from June 1964, Military Intelligence has been given political assignments on elections and post-election repercussions."

Bhutto on ISI

Bhutto, in the book *If I am Assassinated* writes extracts of the White Paper issued by the Zia administration that it "demonstrates its piety with crocodile tears on the role of the intelligence agencies of the State as a political arm of the government of Pakistan People's Party." He writes that on page 195, the White Papers registers it concern in the following words.. "The role of the intelligence agencies of the State as a political arm of the PPP regime, particularly in relation to the general elections, raises many disconcerting questions.

When politics permeates such sensitive institutions as the Intelligence Bureau or the ISI, it naturally deflects them from their prime concern with the State's external and internal security. Political bias against dissenting political parties which are a very necessary component of a democratic society, also tends to complicate and distort the task of State security."

Bhutto refutes the allegations and writes that Lt Gen G Jilanl was DG of ISI before he became President of Pakistan on 20 Dec 1971, that except for him, "all the officials incharge of intelligence at the federal level were arrested on the night of the coup, or within a month of it," that Jilanl was "not touched but on the contrary was sent to the Defence Ministry as its Secretary."

He further adds, "This question must be considered in conjunction with Lt Gen Jilanl's successful effort in influencing me to consider the then Maj Gen Zia-ui-Haq for the post of the Chief of Staff in suppression of about six Generals.

This is only a fraction of the story. But even with this *minimum disclosure* I would like to ask who exploited whom? Did the Military Intelligence Chief and his Chief of Staff exploit me or I exploited them?".

Undoubtedly Bhutto suffered at the hands of the ISI, but he cannot be absolved of his contribution to the breeding of this Frankenstein. Of his own admission, he mooted the suggestion for "the merger of Central Intelligence Agencies into one integrated intelligence department divided into two categories (i) internal and (ii) external. Obviously, he conceived a greater role for the ISI, hoping to keep his position secure by placating the military's most powerful army, but the chicks came home to roost. It was Zuifiqar, who legalised the ISI's involvement in domestic surveillance, for which he paid heavily. Benazir, too, had wrecked her reputation and suffered a smash-up when she tried to take on the ISI. Today, she is an ardent supporter of the organisation and a collaborator of its misdemeanours.

Proxy War in Kashmir

The extent of Pakistani and Afghan influence on the Islamic transformation of the Kashmiri insurgency is quite clear. In mid-Eighties, Islamic revivalism had taken a "radical political stance", slogans advocating establishment of an Islamic state were publicly raised and received with growing popularity. The population came under the influence of the leadership of Jamaati-islami and Khomeinists. By 1984, an Islamic radicalisation had developed that saw the rise of such movements as JKLF, Kashmir Liberation Front, the Mahaz-e-Azadi and the Liberation League.

By 1985, Jamaat-e-lsiami and Al-Jihad movements had become influential in Kashmir politics. Islamic indoctrination was provided by Jamaat-isiami of Pakistan". This is the same organisation about whose leaders Bhutto had written that, "they show a total ignorance of Islam and betray an un-islamic mentality", they "follow the ways of *jahiliyat* (imbecility)" and accused them of denouncing *Qaid-i-Azam* as*Kafir-e-Azam.*

Al Jihad took inspiration from the ideology of the Iranian revolution. It publicly pronounced that "Islamic revolution" was the only way to liberate Kashmir. In a short span of a few years, "there was a marked erosion of the secular Kashmiri personality and a Muslim identity with fundamentalist overtones started emerging rapidly." It lent justification to give the movement "a pan-Islamic character and an extra territorial dimension."

In the early stages, the ISI used *Mujahideen* infrastructure to help the Kashmiri and Sikh separatists. "At times the assistance was funnelled through Afghan rebel leader Gulbuddin Hekmatyar's Hizb-i-isiami group, thus providing 1siamabad with deniability."

The report submitted by the task force to the American Congress mentions creation of a special force, which made its debut in July 1991 and within months perpetuated communal frenzy and accelerated militancy. This was the time when Pak sponsored terrorism was at its peak. The novel feature of the special force is that it has been drawn from those with operational experience in Afghanistan. Officered by mainly Punjabis, the cadre is highly motivated and willing to undertake daring assignments.

They have let loose agents provocateur, who freely mingle with government functionaries in the Valley and have been known to use Indian army and police uniforms. Recent events show that they have been effective in creating bad blood between the two arms of the security outfit, pitching one against the other. A hot ploy is to commit atrocities the garb of the security forces, so that the finger of accusation is pointed in the wrong direction.

The report points out that about 20,000 young Kashmiris have been trained and armed in POK in recent years. It dwells at length over the Pakistani involvement in stoking the fire of terrorism and insurgency in Kashmir. "Indeed the very size of the Pakistani training programme is telling," it observes; and goes on to describe the breakdown of the number of trainees in the ISI run camps and their cabal affiliation.

In the manner of Maoist classical approach, 1987 to 1989 marked the first stage of insurgency. It aimed at seeding discontent and creating a nucleus of Islamic militancy; and was characterised by sporadic uncoordinated attacks on soft targets. The insurgents adopted hit and run tactics and avoided direct confrontation with the security forces. "Only expendable, barely trained terrorists were committed." Had the Indian authorities dealt with the insurgents more firmly and nipped the secessionist movement in the bud, the ISI would have suffered a dismal defeat, but the Government dilly-dallied; worst, it openly aired differences within its own ranks on the approach to be adopted. This led to the second stage, more professionalized and better co-ordinated. The assassination of Mirwaiz provided the right kind of opportunity for garnering active support for the terrorists.

In early 1992, the ISI had established a common command over the disparate military arms of organisations that had mushroomed, true to the example set by the *Mujahideen* of Afghanistan and the general pattern of Islamic militancy elsewhere. It succeeded in the fall of 1991, in mediating and settling an agreement between the military arms of the Hizb-ul- Mujahideen, the Allah Tigers and the Ikhwan-ul-Musalmeen to launch joint and co-ordinated operations. Though somewhat tenuous, the ISI control helped in funnelling arms, ammunition and money to the militants, besides conducting training and indoctrination programmes. The training campus had started turning out more hardened and motivated gangs, well-versed in the use of sophisticated weapons, explosives and radio sets. Whereas a total of 390 cases of terrorism were reported in 1988, the number spurted to 4,971 in 1992. There was a substantial increase in the incidents against the security forces from 6 in 1988 to a high of 3,413 in 1992. The quality and the quantity of arms captured by the security forces, too, is indicative of the growing involution of the ISI. In 1988, only 34 AK-47s (or its later versions), were recovered; the figure went up to a whopping 3,775 in 1992.

The second stage was also marked by the setting up of a number of broadcasting stations in POK. These spewed communal venom and created a "spiral of hatred and violence between the security forces and the masses." Gremlin broadcasts and mischievous propaganda led to influencing the gullible and the devout, who came out on the streets with increased frequency and virulence. Sada-i-Hurriet became the instrument for hatching and mongering rumours. The fare that it dished out in local languages, is the fertile product of ISI propaganda mill. A notable achievement of the ISI is the influencing of the foreign media like AFP and BBC, whose misrepresentation of happenings in India has seriously affected peace and serenity of minorities and led to escalation of tension in the Valley.

THE RESPONSE TO TERROR

The type of modernity in which we currently find ourselves is, in a Zizekian sense, one where we have a series of competing claims as to both the validity and location of the Real – and a series of competing claims as to what are acceptable actions to institute its recognition by the wider population. Fundamentalist terror sees what it seeks to destroy as chaotic, as unnecessary, as an affront to what is Real, what is ordered, what is necessary. Fundamentalist terror is the violence of the Real in the service of what is seen as the *necessary alternative*. The type of symbolic violence undertaken is a reflection of the type of claims of reality being made. Symbolic action as has been undertaken so far in New

Zealand reflects a society that is secular by inclination. The Real is contained in symbolic action that can be reported and represented as secular in effect and motivation. Other acts of symbolic action in New Zealand such as desecration of Jewish graves, and graffiti attacks and vandalism of mosques and synagogues can, in a secular society, be contained as criminal acts of a non-legitimate extreme minority. The challenge presented by Destiny Church is not its symbolic nature, but rather the media response that gives credibility to religiously motivated symbolic events as being effective – and as being a means of effecting a form of legitimacy. Yet paradoxically, what will keep Destiny under control is its obsession with a gospel of prosperity – they will not seek to destroy the type of society that they believe will reward them. The danger to a country like New Zealand is the recourse to symbolic violence by those marginalized by both belief and culture – and yet given postmodern tolerance for their intolerant beliefs. The Real of the modern secular pluralist state is ever open to the challenge of the competing modernity of the religious Real that understands the nature and efficacy of symbolic violence. As Paul Piccone and Gary Ulmen noted in response to September 11: The first thing that will have to go is the criticism of the concept of tolerance for the intolerant – and therefore of its pseudo-universalism. Tolerance is a particular western value, which applies only to those who practice it. It excludes not only those who reject it, but also those who tolerate its rejection.

The religion of terror is linked to the religion of modernity, the belief in the pluralist secular nation state, the belief in a future that unfolds through rationality and progress – and in particular to a distinct form of western modernity. The failure of the postmodern can now be seen as the failure of the extension of tolerance to the intolerant, to those who seek to reject that which enables them to dissent. The recourse to symbolic violence is the challenge of the transgression of the taboo of intolerance; that which seeks a response that will assert the validity of the claims of the Real being made by the terrorist. As Baudrillard notes: "The tactic of the terrorist model is to provoke a surplus of reality and to make the whole system collapse under it".

To oppose the surplus of the reality of taboo and transgression that is to be found in the act of terror, the system under attack needs an alternative Real that can neutralise any attempts to impose any religious Real upon the general public and the nation. This occurs either by the symbolic actions that terrorise the liberal State's fear of being viewed as intolerant, or in specific actions that by act of violence seek to spread the terror of the Real through the *religare* of the mass media and so constitute the grounds for a new *religare* of terror. The challenge is that it is the freedom of the mass media that allows the circulation of the spectacle of terror – yet to limit the spectacle is to enforce the control of image and truth of the kind sought by the fundamentalist terrorist.

Contemporary terrorism is not a challenge against modernity, but rather a challenge that rejects the offer of postmodernity, an offer made by the post-Christian West and yet rejected by those who that West sought to include. What is offered in the act of fundamentalist terror is the challenge of an alternative modernity, an alternative way of ordering the chaos of life, an alternative belief system that uses the synthesis of mass media and terror to provide a new *religare* of terror that, in our response, serves to validate, from the point of view of the terrorist, the sacred necessity and justification for the act of terror: "We realized from our defence and fighting against the American enemy that, in combat, they mainly depend on psychological warfare. This is in light of the huge media machine they have".

To oppose the *religare* of terror the state may opt to secularize symbolic recourse as criminal behaviour, as has been the case in New Zealand, in effect trying to neutralize terrorism claims to efficacy as religious act and as *religare,* through a response of indifference. Secondly, it may be recognized that the privatization of belief and culture that occurs in modernity can also serve to allow the legitimization of intolerance within those groups. A cosmopolitan society is therefore confronted with the reality that calls for religious and cultural difference which can locate and express themselves in statements and actions of intolerance. Thirdly, this means that the secular *religare* of a cosmopolitan society *will* result in symbolic acts by those who seek to reject it. With the increasing recourse to religion as a form of identity politics (beliefs and communities as tangible *religare*), the state's dismissal of these to the privatist sphere may force the recourse to further symbolic action and this will be seen by some as a necessary risk. The alternative will be understood as responding *as if* the global*religare* of terror paradoxically legitimizes the unnecessary ornamentation of communal religious expression *within* the public sphere.

As Baudrillard notes, already the West is responding to "the spectre of terrorism" by terrorizing itself. In effect we are unsure how to respond to what he notes is the inversion of the master and slave relationship because the non-terrorist is "deprived of death and destiny" while the terrorists, the ones who control death, are the symbolic master. The western terrorising of "itself" occurs when, seeking to remain "tolerant" it provides the symbolic space for the terrorist "master" impose a hyper-real condition of REAL EVENT-DEATH as a permanent condition of the *religare* of fear and "*eschaton* expectation" – the "crystallization" of "all the ingredients in suspension".

The dilemma for the secular, cosmopolitan society is therefore when the private belief attempts to act within the public domain in a manner that seeks to impose its particular values and identity *upon all* within the society, this is particularly true of any recourse to religious fundamentalism. To avoid the self-terrorism that is the common response, perhaps in the end all private beliefs are to be equally unequal – and so exist in a form of oppositional equality. This is because in a Loosian-derived modernity, unnecessary ornamentation is itself the location of definition in a pluralist society.

To proceed from locating *all* religious identity as unnecessary ornamentation is perhaps the only way to achieve equality, but also the groundwork toward the articulation of a pragmatic common narrative of modern identity. To privatize religion may protect an individual's identity, but it may also impede it. So, on the one hand the state may attempt to reply to fundamentalist terrorism with indifference. But what about the terrorism of the state and the uncertainty that the state – terror relationship bring to any discussion of either?

Jean-Luc Nancy, who raises the question of "what is to be done?" also offers a possibility which in its articulation of the necessity of the provisional possibility is a possible (non)solution:

Perhaps though, we know one thing at least: 'What is to be done?' means for us, how to make a world for which all is not already done (played out, finished, enshrined in a destiny), nor still entirely to do (in the future for always future tomorrows).

This challenge sits against the claims of necessity and certainty, the dualist battle that "terror" and "the war on terror" encompass. That this is a war of rhetoric – a rhetorical war – is also beyond a doubt. This is a point acknowledged by Kevin Roberts, CEO Worldwide of SAATCHI & SAATCHI Ideas Company in his recent "presentation to various U.S. Defense Intelligence Agencies". Robert's claim was the need for the rebranding of the rhetoric of "the War on terror", with the aim to create a new "loyalty beyond Reason", what Roberts calls a Lovemark: "these are brands that make deep emotional connections with consumers. Passionate connections that go inside people's lives and make a difference". These are brands that have "High Love, High Respect" such as Harley Davidson, Apple and JFK. For Roberts "brand America" currently has "High Respect, Low Love". His rebranding of "brand America" and of the "War on terror" is based on his "Lovemark" credo: "Mystery, Sensuality and Intimacy". This could be termed the seduction, the eroticism of the brand, the pornography of global capital.

Roberts' rebranding is to what he terms the "fight for a better world", a fight launched alongside the war on terror that seeks to tackle geopolitical issues such as "global AIDS, malnutrition and malaria". But Roberts' call "to create America as a lovemark" is a response that needs to be added to the already empty rhetoric that "terror" inspires. This is capitalism as hyper-real benevolence, a simulacrum of compassion that is pushing a global product. It merely swerves to emphasise Zillah Eisenstein's critique that: "Anti-terrorism rhetoric fits well with global capitalism ...there is no single country that houses terrorism...or capitalism. Both are networked transnationally.

What this demonstrates is that the *religare,* the religion of terror has already become just another product, something to be consumed in a form of globalization. Baudrillard encourages us to think about the problem of fundamentalist terrorism by reversing several of our standard assumptions. What if it were Islam, he asks, that were spreading through the West and rising to dominate the globe? Baudrillard tells us that if this were the case then "...terrorism would rise against Islam, for it is the world, the globe itself, which resists globalization".

What we need to consider, perhaps even confront, is the challenge that the *religare* of globalization is the *religare* of terror which is both product and consumption of capitalism and its other – terror. For terror is the inside of capitalism; that which acts as perhaps the "lovemark" of the inverted fight against the global. This link of religion, modernity and capitalism was noted by Marx in his call that "the criticism of religion is the prerequisite of all criticism". One could perhaps invert and expand it and say also that "the religion of criticism is the prerequisite of all terror". This dualism is what perhaps sits under all questions involving the modern, capitalist state and terrorism. Both the state and terror are built on certainties – yet both are certainties under attack from their other within the *religare* of the global. As Nancy has also noted: "Where certainties come apart, there too gathers the strength that no certainty can match.

The collapse of certainty is perhaps the collapse of the real, or rather the collapse of the belief in the real, a collapse that forces a struggle to assert the claim of the real (terror/war on terror) over and against the uncertainty and the indifference that the collapse of the real engenders. As Baudrillard notes: "There is no corpse of the real, and with good reason: the real is not dead, it has disappeared.

The unacceptability of terror is only as unacceptable as the *religare* of modernity, of the global, of global capital, as the drive to non-ornamentation. All are drives for the real arising out of claims of certainty as to the location and representation of the real. The *religare* of the real is the religion of terror – and of the war waged against it – a war of mutual rhetoric that by transgressive public religion/*religare* and public death affirm the Manichean centrality of modernity itself. Baudrillard's aphorism that "He does not have room for both the world and for its double – but no one knows which will have the last word" sits under any consideration of a response. Perhaps the only response is not to fall into the impatience of desiring a response, for out of impatience could possibility eventuate that which we do – but deny – desire:

> Impatience is a millenarian passion which desires the immediacy of the end. Now today, wherever time has been abolished by the operation of 'real time', events no longer come to maturity, either immediately or with a delay. But impatience is not consoled by that: having nothing left to devour, it devours the remains of the real.

The immediacy of the end, the desire to immediately end "terror/the war on terror" or that which terror strikes at, are reminiscent of the drive to hygiene of futurism, the banishing of ornament, the self-implosion of Modernity at Pruitt-Igoe. The state that desires the immediate end to terror by self-terrorising itself is itself devouring what it believes is the remains of the real (itself as bureaucratic state) out of a millennial passion for the end. This self-terror of the self-devouring response has, as Baudrillard notes, its immediate prior expression in the West's hyper-real Iranian *Fatwa* it carried out for the Iranian state on Salman Rushdie: "The Iranian strategy consists in inflecting Western culture with fear, duplicity and self-pity".

Perhaps the issue is the centrality of the Loosian modernist rejection of disorder – a pursuit of order as *religare* that terror seeks to deny and discredit. Writing of the 1988 Libyan terror bombing of the plane over Lockerbie, Baudrillard notes: "What fascinates thought is this terrorist enchanting of things, the symbolic disorder of which terrorism is merely the visible epicentre".

The choice is therefore a degree of no-choice, the enchanting of terror by the state, the enchantment of terror by the terrorist, both symbolize a disorder against the Loosian claims of the realised real in ordered modernity, in the systems of order that the bureaucratic state now activates to self-terrorise itself, in effect to institute its internal *Fatwas* on its own citizens in the recognition that: "Every society must choose itself an enemy, but it must not try to exterminate it".

The state and the self-instituting terrorist act both have each other as enemy, but cannot act for a final extermination, a fulfilled millennial, apocalyptic passion for then their claims of and for the real are finished. The act of extermination is the internal destructive act of Pruitt-Igoe, the real terror is that turned by the state upon itself, to clear the space for the self-transcendence of its prior claim for the real.

As the French novelist Frederic Beigbeder notes in his mediation on the final hours of the twin towers: "Since September 11, 2001, reality has not only outstripped fiction, it's destroying it. It's impossible to write about this subject, and yet impossible to write about anything else. Nothing else touches us". The Western *Fatwa* has been extended – we all now live as Rushdie: self-imprisoned not by the original action but by our (Western) reaction to the original event-death. The Irony is that the modern Western dismissal of the ornamentation of religion has been supplanted by a *religare* of terror that ornaments us continually in the hyper-real self-*Fatwa*. Maybe our best case scenario is to hope that Baudrillard is right when he says: "terror is dissipated by irony" Neither are in short supply today.

FUTURE ENGAGEMENT WITH THE ISI

When interviewed about the relationship between the West and Pakistan and the ongoing conflict in Afghanistan, the bestselling author Steven Coll stated:

This could not be a more complicated war. If you think about it, the United States is essentially waging a war against its own ally. The Taliban are a proxy of the government of Pakistan [orchestrated by the ISI]. We are an ally of the government of Pakistan. We are fighting the Taliban. In the end, the Taliban will be defeated strategically when the government of Pakistan makes a strategic decision that its future does not lie in partnership with Islamic extremists. (2009)

Coll pinpoints the root of current and future problems in dealing with the ISI and their clandestine terrorist support networks. In 2009, the U.S. provided close to $6.5 billion dollars in aid to the Pakistani government; $300 million of that was dedicated to military spending (Mohammad). The West is figuratively caught between a rock and a hard place. It requires the assistance of Pakistan to successfully prosecute counter-terrorism campaigns in Southwest Asia. Yet, the ISI has infiltrated all ranks of Pakistan's military structure and leverages sympathizers and supporters throughout the Pakistani population. A large amount of that military aid is falling into the hands of the sponsors of the exact networks the West is attempting to defeat. On February 16, 2010 the Taliban's second in command, Mullah Baradar, was captured in a raid conducted jointly by the ISI and the U.S. Western leaders hoped that this would be a catalyst for strengthening the cooperation between the ISI and Western intelligence agencies and serve as an indication that the ISI would begin dismissing its historical involvement with militants. However, after a close examination into the raid, the New York Times provided: Relations between the intelligence services, [CIA and ISI], of the United States and Pakistan have long been marred by suspicions that Pakistan has sheltered the Afghan Taliban. The Pakistanis have long denied it. New details of the raid indicate that the arrest of the No. 2 Taliban leader was not necessarily the result of a new determination by Pakistan to go after the Taliban, or a bid to improve its strategic position in the region. Rather, it may be something more prosaic: "a lucky accident..." (Shane and Schmitt) Upon Baradar's capture, ISI officers delayed allowing U.S. intelligence officers to question him and were hesitant in sharing news and information about his detention with the Pakistani press (in fear of casting themselves in a pro-Western light).

The ISI will continue to act out of its own interest. It has grown in size from its inception and now forms a state within the Pakistani state. While it serves as an intelligence agency of the Pakistani government, the Pakistani government is largely unable to control its actions or relationships with terrorist organizations, both domestic and abroad. Ongoing operations to defeat extremists and terrorists places the ISI at a crossroads with Western intelligence agencies and irregular warfare personnel. Without a complete transformation of the ISI's motivations, allegiances, extremist slant, and structure, it will continue to exist as more of an enemy to the West than an ally.

Conclusion

The historic actions of the ISI in sponsoring organizations like al-Qaeda, JEM, LET and HUM, as well as their utilization of the Taliban as a proxy for foreign policy, signals that the ISI is a significant state sponsor of terrorism. "Since Pakistan has terrorism, nuclear weapons, religious extremism, economic instability, and political volatility, easy [foreign policy] answers provide little guidance in a dangerous, fluid environment. If, due to ISI sins of omission or commission, terrorists acquire Pakistani nuclear weapons and there is a nuclear incident or nuclear war, the consequences will be unthinkable" (Roberts 109). These variables set the ISI's sponsorship apart from other international sponsors and make it definitively the most dangerous.

A careful policy of continued engagement with the ISI and accountability of Western funding to Pakistan will be essential to secure future stability in the region.

The ISI will continue to be a clandestine sponsor of worldwide extremism and transnational terrorism. The fragile nature of Pakistani politics, the existence of deeply entrenched Islamic foundations, and insecurity surrounding the Pakistani nuclear arsenal make the ISI the foremost terrorist threat and non-state sponsor of terrorism in the international community. The ISI masquerades as a controllable tool of the Pakistani government while covertly supporting enemies of the international community – conclusively acting as a threat to international stability and as a fifth column within the Pakistani state.

AN IDEOLOGY BASED ON VIOLENCE AND TERROR

While racist groups that represent racism and xenophobia come together under the umbrella of the Ku Klux Klan in America, the neo-Nazis perform the same role in Europe. European racism began with the skinheads in Great Britain, and turned into a neo-Nazi movement in the 1990s. The main characteristics of these groups which define themselves as neo-Nazis are the way that, just like the Ku Klux Klan, they maintain the superiority of the white race and attack foreigners and those living in poorer areas.

Neo-Nazi movements have grown increasingly powerful over the last 10 years, and their sphere of influence has widened considerably. Their members now number around 70,000. The neo-Nazis have set themselves various targets in different countries. According to one study, Turks in Germany, Gypsies in Hungary, Slovakia and the Czech Republic, Asians in Great Britain, North Africans in France and Northeasterners in Brazil, are among their slated victims. The neo-Nazis' distinguishing characteristics are violence, hatred, intimidation, the use of threat and destruction.

According to official German figures, in 1997 alone there were 10,037 incidents linked to racism and xenophobia. The figure for 2000 was more than 10,000. In Britain, there were 10,982 racism-linked incidents between April and September alone. More than half of these crimes consisted of threats, menaces and intimidation. The rest were made up of murders, assaults, vandalism of homes and businesses, etc.

Louis Beam and William Pierce, extreme right-wing American ideologues, share a very important place in the neo-Nazi movement that developed during the 1990s. The concepts of "leaderless resistance" and "white revolution" put forward by these men have now come to dominate the thought of the neo-Nazi movement. At the root of various acts of terror, such as bombings, looting, and the destruction of workplaces in numerous countries of the world, can continually be found their concept of "leaderless resistance." According to their idea, neo-Nazi actions aught to be carried out on either an individual basis or else by very small gangs.

The books *Hunter* and *The Turner Diaries* by William Pierce are regarded as the principle inspiration behind neo-Nazi terror. The pamphlet *A Practical Guide to Aryan Revolution* by the French Nationalist Socialist Movement, which took those books as its theoretical basis, contains all the information a neo-Nazi would require. The pamphlet is a detailed, practical terrorist handbook, divided into such chapter headings as *Methods of Covert Direct Action, Escape and Evasion, Assasination, Terror Bombing, Sabotage,*

Racial War, How To Create A Revolutionary Situation, and Rules of Engagement – Regulations Concerning the Conduct of Soldiers of the Aryan Liberation Army.

Even if they do not play an active role within these groups, many people nevertheless support fascism and are influenced by these books. *The Turner Diaries,* for instance, describe how one underground group organized against the state and what kind of activities it engaged in. In his defense, a man by the name of John William King, who killed a Black man named James Byrd Jr. in 1998 by tying him and dragging him behind his pick-up truck, was reported to having said, "We're going to start The Turner Diaries early."

Following the 1993 Oklahoma bombing by Timothy McVeigh, attention turned to William Pierce's book *Hunter,* in which Pierce described the actions of a bomber who acted alone. The hero of the book was not supported by any group or organization, but consciously carried out a terrorist attack single-handedly, just as Timothy McVeigh did.

The Oklahoma Bomber Was a Neo-Nazi

Up until September 11, 2001, the worst terrorist attack the American people had witnessed was that of on federal building in Oklahoma by Timothy McVeigh, as a result of which 168 people lost their lives, including a number of children. What is interesting about that bombing is that Timothy McVeigh was both the member of a deviant cult as well as a neo-Nazi.

McVeigh claimed to have carried out that bombing in revenge for David Koresh and his followers who burned to death on a farm in 1993. According to McVeigh, Koresh and the cult members did not kill themselves, but were actually murdered by the American state. He therefore decided to take revenge on that state, and planned to bomb the people working in its name in the Federal Building. Exactly two years after the deaths of Koresh and his cult followers, on the second anniversary in fact, McVeigh cold-bloodedly parked a lorry full of explosives in front of the Federal Building and the rest is history. After the attack, McVeigh was helped by another neo-Nazi, Terry Nichols. The most important fact to recognize about those who supported Nichols and McVeigh before the attack, who helped locate the explosives and knew what McVeigh was up to, is that they were all neo-Nazis.

Shortly before his execution, McVeigh sent a letter to *The Buffalo News* in which he said he was not sorry about the bombing, which he saw as a "legit tactic," in his solitary war against the federal government. That attack, the product of a disturbed mind, is once again an appalling indication of what terrible destruction the movements we are presently discussing can wreak on people and society.

As we should now be able to recognize from these numerous examples, those who are caught up in the system of the Antichrist believe it is entirely justified to discriminate between people on the grounds of race, language and gender, and to exercise brutality against them. What is more, that discrimination between communities can turn into the type of hysteria that leads to war and destruction. People are attacked solely because of their language, religion or race, and needlessly suffer all sorts of abuse. One of the reasons for this, as is made clear in the Qur'an, is that the Devil portrays "fanatical rage" as right and honorable. Most of the groups who at the present are encouraging terrorism, or who carry such acts, are caught up by this temptation, and base their attacks on racist statements. It is clear from the following verse exactly to what extent such racist provocation violates the principles of Islam:

Those who disbelieve filled their hearts with fanatical rage—the fanatical rage of the Time of Ignorance—and God sent down serenity to His Messenger and to the believers, and obliged them to respect the formula of heedfulness which they had most right to and were most entitled to. God has knowledge of all things. (Qur'an, 48:26)

The different peoples of the world have been created in order for human beings to come to know each other, to have good relations with each other, not to be enemies of one another. In the Qur'an, God has revealed that the ideology of the "master race," which foments the climate of terror desired by the Antichrist, is utterly false. Only better morality proffers societies, cultures or individuals with superiority. It is of absolutely no importance what race people belong to, what language they speak, or what color their skins are. Trying to ascribe superiority on the basis of such values, and harboring feelings of hatred towards other societies, are products of the ideology of the Antichrist. This is how God has revealed that the differences between races are a means by which friendship and cultural exchange can be brought about, and that superiority depends solely on piety, in other words, on faith and morality:

Mankind! We created you from a male and female, and made you into peoples and tribes so that you might come to know each other.The noblest among you in God's sight is the one who best performs his duty. God is All-Knowing, All-Aware. (Qur'an, 49: 13)

SATANISM; THE TERROR OF THE DEVIL

Satanism is a perverted ideology that makes violence and savagery a ritual in its creed. Satanists, who describe themselves as such, make deeds of inhumanity and brutality into acts of worship.

When the word Satanism is mentioned most people think merely of its widespread psychological influence on young people, and regard it as a kind of insignificant mystical movement. Also, due to the influence of the media, they may think of Satanists as performing strange rituals, much unlike what ordinary and well-balanced people would otherwise do. It is true that Satanists are part of a culture of violence and perform strange and horrible rites, yet, what most people fail to see is that Satanism is a materialist and atheist ideology that supports violence and which dates back to the 1800s. Furthermore, the ideology has a large number of followers throughout the world.

The fundamental principle of Satanism is that it rejects all religious values, takes the Devil as its deity, and claims that hell is a kind of salvation. According to the belief of Satanism, people have no responsibilities, apart from that of following their own desires. If his desires lead a person to anger, hatred, revenge, deceit, theft, the harming others or even murder, then that is acceptable. The basic logic that Satanism relies on, in support of that belief, is the claim that the avoidance of evil is a kind of insincerity. In other words, this perverted belief maintains that if his desires impel someone to kill another, and if he acts according to that impulse, then he has behaved sincerely.

Virtues such as love, tolerance, patience and forgiveness, which are highly esteemed by most people, and are elements of the true morality, are loathed by Satanists. This deviant ideology maintains that there should be no restrictions on evil and such feelings as hatred, anger and vengeance. Article 5 of *The Satanic Bible,* widely regarded as the fundamental textbook of Satanism, states, instead of the biblical principle that says "To him who strikes you on the cheek, offer the other also." that "Satan represents vengeance, instead of turning the other cheek." Elsewhere in that same book appears the commandment:

Hate your enemies with a whole heart, and if a man smite you on one cheek, SMASH him on the other!

It is obvious that according to such thinking it will be impossible to prevent any kind wickedness. Such an atmosphere will inevitably lead to chaos and strife. It is impossible to speak of order, peace, stability, security, forgiveness or tolerance in any society in which people do not listen to the voice of their consciences, and are thus unable to distinguish between good and bad, and to use their will and judgment to act for good. In an environment of that sort, anyone who feels anger towards somebody else will be unable to restrain that anger and behave with moderation, and will inevitably seek his revenge. Alternatively, instead of being patient in times of need and poverty, and attempting to address those needs in a sensible manner, these people will resort to theft and other sorts of crime. Satanism is their justification for doing so.

The kind of society proposed by the ideology of Satanism recognizes no rules and no bounds. Its aim is the free expression of selfish desires and evil. In his book *The Satanic Bible,* Anton LaVey, regarded as the founder of modern Satanism, recommends to his followers that they live by and promote wickedness as they so please. In an interview, LaVey even said: "I feel laws are, obviously, made to be broken ... I see nothing wrong with robbing somebody on the street. Satanism's refusal to recognize any bounds does not stop there, of course. People would not only harm themselves and those around them, but would direct their hostility and anger at all.

That refusal to recognize any limits, moreover, leads to the regard of violence as an intrinsic part of life. According to Satanism, violence is a fact of nature, and thus inescapable. Therefore, this distorted view maintains that it is perfectly permissible for people to resort to violence. Since any attempt to prevent or minimize violence is a violation of what is natural, any attempt to do so is futile, and it is therefore illogical to do so.

As we have seen, Satanism holds utterly perverse beliefs, which encourage people to be aggressive, to commit murder, and even mass slaughter. In America in particular, academics have established that Satanism lies at the root of national terror, and that serious steps need to be taken in order to deal with it. One of these academics is Carl Roschke, a professor at Denver University, who has stressed the importance of the subject in the words, "We're really dealing with the way satanic ideology has become a basis for domestic terrorism." Roschke says that the most important step in the war to be waged against Satanism is to make it clear that its followers are not just "harmless wackoes," but that when their crimes are examined, one can understand just how harmful someone claiming to be a Satanist can be. There is no doubt that the most important fight against a movement of this sort must be ideological. That being the case, we must establish which ideologies Satanism is founded on.

Darwinism is the Ideological Basis of Satanism

One of the most common ways Satanists use to describe themselves, in their books, magazines and publications, as well as their websites, is to regard man as a "kind of developed animal," and to maintain that "only the fittest can survive." This is the most important piece of evidence to corroborate that Darwinism lies at the very root of the Satanists' beliefs. In fact, many Satanists do not hesitate to admit the fact. In *A Description of Satanism*, a Satanist writer describes the ideology in these terms:

...First of all, Humans are social animals... all people and animals share a common source in mere biology. Satanism is the belief that Humans are nothing more than higher animals—we have no special place in creation other than being lucky to have evolved and survived...

Another Satanist publication, *The Church of Satan,* describes how they believe that human beings are a kind of developed animal:

Since Satanism stands for acceptance of Man as an animal, there have often been creators in many past cultures who embraced this insight and explored it in the context of their society, thus we seek out these artistic philosophical expressions and see them to be the roots of our current awareness.

It is clear from the preceding that Satanism regards Darwin's theory, that human beings evolved from animals, as the source of its own ideological "awareness." The introduction to an interview with Anton LaVey, carried in the music journal *MF Magazine,* describes the relationship between Satanism and Darwinism:

In the late 1960s, Anton LaVey brought forth an easily understandable doctrine of social Darwinism, and strong positive thinking (magic) to the growing mass of individuals sick of both hippieism and the stagnant morals of Christianity.

Magister Peter H. Gilmore, a priest of the Church of Satan, describes this perverted religion in the following terms:

... Let us instead look at contemporary Satanism for what it really is: a brutal religion of elitism and social Darwinism that seeks to re-establish the reign of the able over the idiotic, of swift justice over injustice, and for a wholesale rejection of egalitarianism as a myth that has crippled the advancement of the human species for the last two thousand years.

Of course, the idea of justice, as set out above, has absolutely no resemblance to the notion of justice as we know it should be, that is, established on the principle of equality. The above version is a Satanist idea of justice, and as will be seen from what follows, it is a version that endows anyone who regards himself as superior to others to usurp all such powers and rights.

The way Satanism shares so many parallels with Social Darwinism, which regards Western society as superior to others, has led to cooperation between it and a number of other racist and chauvinistic movements, especially fascism. One can find many individuals who believed in Satanism among the ranks of Hitler's National Socialists and Mussolini's Blackshirts. Anton LaVey makes this reference to that collaboration:

It's an unholy alliance. Many different types of such people have made contact with us in the past. The anti-Christian strength of National Socialist Germany is part of the appeal to Satanists—the drama, the lighting, the choreography with which they moved millions of people.39

Darwinism is the primary ground shared between these tendencies and Satanism. Social Darwinism, which lies at the heart of all these deviant ideologies, is defended by Satanists as follows:

The principle of the survival of the strong is advocated on all levels of society, from allowing an individual to stand or fall, to even letting those nations that cannot handle themselves take the consequences of this inability... There would be a concomitant reduction in the world's population as the weak are allowed to experience the consequences of social Darwinism. Thus has nature always acted to cleanse and strengthen her children... We embrace reality and do not try to transform it into some utopia that is contrary to the very fabric of existence.

Another expression of the Satanists' attachment to Social Darwinism is their fierce support for the theory of eugenics, itself the product of fascism. The theory of eugenics maintained that the sick and the crippled ought to be eliminated from society, and the number of healthy individuals increased through breeding. The theory was most prominently implemented in Nazi Germany. According to the theory of eugenics, in the same way that healthy animal stock is bred by mating healthy species, by this way a race of humans also be improved. Those elements obstructing such improvement (the sick, crippled, mentally handicapped etc.) need to be eradicated. When this line of thinking was adopted in Nazi Germany, tens of thousands of people with genetic and mental diseases were slaughtered ruthlessly.

Satanism is also in favor of the same terrible mercilessness. Their own publications reveal their view on eugenics:

Satanists also seek to enhance the laws of nature by concentrating on fostering the practice of eugenics... It is the practice of encouraging people of talent and ability to reproduce, to enrich the gene pool from which our species can grow. This was commonly practiced throughout the world... Until the genetic code is cracked and we can choose the character of our offspring at will, Satanists seek to mate the best with the best.

The Perverse Rites of Satanism

Black masses, and the terrible things that are conducted during them, is what most often comes to peoples' minds whenever Satanism is mentioned. Yet, many people believe that it is make-believe only portrayed in films, and that nothing of the sort actually takes place in real life. However, the terrible scenes we are used to watching in films are really parts and aspects of Satanist masses and rituals.

The real purpose behind these rituals is to make contact with the Devil and learn his so-called teachings. In order to see just how important these devilish rites are in Satanism, a brief look at their own books and websites is more than sufficient. The common feature of these publications is the way they devote considerable space to gloomy subjects and insist on the importance of the black mass. In a well-known Satanist website, which carries various Satanist messages for the under-18s, these so-called masses are emphasized as being one of the fundamental elements of Satanism, and that young people who cannot attend group ceremonies should nevertheless hold such services on their own. The details of the services these young people are instructed to hold are then given:

Don't be disturbed or frightened or think you're crazy when you feel contacted by the Dark Ones... Approach the Dark Masters with the proper degree of respect and decorum—that's what rituals are for, to establish a relationship... You don't need everything mentioned in Dr. LaVey's books to do an effective ritual. Maybe you don't have the money to obtain, or the private space to store, items such as swords, chalices, black robes, gongs and elaborate altars. Here is a powerful ritual you can perform... Light the candle and set it before you... As you gaze at the flame, say in your mind or out loud, "I am ready, oh, Dark Lord. I feel your strength within me and wish to honor you in my life. I am one of the Devil's Own. Hail Satan!"... This is a simple way of conjuring Satan into your life.

One can recognize such perversion, immorality and savagery in any society that takes Satan as its guide. For Satanists, these things are inspired by the Devil himself, and must be adhered to. Satanists, who do adhere to them, fall into forms of sexual perversions, torture humans as well as animals, and even perform such disgusting things as the drinking of the blood of the creatures or people they kill. In many countries of the world, young people who describe themselves as Satanists hold drug-parties at which all kinds of immorality and perversion take place, and which frequently end in the killing of one of their number in the Devil's name.

The way Satanists attach such importance to the shedding of blood at their rituals is a small-scale example of the plan Satan has for mankind. Satan hates mankind, and wants to inflict as much suffering on it as possible. It is therefore his aim to fill the world with bloodshed. The ideologies of the Antichrist we discussed earlier, such as fascism, racism and communism, all serve his purpose. All the wars, massacres, killings, and acts of terrorism, linked to these and similar atheistic ideologies, are all "Satanic masses" aimed at satisfying the Devil's lust for blood.

Those who openly describe themselves as Satanists carry out the shedding of blood as an act of worship. Those who incite terror and anarchy in the world are actually performing the same rite, in a more secret but with far wider ramifications. In short, the Devil, and the system of the Antichrist established by him for the world are using those they have managed to take in and are trying to turn the world into a brutal battleground.

Satanism is an Ideology That Has Already Been Defeated

We need to bear in mind the Satanists' own views when considering the threat posed by it. When Satanists are asked how many of them there are, they claim to have large numbers of followers, because there are many people who actually live by the tenets of Satanism without being aware of the fact. In a way, that is actually the case. Many people, consciously or unconsciously, share the views of the Satanists. That is because, refusing to listen to the voice of one's conscience, or to live by proper morality, therefore following one's own desires, is the same as obeying the commands of the Devil. When one considers all the destruction caused by Satanists up to the present day, it is quite clear in what a terrible state a society consisting of such people is going to end up to be.

The claim that man is a species of animal, on which Satanism is founded, is utter nonsense. Mankind did not come into being as the result of blind chance. The Creator of mankind, and of the order and splendor of the entire universe, is the infinitely powerful, superior and All-Wise God, who has no weaknesses of any kind. He created man with the ability to think and reason, to distinguish between right and wrong, and also with a responsibility towards his Creator. Just as each individual's ego direct him towards evil, so his conscience protects him from it, and commands him to turn away from it. It is man's duty to listen to the voice of his conscience, not to his ego and adopt the kind of morality that is pleasing to God. That morality will not only allow the individual concerned, and the society in which he lives, to enjoy a peaceful and secure existence, but will also, by the will of God, lead to the sublimest reward in the hereafter.

One important fact that must not be lost sight of is that the life Satan offers, which he dresses up to appear so very attractive, is mere deception. Satan may make all kinds of promises about the possibilities of the life of this world, and may try to turn people away form the true path, yet, it must not be forgotten that the road he beckons man to follow will only lead to ultimate destruction for those who take it. That is because Satan and his followers have already been defeated. As God explains in a verse:

... What they call on is an arrogant Satan whom God has cursed. He said, "I will take a certain fixed proportion of Your servants. I will lead them astray and fill them with false hopes.

I will command them and they will cut off cattle's ears. I will command them and they will change God's creation." Anyone who takes the Devil as his protector in place of God has clearly lost everything. (Qur'an, 4: 117-119)

RACIST TERROR

World War II was madness sparked off by a racist and fascist ideology. Violence and conflict, the so-called sacred values of these ideologies, briskly infected the entire world, leading to 55 million people falling victim to fascist savagery. Though the fact that victory fell upon the Allies meant that fascism was defeated, it did not disappear. It merely went underground. As a whole, there has been a discernable rise in the number of racist and fascist organizations and acts of violence in the world over the last 10 years. While Europe battles with acts of violence perpetrated by neo-Nazis, the United States has had to deal with a resurgence of the Ku Klux Klan and similar "white supremacy" organizations. Today, both the neo-Nazis and the members of the Ku Klux Klan are carrying out attacks and encouraging their members to commits acts of terror and violence.

Many people may imagine that the Ku Klux Klan had carried out most of its attacks on and oppression of Blacks merely in the 1920s and 1930s, but that in modern times it had been consigned to the waste bin of history. The Klan is still alive, however. Today, in the United States as a whole, there are a great many Ku Klux Klan churches, even if they happen to go by other names, and many racist organizations linked to that church's teachings. That church and the organizations linked to it are not just against Blacks, but oppose all non-European races, especially the Muslims living in America, believing that a concerted struggle needs to be waged against them. That "struggle" includes the formation of armed units.

It is no secret that the basis of the Klan's teachings is that European whites are superior to all other races, and that the white race should never be polluted by those others. In order to prevent such contamination, other races must not be permitted to live in areas inhabited by the white race. The idea is that the other races have no right to the kinds of opportunities enjoyed by the whites. These races are regarded as parasites trying to contaminate the purity and superiority of the whites, and it is believed that all kinds of measures need to be taken to oppose them. These views of the Klan are the basis for the attacks carried out against other races in America. At the root of these ideas, lies hatred and aggression instead of love, tolerance and dialogue.

The so-called scientific justification for the concept of the superiority of the white race is Darwin's theory of evolution. Darwin had suggested that certain races, the European race for instance, had progressed further than other races during the evolutionary process. Those outside these advanced races were in his view primitive creatures little better than apes. To put it another way, while some races had made enormous evolutionary progress, others were still at a level not far removed from man's primitive ancestor, the ape. Darwin indulged in racist speculation about the future, and wrote:

At some future period, not very distant as measured by centuries, the civilised races of man will almost certainly exterminate, and replace, the savage races throughout the world. At the same time the anthropomorphous (manlike) apes, ...will no doubt be exterminated. The break between man and his nearest allies will then be wider.

These racist views of Darwin's became an important justification used in the service of the colonialist powers of the time to disguise their own brutality. The claim that Darwin put forward to demonstrate his theory is extremely interesting in the point of view of revealing his ignorance and prejudice. In a letter to a scientist named W. Graham in 1881, Darwin cited the Turkish nation as a proof of his theory. According to this nonsense of Darwin's, the Turkish nation was one of those backward peoples that would soon disappear:

I could show fight on natural selection having done and doing more for the progress of civilization than you seem inclined to admit. Remember what risk the nations of Europe ran, not so many centuries ago of being overwhelmed by the Turks, and how ridiculous such an idea now is! The more civilised so-called

Caucasian races have beaten the Turkish hollow in the struggle for existence. Looking to the world at no very distant date, what an endless number of the lower races will have been eliminated by the higher civilized races throughout the world.16

Even today we still hear of churches belonging to Blacks in various states in America being burned, of attacks on mosques and synagogues, and assaults of members of other races. Following the terrorist attack on the World Trade Center on September 11, 2001, in particular, certain circles influenced by this and similar organizations stepped up their attacks. Businesses, mosques and associations belonging to Muslims in a number of states were attacked. Muslim students were not allowed into school, and Muslim children were assaulted in the streets. Everyone not totally devoid of reason and logic knows that the Islamic world, and innocent Muslim civilian and children in particular, cannot be held responsible for those ruthless attacks. (In fact, following September 11, there emerged a significant reaction, on the part of those with intelligence and common sense, which instead began to look into Islam. There was also an increase in the number of people turning to Islam). On the other hand, the situation was merely one indication of what a menace the encouragement of hatred based on race or belief could pose.

Members of the Klan do not agree, however. They are busily preparing for a great war between the races, which they believe will take place in the 21st century.

The Dimensions of Racism in America

The Ku Klux Klan was established in the 1870s, and became very powerful in America in the wake of the First World War. By the 1920s, it had some 3-4 million members.17

Like those of all other racist ideologies, the ideological roots of the teachings of the Klan, which start from the premise that "We will slaughter our enemies when the war to protect the white race begins," is the view that the white race is at the top of the evolutionary scale, while other races are to be located further down, for which reason they merit all kinds of inhuman treatment. A great number of people in America still hold to this view. It is fair to say that these groups, organized under different names, such as the National Alliance, the World Church of the Creator and Arian Nation, actually operate under the umbrella of the Ku Klux Klan.

The most important common factor between the views of these organizations, some of which we shall be looking at below, is that they have no qualms about using violence to achieve their aims, but rather often regard violence and aggression as necessary.

World Church of the Creator (WCOTC)

The WCOTC is one of those active racist organizations in America that is growing stronger by the day. This deviant organization denies the existence of God, the day of judgment, heaven and hell, and also has a large number of followers outside the United States. The idea of the superiority of the white race constitutes the basis of the organization's ideology. On its web site, Ben Klassen, the founder of this racist group, has this to say about their ideology:

> *[The] objective [of our religion] would be: The Survival, Expansion and Advancement of the White Race. It [our religion] is based on love—love for the White Race.... We, therefore, reject ...angels and devils and gods.... Our Golden Rule briefly can be summarized as follows: That which is good for the White Race is the highest virtue; that which is bad for the White Race is the ultimate sin... Nature tells us to take care of our own kind and only our own kind. We do not regard any of the mud races to be our own kind... The niggers, undoubtedly, are at the very bottom of the ladder, not far above monkeys and chimpanzees... We have no intention of helping the mud races prosper, multiply, and crowd us off the limited space of this planet.*

This perverse idea, as we have seen, is treated as a religion by its followers, its members subscribing to it wholly. However, it is totally unfounded, of course, to call this perversity a religion. We would be more correct in calling it a brand of Social Darwinism, the fundamental teaching of which is the future struggle against other races. That notion is actually referred to by the slogan

"Rahowa," (Racial Holy War), and is regarded by the group as one of its core values. In another address, Ben Klassen informed his followers what Rahowa actually means, and felt no scruples about calling them to take up arms:

RAHOWA! In this one word we sum up the total goal and program of not only the Church of the Creator, but of the total White Race, and it is this: We take up the challenge. We gird for total war against the Jews and the rest of the goddamned mud races of the world—politically, militantly, financially, morally and religiously. In fact we regard it as the heart of our religious creed, and as the most sacred credo of all. We regard it as a holy war to the finish—a racial holy war.

The expected war between the races is one of the major aims of Klan organizations. The subject is stressed at just about every meeting. During speeches, Klan members are filled with enthusiasm for the war, and many references to it are made in their writings. Incitement towards this war, which has now assumed mythical status among them, is frequently to be seen in Klan publications. For instance, the journal *Knight-Ridder*, which covered a national rally held in Columbia, included the following lines:

King is the leader of the Christian Knights, who dreams of a resurgent Ku Klux Klan... He points down the street where both he and a neighbor decorate their front yards with robed Klansmen yard statues. He says: "A race war is coming. The Klan is the only hope for the white race."20

As is the case with many racist organizations, Rahowa is founded fundamentally on the belief in evolution. Such a degree of hostility towards other races, and the lack of any compunction over the using of violence as a means, are all the result of the belief in the theory of evolution. Nothing can prevent anyone who regards somebody else as an animal from abusing, attacking and, if necessary, killing that individual.

The following words of Matt Hale, who became leader of the organization after Ben Klassen, are just one example of the close connection between the idea which they treat as a religion and belief in evolution:

But we *are* animals. That's the thing. We don't accept this idea that just because we can think and speak and walk on two legs that we are not bound by nature's laws. We are.

These words are an indication of the organization's peculiar, unique view of religion. Naturally, that religion has absolutely nothing to do with Christianity, which promotes humility, love and tolerance. And, the leaders of the organization do not hesitate to admit the fact. The following extract from an interview with Matt Hale nicely sums up their view of religion:

Rather than a religion such as Christianity, which tells them to love their enemies, love the meek and the inferior. We need a religion, which exalts our own people and our own people alone... So we need to recognize this and do away with the idea that all men are created equal and idiotic notions of that kind... what we believe in doing is ending all aid to all non-white races. We believe that without this aid the non-white races would very quickly shrink their own numbers. They could not feed themselves... We believe that a perfect world is much more possible by having only white people, white racial comrades around the world. And we believe that once the non-white races are gone, and the white race is united with a pro living, a pro-life creed such as Creativity, there will be peace and prosperity for our white people.

Yet those who maintain the superiority of one race, and believe that their characteristics make them superior to others, are ignoring one very important truth. None of these values are permanent. Every human being, be he a believer or an unbeliever, will sooner or later die, leaving behind everything that he possessed in this world, and render account for himself to our Lord. On that day, nobody will be able to help anyone else, nobody's race, color or ancestry will be of the slightest importance, nothing he possessed in this world will be of the slightest advantage to him, and nobody will be able to put forward any excuses to justify his actions. God describes this in a verse:

Then when the Trumpet is blown, no ties of kinship will exist between them on that day, nor may they question one another. (Qur'an, 23: 101)

Klan Teachings

The following articles were taken from a speech by Matt Hale at a Klan rally on January 14, 2001:

Saying the races are equal is an insult to our race.

We despise and abhor integration, interracial marriage and the flooding of this country with non-White hoards.

Interracial marriage is a sin against our people.

The Civil Rights movement was wrong for us. It was wrong for our interests.

The white race is intellectually superior to all other races.

When we have our day, when we are in power in this world as we wish to be, as we will be, certainly we will subsidize the best of our race, the most intelligent of our race to have the most children.

The future is going to be one in which we have a land that is White and we will repatriate the other races.

They would be pushed on the boats by force—within the law! That's going to be the law.

Non-Whites are absolutely irrelevant. If they were lying in a pool of blood, it would be absolutely irrelevant. It simply means nothing to me. What I care about is my own racial family.

The brain makes the races different. The races have different shapes and sizes of brains.

On why most serial killers have been White ... White people plan what they do. White people actually think. Most of the crimes that Blacks commit are impulsive.

White people think about the crime they are going to commit. White people are involved in this type of crime because it takes a lot of planning.

These words strikingly reveal the thinking of a Klan member. This mentality is of such a kind that even the acts of a serial murder can become the cause for boasting, and savagery justified in the name of racial superiority.

The National Alliance

One of the fascist organizations enjoying increasing support from young people in America is the National Alliance. The organization was first founded in 1970 by Dr. William Pierce, a young professor of physics at Oregon State University, as the National Youth Alliance.

Its outstanding characteristic was the way it targeted colleges and universities. Age of membership was restricted to 30 and under. Later, however, that age barrier was lifted and a new organization was created called the National Alliance. One of the principle objectives of this organization attaches great importance to the rearing up of young people with racist ideas. That, it is believed, will enable future generations to emerge in the awareness of racial superiority. Like all other racist groups, the National Alliance aims to defend the superiority of the white race under all circumstances. Dr. Pierce summed up this objective during an interview he gave in 1997:

Ultimately, we must separate ourselves from the Blacks and other non-Whites and keep ourselves separate, no matter what it takes to accomplish this... Eventually we must hunt them down and get rid of them.

That, of course, is not the only similarity between the National Alliance and other fascist organizations. As with others who believe in the theory of evolution, it is also prominent in the National Alliance. No matter how much organization members may claim to be religious, their statements reveal their beliefs to be totally opposed to religion. In general, they will state the following:

We see ourselves as integral with a unitary world around us, which evolves according to natural law. In the simplest words: There is only one reality, which we call Nature: ...We are part of Nature and subject to Nature's laws. Within the scope of these laws we are able to determine our own destiny... In other words, we ourselves are responsible for everything over which we have the power of choice: in particular, for the state of our environment and for the destiny of our race. This view may be contrasted with the Semitic view.

As we have seen, the use of religious principles in speeches by fascist and racist groups, and their efforts to portray themselves as people who live by the morality of religion, are nothing more than a sham tactic. Studies and researches by sociologists and academics have emphasized this fact. One of these academics is Jack Levin, director for the study of Violence and Social Conflict at Boston's Northeastern University. Levin states that the reason the groups use biblical references is to "lend an air of religious credibility" to their message of hate.

THE WEB OF TERROR: EROSION & ENCIRCLEMENT

The primary focus and target of the armies of *mujahiddeen*, and their suicidal hard core, the *fidayeen*, who pour out of the *madrassas* and Pakistani terrorist training camps, at present, is the Indian State of Jammu & Kashmir (J&K). The leadership of the terrorist movement in J&K passed out of the hands of local militants, and to groups created by and based in Pakistan as far back as in 1993, when the most powerful terrorist group indigenous to the State, the Jammu & Kashmir Liberation Front (JKLF) led by Yasin Malik, chose to give up arms and seek a 'political solution' to its grievances. The JKLF still demands Kashmiri 'Independence', and is strongly opposed to any amalgamation with Pakistan. The Pakistan-based groups, quite naturally, are far more amenable to a merger with that country.

Terrorist groupings enjoyed substantial mass support, particularly in the Kashmir Valley, as long as the movement for secession remained indigenous. Progressively, however, a process of disillusionment with the activities of Pakistan sponsored militants has combined with exhaustion to diminish this base, and terrorism is now sustained purely on inputs – ideologies, material, and increasing numbers of men – from across the border. The currently most active terrorist groups in the State are each headquartered in Pakistan, and include the Hizb-ul-Mujahiddeen (HuM) , linked to the JEI in Pakistan; Lashkar-e-Toiba (LeT), the armed wing of the Markaz-ad-Da'awa-wal-Irshad; the Harkat-ul-Jehad-e-Islami (HuJI) and the Harkat-ul-Mujahiddeen (formerly the Harkat-ul-Ansar), linked to the JUP, the Pakistan Tablighi

Jamaat and to the Hizb-e-Islami of Afghanistan; al Badr; and the recently formed Jaish-e-Muhammad (JeM). There are another score of minor and dormant groupings, also located in Pakistan. The umbrella Muttahida Jehad Council coordinates the activities of 13 of the most prominent terrorist factions (14 till the HuM was expelled for declaring a brief unilateral ceasefire in July 2000).

The years 1997, 1998 and the first half of 1999 had seen a gradual decline in violence and fatalities in J&K, but there was a radical escalation after the Kargil War of May-July 1999. The trends underwent a further deterioration after two ceasefires – the first announced unilaterally by the Hizb-ul-Mujahiddeen in July 2000, and the second, again unilaterally, by the Indian Prime Minister, A.B. Vajpayee, in November 2000 – as the possibility of an emerging peace process threatened the entrenched interests and ideological ambitions of the extremist Islamist groups in Pakistan, and of their official sponsors there. A total of 26,226 persons have died in this conflict between 1988 and 2000. These include 10,285 civilians, 12,375 terrorists, and 2,566 security force (SF) personnel. Among the civilian fatalities, 8,712 (nearly 85 per cent) have been Muslims.

The conflict in Kashmir has been substantially documented in the context of Pakistan's strategy and "overriding interest... to achieve internal security by provoking instability among its neighbors." There is, however, comparatively little understanding of the extremist or pan-Islamic agenda in the rest of South Asia, and of its integral links to the strategies and tactics that prepared the ground for terrorism in Kashmir.

As with much of South Asia, the culture and religious practices of the Muslims of Kashmir had little in common with the rigid and distorted version of Wahabbi Islam – with its ideological source in Saudi Arabia – that is the dominant ideological force among contemporary extremist Islamists. Kashmiri Islam was seeped with the mysticism and values of the devotional Sufi order, and the Kashmir Valley was, indeed, held up as a unique and inspirational example of secular values at the time of Partition and Independence, and in the decades that followed. The emergence of terrorism in the State was preceded by decades of religious mobilization and reorientation centered primarily in the mosques in the Valley, and when terror broke out in the late 1980s, it was the mosques and the *madrassas* that provided the motivation, the moral sanction, and the initial impetus, not only to the violence, but to the near complete ethnic cleansing of the Valley of its Kashmiri Pandit minority. It is interesting that, among the priority targets of the terrorists was the network of secular school, most of which were shut down under threat, especially in rural areas, progressively forcing the children into the only surviving 'educational' institution – the *madrassa* – the 'schools of hate' that created new 'supply lines' for *Jihad*.

There is, today, a sustained effort – with mixed results – to replicate these processes of religious mobilization and an extremist Islamist reorientation throughout South Asia. In India, while there have been several political factors and events contributing to higher levels of communal polarization, general communal conflict – expressed in the incidence of communal riots – has been on a decline. Political parties are yet to abandon the electoral strategy of exploiting religious sentiments and insecurities, but the mass base and credibility of those who seek to do so has suffered steady erosion. Nevertheless, the intent and strategy of Pakistan's covert agencies and extremist religious groupings is increasingly apparent in a wide range of activities intended to provoke communal confrontations, engineer terrorist incidents, and recruit soldiers for a pan-Islamic *Jihad* in pockets of Muslim populations across India. This is compounded by a process of 'encirclement' and massive demographic shifts that deepen the danger, particularly along India's Eastern borders.

During a three-day annual congregation of the members of the Markaz-ad-Da'awa-wal-Irshad at Muridke near Lahore on February 6, 2000, the Amir (head) of the Markaz, Hafiz Mohammad Saeed, declared that Kashmir was a 'gateway to capture India' and that it was the aim of the Markaz and its military wing, the Lashkar-e-Toiba, to engineer India's disintegration. Saeed added that his organization's campaign in Hyderabad (Andhra Pradesh) and Junagadh (Gujarat) were among the highest priorities. Abdul Rahman Makki, the LeT's ideologue, expanded on this theme, proclaiming that the group had opened a new unit in Hyderabad to liberate the Indian city from "un-Islamic Indian rule". These declarations are, at once, an expression of the pan-Islamic ambitions shared by all extremist Islamist groups operating in the region, and a reiteration of Pakistan's larger strategy of destabilization beyond the scope of the supposed 'core issue' of Kashmir.

Within this larger design was a series of 13 bomb blasts in various churches in Andhra Pradesh, Karnataka and Goa between May and July 2000, executed by an obscure Islamic sect created in 1924, the Deendar Anjuman. The Anjuman is headed by Zia-ul-Hassan, the son of its founder, who is based in Peshawar, Pakistan, where the sect goes by the name Anjuman Hizbullah. Hassan is also said to have floated a militant organization, the Jamat-e-Hizb-ul-Mujahiddeen in Pakistan, in order to 'capture India and spread Islam'. Intelligence sources indicate that Hassan is bankrolled by the ISI, and the Indian Union Home Minister stated in Parliament that linkages between the Deendar Anjuman and Pakistan's covert intelligence agency had been established by investigators. Investigations have exposed a network of the Anjuman's subversive activities extending across several small towns and urban centres, including Nuzvid, Atmakur, Kurukunda, Palem, Vijayawada, Khammam and Nandyal in Andhra Pradesh; and Batakurki, Ramdurg and Hubli in Karnataka.

Another series of 19 explosions had earlier, on February 14, 1998, left over 50 dead and more than 200 injured in the Coimbatore district of Tamil Nadu. While the Al Umma group, founded by S.A. Basha, investigations and subsequent arrests exposed the involvement of a wide network of extremist Islamist organization across South India, including the Indian Muslim Mohammadi Mujahideen, the Tanzim Islahul Muslimeen, the Jihad Committee in Tamil Nadu; and the Islamic Sevak Sangh, subsequently banned and revived as the People's Democratic Party (PDP), headed by Abdul Nasser Madani. ISI agents, including Azam Ghauri (who was subsequently shot dead in an encounter with the police at Jagityal, Karimnagar District, Andhra Pradesh, on April 6, 2000), Saleem Junaid, Farooq Ahmed and Mohammad Mansoor. By far the most dramatic serial blasts engineered by the ISI took place in Bombay on March 12, 1993, and these revealed a unique pattern of operation that has gradually consolidated itself over the years – the use of organized criminal networks to execute terrorist strikes. Nearly 1,800 kilograms of RDX and a large number of detonators and small arms had been smuggled through the West coast of India prior to these blasts, which killed over 300 persons and targeted critical commercial infrastructure, including the country's largest stock exchange at Dalal Street. The explosions were executed by the notorious D-Company headed by Dawood Ibrahim. Ibrahim now lives in Karachi, and runs India's largest criminal empire through aides located outside India, and primarily in the Middle East.

India's Northeast is another interesting area of emerging Islamist militancy, and here it combines with major demographic shifts that hold significant dangers for the future. Illegal migration on a large scale across the border from Bangladesh is the most potent single factor in the destabilisation of this region. In November 1998, the Governor of Assam, Lt. Gen. (Retd.) S.K. Sinha, submitted a report to the Indian President which estimated the total volume of this infiltration at six million people. Most of this increase was concentrated in a few areas, with a dramatic impact on the local demography and, hence, politics. According to the report, four districts of Assam – Dhubri, Goalpara, Barpeta, Hailakandi – had been transformed into Muslim majority districts by 1991 as a result of this mass infiltration. Another two districts – Nagaon and Karimganj – would have had a Muslim majority since 1998 and yet another district, Morigaon, is fast approaching this position. This demographic destabilization, combined with the widespread violence and political instability in the region has created a unique recruiting ground for the Islamists, and there has been a veritable efflorescence of Muslim terrorist groups operating along India's borders with Bangladesh in the Northeast. In Assam alone, there are over 15 terrorist groups operating under an Islamic banner, and the ISI's role in funding and arming these groups has now been fairly well documented.

Serial bombings and overt terrorist movements, however, cannot be a measure of the penetration that has been achieved by the extremist Islamists and their state sponsors. Acts of terror – especially on a large scale – represent the culmination of years of preparation that are reflected in motivation, mobilization and organizational development. Evidence of these processes is mounting throughout India, and is reflected in the number, both of fundamentalist and of subversive groups in existence, and the geographical spread of their activities. The most prominent of these include the Jamaat-e-Islami Hind (JEI Hind), the All India Milli Council (AIMC), All India Jihad Committee (AIJC), the People's Democratic Party (PDP, formerly the Islamic Sewak Sangh), All India Muslim Federation (AIMF), Muslim United Front (MUF), Tamil Nadu Muslim Munnetra Kazhagam (TNMMK), National Development Front (Kerala), Tabligh Jamaat, Students Islamic Movement of India (SIMI), Students Islamic Organisations (SIO), Al Umma, Al Jihad, and the Muslim Sena Sanghathan, Ikhwan-ul-Muslameen, Islami Inqalabi Mahaz, Tanzim Isla-ul-Muslameen, and the Minorities United Front, among others.

Each of these organizations runs one or more non-governmental organization (NGO), many of which have offices abroad. Very substantial funds are received, and a range of interactions, including frequent 'Tablighi conferences' with foreign delegations, are organized. The flow of funds is primarily through what are known as *hawala* (illegal) channels, and while Pakistan largely defines the patterns of use and the beneficiaries, the preponderance of such transfers originate in Saudi Arabia, Kuwait, United Arab Emirates, Qatar and Oman. Thus, very substantial transfers of foreign funds generated under the pretext of providing relief to the Coimbatore riot victims are believed to have been used for the Coimbatore blasts.

The range, the volume and the persistence of such subversive activity throughout the country is more a measure of Pakistan's tenacity and the intensity of the extremist Islamist vision, than it is of the present impact these activities have had on the larger Muslim community in India. The tragic loss of life, the wasted human and developmental resources, and the atmosphere of fear and suspicion that sporadic incidents of terrorism generate notwithstanding, India has the flexibility, the resilience and the political space to absorb a level of subversive and extremist Islamist activities significantly higher than the present. Nevertheless, the sheer lethality of weaponry and explosives, the possibility of an escalation to a new generation of Chemical and Biological Weapons, and the inherent uncertainty of the politics of a complex society characterized by immense religious and cultural diversity, make the existing risks and levels of activity unacceptable. These risks are even greater and less acceptable in countries where such space is wanting, where political instability is at higher levels, and where the roots of democracy are yet to take firm hold of the soil.

Islamist subversion threatens peace and regime stability more immediately in neighboring Bangladesh, where religious extremism has emerged as a major threat to the prevailing political order and to internal security. There are grave and immediate dangers to peace and stability in Bangladesh: the revival of the activities of the Jamaat-e-Islami, the return to Bangladesh and its politics of Pakistan-backed elements who collaborated closely with the genocidal campaign of 1971 in what was then East Pakistan, the rising rhetoric of Islamic *Hukumat* (rule), and the deepening linkages between militant Bangladeshi groups and the extremist Islamists in Pakistan, Afghanistan and West Asia. Here again, the pattern of funding, subversion and mobilization through the mosque and the *madrassa* is clearly in evidence. Prior to Independence, there were 1,467 *madrassas* in Bangladesh. Their number has currently risen to over 6,500, with more than 90,000 teachers and about 1.8 million students. A large number of these institutions have been established as a result of massive foreign aid, primarily from Gulf countries, and largely unmediated by official channels. Bangladesh's *madrassas* are the chief recruiting ground for Islamic militant groups, including several that are linked to Pakistan and also to Osama Bin Laden's *Al Qaida*. The latter category includes the Harkat-ul-Jehad-e-Islami, which was established by Shawkat Osman, alias Sheikh Farid in 1992 with Bin Laden's backing, and which has an estimated strength of about 15,000. The Harkat maintains six camps in the hilly areas of Chittagong, where the cadres are given arms training. Several hundred recruits have also been trained in Afghanistan. The cadres, recruited mainly from among students of various *madrassas*, style themselves as the 'Bangladeshi Taliban.' Reports suggest that foreign-aided religious fanatics are actively conspiring to establish 'Islamic *hukumat*' by waging war and killing progressive intellectuals, as well as various minority groups and 'heretical' sects, such as the Ahmadiyas.

In addition to the JEI, the prominent fundamentalist Islamist political parties in Bangladesh include the Muslim Leagure, Tabligh Jamaat, Jamaat-e-Tulba and Jamaat-ul-Muderessin. One significant pro-Iranian group, the Islamic Shasantantra Andolan (Movement for Islamic Constitution), is also active. The subversive activities of the ISI and foreign extremist Islamist agencies in Bangladesh increased radically after Sheikh Hasina's broadly secular Awami League came to power in June 1996, and this has contributed to an upsurge in militant and fundamentalist political activity. Superimposed over a history of military coups, a politics dominated by the rhetoric of Islam, and increasing international linkages, including networks with insurgent groups operating in India's Northeast, extremist Islamic militancy constitutes the most serious existing internal security threat in Bangladesh.

The security agencies of the infant democracy of Nepal are also being challenged by rising extremist Islamist activity, despite the fact that Muslims constitute a bare three percent of the population. Such activity is, presently, primarily directed against India, but its linkages with organized criminal operations and the destabilization of pockets of Muslim concentrations in the Terai region bordering India are a cause of increasing concern for Kathmandu. A succession of recent reports has documented increasing activities of the ISI and by the Pakistan Embassy at Kathmandu involving strong organized criminal networks and prominent political leaders in a range of activities targeting India and reinforcing the Islamist agenda within Nepal. The Muslim pockets of the Terai, especially Bardiya, Banke, Rupendehi and the Parsa-Morang belt have seen increasing '*Tablighi*' activities, and the construction of mosques and *madrassas* with financial flows from Pakistan – often directly from the Embassy at Kathmandu – from Saudi Arabia and from a range of pan-Islamic organizations.

Over the past two decades, more than 275 mosques and *madrassas* have been built in just the four districts of Rupandehi, Banke, Kapilvastu and Bardiya. There are some 15 major *tablighi/* fundamentalist organizations in Nepal, and at least five of these are well within the ambit of Pakistan's influence and control. These include the Jamaat-e-Millat-e-Islamia; the Nepal Islamic Yuba Sangh; the Nepal Muslim League; the Nepal Muslim Ekta Sangh; and the Democratic Muslim Welfare Association. Nepal is, consequently, emerging as an important 'staging post' for Pakistan's strategy of erosion and encirclement against India, and is increasingly the preferred route for terrorists movements to various areas of low-intensity conflict in J&K and the Northeast. In Sri Lanka, the Muslim community and emerging fundamentalist forces have generally aligned themselves with the interests of the government. The Island nation's Muslim population is mainly Tamil, but has been driven out of the ethnically cleansed northern areas controlled by the Liberation Tigers of Tamil Eelam (LTTE), and is now concentrated along the eastern coast, the north-west coast, Kandy and suburban Colombo. Islamic fundamentalist mobilization in Sri Lanka began after a succession of attacks on the Muslims by the LTTE in the early 1990s, after which the government decided to arm the Muslim youth for self-defence. The conflict between Hindu and Muslim Tamils resulted in the polarization of mindsets on the issue of religious identity. There are, today, nearly a dozen Muslim fundamentalist organizations in Sri Lanka who are funded by foreign countries, primarily Saudi Arabia, with at least two political parties drawing significant support from Iran.

7

Madrassas and Islamic Militancy

The *madrassas* are obviously institutions which have a blueprint of society in their mind. What needs explanation is that the *madrassas,* which were basically conservative institutions before the Afghan-Soviet War of the nineteen eighties, are both ideologically activist and sometimes militant. This, indeed, is the major change which seems to have occurred in the Pakistani religious establishment. The British conquest was opposed with some armed resistance but mostly the *ulema* retreated into their *madrassas* where orthodoxy, conserving the legacy of the past, was the order of the day.

Folk Islam in South Asia was mystical, ritualistic and superstitious. The Barelvi sub-sect, which was very popular, supported extreme reverence for saints and rituals—such as the distribution of sweetmeats (*halwa*) on certain sacred days. This type of Islam—low church as it may be called—was challenged by the Deobandis, the Ahl-i-Hadith and the Jama't-i-Islami because none of these believed in the intercession of saints, the distribution of food on fixed days or other practices of folk Islam.

These strict religious groups found unsuspected allies among the modernist Muslims and the Westernized or secular urban people who were in a Muslim culture but whose world view was Western. All these people opposed mysticism and folk Islam too which they considered irrational and retrogressive. The result of these tendencies was that Islam came to be defined more and more in legalistic terms and the conservative point of view come to be replaced slowly by the revivalist one.

As the Pakistani *ulema* came to be drawn more and more into the ideology of the state (by becoming teachers of Arabic in ordinary schools or minor bureaucrats, for instance, they became politicized. They started thinking of how they could pursue power to make the society Islamic as they understood the term. The Iranian revolution of 1979, the defeat of the Soviet Union in Afghanistan in the late eighties and later the rise of the Taliban convinced the Pakistani *ulema* that Islam could be a power in its own right. In short, the *ulema* were drifting from conservatism to revivalism and activism. Surely the Deobandi and Ahl-i-Hadith *ulema* were more consciously revivalist as were the Shia *ulema* but, on the whole, the character of Islam, as preached in Pakistan, has undergone a tremendous change on the whole.

So, while the basic texts of the Dars-i-Nizami remain the same, what has changed is that the *ulema* are more conscious of world affairs which they see and describe with reference to the crusades. Indeed, Karen Armstrong in her book on the impact of the crusades on the world states clearly that 'The wars in the Middle East today are becoming more like the Crusades in this respect, especially in the religious escalation on both sides of the conflict' (Armstrong 1988: 530). And, it is not just the Israel-Arab conflict but other wars in the Muslim world which are seen in religious terms. Thus, even before Huntington presented his thesis about the 'clash of civilizations', the *imams* of Pakistani mosques used to describe world affairs with reference to such a theory in mind. This political conciseness invoking the name of Kashmir and Palestine in Pakistan, has permeated much of the religious establishment and the middle class in Pakistan. Thus, not just the *madrassa* teachers and students but people from secular institutions belonging to the lower-middle and middle classes respond to political Islam. Such people see the United States in particular and the West in general as the major forces for oppression and injustice in the world. According to Peter L. Bergen, author of a book on Osama bin Laden and his al-Qaeda group: 'nowhere is bin Laden more popular than in Pakistan's *madrassas,* religious schools from which the

Taliban draw many of its recruits' (Bergen 2001: 150). While it is not clear how Bergen obtained this information, my own impression is that it is largely correct but that bin Laden is popular among a number of non-madrassa educated young Muslims, especially the politically-aware ones, too.

Madrassas Militant

All *madrassas* are not militant. Those which are became militant when they were used by the Pakistani state to fight in Afghanistan during the Soviet occupation and then in Kashmir so as to force India to leave the state. Pakistan's claim on Kashmir, as discussed by many including Alastair Lamb (1977), has led to conflict with India and the Islamic militants or *Jihadis,* who have entered the fray since 1989. The United States indirectly, and sometimes directly, helped in creating militancy among the clergy. For instance, special textbooks in Darri (Afghan Persian) and Pashto were written at the University of Nebraska-Omaha with a USAID grant in the 1980s (Stephens and Ottaway 2002: Sec A, p. 1). American arms and money flowed to Afghanistan through Pakistan's Inter services Intelligence as several books indicate. At that time all this was done to defeat the Soviet Union. The fact that till January 2002, where General Pervez Musharraf clamped down on Islamic militants, lists published by fighting group included *madrassa* and non-madrassa students, suggests that at least some *madrassas* did send their students to fight in Kashmir. This has been reduced considerably though *The Herald,* one of the most prestigious monthlies from Karachi, tells us in its July 2005 issue that 'hundreds of young boys between the ages of 13 and 15 years make ready cannon fodder for violent militant campaigns'. These young boys, who do not necessarily belong to *madrassas,* belong to private armies—there are said to be fifteen of them—raised by different religious-political parties. The *Herald's* implication is that, at some covert level, the state is still supporting these militant outfits so that they can be used to fight in Kashmir if the peace process fails.

However, while Pakistan's military kept using the militant Islamists in Kashmir, the United States was much alarmed by them—not without reason as the events of Nine Eleven demonstrated later. The Americans then tried to understand the *madrassas* better. P.W. Singer, an analyst in the Brookings Institute who has been referred to earlier, wrote that there were 10-15 percent 'radical' *madrassas* which teach anti-American rhetoric, terrorism and even impart military training (Singer 2001). No proof for these claims was offered. However, fighters from Afghanistan, Kashmir and even Chechnya did come to the *madrassas* and may have talked with students inspiring them to fight against those whom they saw as the enemies of Islam.

More significantly, the private armed groups or armies associated with religious parties or acting on their own, mentioned earlier, train both *madrassa* and other school dropouts. They were financed by the intelligence agencies of Pakistan as the *Herald, Newsline, Friday Times* and a number of Pakistani publications have written repeatedly in the past few years. Some of these armies such as Lashkar-e-Tayyaba, Jaish-e-Mohammed and Harkat-ul-Mujahidin—print militant literature which circulates among the *madrassas* and other institutions.

Militancy and Islamist Fighters in Madarsaa

Islamic militancy is going on in many parts of the world notable among which are Palestine, Chechnya, the Phillipines, Afghanistan, Kashmir and parts of Central Asia. However, what is surprising to many people is that secular institutions and Western countries also produce Islamic militants. As Olivier Roy points out, most young Islamist militants are trained in secular institutions. He quotes many names of the 9/11 militants concluding that: None (except for the Saudis) was educated in a Muslim religious school and Jarrah even attended a Lebanese Christian School. Most of them studied technology, computing, or town planning, as the World Trade Center pilots had done (Roy 2004: 310). This seems to be true about the angry young British Muslims who struck on 7 Jul 2005 as well as the cadres of the Jama't-i-Islami in Pakistan who support fighting in Kashmir though most of them come from the state education system and not the *madrassas*.

Roy further points out that deterritorialized Muslims in Western countries, being overwhelmed by the dominant culture around them, fall back upon the Islamic identity. They are not guided by traditional texts or the *ulema*; they find their own meanings from the fundamental texts of the faith (the Qur'an and the *hadith*). Their neo-colonial reaction to the injustice of the world order, the irresistible globalization which seems to inundate all civilizations under the banner of Micky Mouse, is to lash out in fury against Western targets and elites in Muslim countries who support Western policies. They use the idiom of Islam but the anger which motivates them comes from a sense of being cheated. There are, of course, pegs to hang this anger on: Palestine, Chechnya, Kashmir, Afghanistan, Iraq, Iran—the list can go on. But essentially Muslim militancy is a reaction to Western injustice, violence and a history of exploitation and domination over Muslims. This can only be reversed by genuinely reversing Western militant policies and a more equitable distribution of global wealth.

In Pakistan, General Musharraf feels that Islamic militancy can be reduced as far as Pakistan's *madrassas* are concerned, if secular subjects are taught in them and if foreigners are not allowed to study there. Let us take both these propositions in turn. What are called secular subjects were taught as *maqulat* in Mughal *madrassas* because one of the functions of these institutions was to produce bureaucrats for the state. What is now being advocated is to add the social sciences, English, computer skills and mathematics to the curricula. General Pervez Musharraf's military government introduced a law called the 'Pakistan Madrassah Education (Establishment and Affiliation of Model Dini Madaris) Board Ordinance 2001 on 18 August 2001. According to the *Education Sector Reforms* (GOP 2002c) three model institutions were established: one each at Karachi, Sukkur and Islamabad. Their curriculum 'includes subjects of English, Mathematics, Computer Science, Economics, Political Science, Law and Pakistan Studies for its different levels (GOP 2002c: 23). These institutions were not welcomed by the *ulema*.

However, some modern subjects have been taught for quite some time in the *madrassas*. The Ahl-i-Hadith *madrassas* have been teaching Pakistan studies, English, Mathematics and General Science a long time (GOP 1988: 85). The Jama't-i-Islami also teachers secular subjects. The larger Deobandi, Barelvi and Shia *madrassas* too have made arrangements for teaching secular subjects including basic computer skills. According to a report in the weekly *The Friday Times* from Lahore the Deobandi Wafaq-ul Madaris has decided to accommodate modern subjects on a larger scale than ever before. They would make the students spend another two years to give a more thorough grounding in the secular subjects. The Wafaq 'has also formed committees to devise ways to capitalize on the government's U.S $ 255 million for the *Madrassa* reform scheme (Mansoor 2003). However, at present, the teaching is done by teachers approved of by the *ulema* or some of the *ulema* themselves. Thus the potential for secularization of the se subjects, which is small in any case, is reduced to nothingness.

I believe that all attempts at secularizing *madrassas* will probably backfire. First, the *madrassas* work on charitable donations so they will not buckle down to the government's fiat. Secondly, they are not the only ones who produce militants. It is poverty and the fighting in Kashmir and elsewhere in the world which does so, so these external conditions—greatly dependent on government policy as they are—must be changed to produce peaceful people. Thirdly, the text books of the so called 'secular' subjects produced by the educational boards in Pakistan are anti-India and glorify armed conflict (Aziz 1993; Saigol 1995; Rahman 2002: 515-524 and Nayyar and Salim 2003). Moreover, the people who will teach them will be selected by the clergy and will be highly politicized Islamists who will be even more fiery in their denunciations of peace, liberal values and the West than even the *ulema* themselves. In any case, as we have observed earlier, Islamists from traditional educational institutions are even more prone to political violence than *madrassa* students. Thus, no amount of 'secularization' of the *madrassas* will eliminate violence.

The other proposal, that of not allowing foreigners to study in the *madrassas* may be more successful. There is now a law introduced to control the entry of foreigners in the *madrassas* and keep check on them. This law—Voluntary Registration and Regulation Ordinance 2002—has, however, been rejected by most of the *madrassas* which want no state interference in their affairs.

Indeed, according to Singer, '4,350, about one tenth, agreed to be registered and the rest simply ignored the statute' (Singer 2001). The number of those who did not register is not known. However, on 29 July 2005 President Musharraf sad in an interview with foreign correspondents that 1400 foreign students would be expelled and visas to aspiring students to denied (*The News* 30 July 2005). If this policy is rigorously enforced, motivated extremists from other parts of the Muslim world may cease entering Pakistan.

PAKISTAN'S LONG DALLIANCE WITH MILITANCY

Many discussions of Pakistan's use of jihadi organizations begin with the 1980s. During this period, General Muhammad Zia-ul-Haq utilized mujahideen forces to undermine the Soviet occupation of Afghanistan. Pakistan, however, has been using proxy forces since attaining independence from the United Kingdom. In October 1947, Pakistan employed Pathan tribesmen to attack the princely state of Kashmir as its monarch vacillated on the question of whether to accede to India or to Pakistan. The rebels quickly advanced on the Kashmiri capital of Srinagar, raping and pillaging along the way. As attacking forces approached Srinagar, a panicked Maharaja Hari Singh appealed to New Delhi for military assistance. The government of India agreed to defend Kashmir if Singh would commit to join the territory to India. He complied, signing an Instrument of Accession on October 28, 1947. Shortly thereafter, a full-scale war erupted, pitting Pakistan-supported and Pakistani regular forces against the Indian military. The conflict ended in stalemate on December 31, 1948, with India controlling approximately two-thirds of Kashmir and Pakistan the remaining third. This division of territory largely set the foundation for decades of Indo—Pak conflict.

Pakistan resorted to irregular forces again in August 1965 by employing militants in an effort to seize the Indian-controlled portion of Kashmir. The militants infiltrated Indian Kashmir to precipitate an uprising, which was to be followed by a Pakistani conventional military operation to seize the territory. The plan presumed widespread Kashmiri support for Pakistan and disaffection with India. This assumption proved to be wrong;

locals promptly alerted the authorities to the presence of the infiltrators, enabling Indian forces to move against them. Despite this failure, Pakistani leaders launched the follow-on, conventional military phase, thereby provoking the second Indo—Pak war. Like the first war, this conflict ended essentially in stalemate. The two parties subsequently agreed to return to the status quo as per the Soviet-brokered Tashkent Agreement of 1966.

In spite of these setbacks in 1947—1948 and 1965, Pakistan's leaders did not lose interest in using militants to help seize control of Indian—administered Kashmir. Indeed, almost immediately after the 1965 war, elements within the Pakistani military started to recruit religious zealots in the Kashmir Valley in hopes of sowing discord and promoting political upheaval within the state. To that end, the Pakistanis started to work with a newly created organization called the Plebiscite Front. While some elements of the Front were willing to limit themselves to the realm of political struggle, others wanted to resort to violence to achieve their goal of merging Kashmir with Pakistan.

These efforts suffered an important setback in the early 1970s, as India cracked down against various jihadi groups. Following Ziaul-Haq's coup in Pakistan and the Soviet invasion of Afghanistan, Islamabad renewed its use of the jihadi option. Zia-ul-Haq presided over the mujahideen campaign in Afghanistan, which played an indispensible role in defeating the Soviet Union. His death during the summer of 1988 in a plane crash prevented him from applying this strategy to Kashmir. When an indigenous uprising erupted in Indian Kashmir in December 1989, however, his successors lost little time in doing so. The Pakistanis initially backed the Jammu and Kashmir Liberation Front (JKLF), a homegrown, notionally secular separatist organization, but such support proved to be shortlived. The JKLF did not wish to join Kashmir to Pakistan. Instead, it sought the creation of an independent Kashmir encompassing both Indian and Pakistani controlled portions of the state. Consequently, the Pakistani military and Inter-Services Intelligence agency (ISI) marginalized the JKLF, redirecting their resources toward more Islamistoriented organizations dedicated to establishing Pakistani control over Indiaadministered Kashmir.

These organizations ranged from the predominantly Kashmiri Hizb-ul-Mujahideen (HuM), to the mostly externally recruited, battlehardened Lashkar-e-Taiba (LeT), whose main goal is to establish an Islamic state in South Asia, and the Jaish-e-Mohammed (JeM), whose main focus is to separate Kashmir from India and join it with Pakistan. Pakistani support for these groups fundamentally transformed the character of the Kashmir insurgency, metamorphosizing it from an indigenous independence struggle, triggered by the malfeasances of Indian rule, to an externally orchestrated effort to attrite Indian resources and seize Jammu and Kashmir for Pakistan.

Over time, Pakistan-backed militants launched increasingly provocative terror operations. On December 13, 2001, for example, LeT and JeM attacked the Indian Parliament while it was in session. Although the terrorists were defeated and no members were harmed, the assault could have resulted in a massacre of India's national legislators. In the wake of this attack, under considerable U.S. pressure, Pakistan undertook cosmetic efforts against organizations such as the LeT and the JeM, briefly incarcerating members of their rank and file. Also, on January 12, 2002, in a nationally televised speech, Musharraf stated that he would not allow Pakistani soil to be used as a launching pad for terror against India or any other country, though he did not rule out the possibility that militant groups might operate from Pakistan-administered Kashmir, which enjoys nominal independence. Despite Musharraf's apparent interest in preventing further terrorism, little changed in practice. Soon thereafter, in May 2002, the LeT were implicated in an attack on the families of soldiers stationed at an Indian military base at Kaluchak in Jammu and Kashmir. The December 2001 parliament assault had led India to undertake a massive military mobilization to coerce Pakistan into ending its support for terrorism. The May 2002 Kaluchak attack brought the two states to the brink of war. For reasons that are the subject of a vigorous debate, they managed to avoid outright conflict during these 2001—2002 crises. Nonetheless, Indo—Pak relations remained fraught as Pakistan failed to completely rein in the jihadi organizations operating on its soil.

In the wake of the 2001—2002 crises, a series of bombings rocked major urban centres across India from Bangalore to New Delhi. Indian authorities attributed several of the attacks to the LeT. Pakistani authorities in some cases ignored the charges, and in others denied any connection with the bombings. Doubts about continued links between Pakistan and anti-Indian terrorism, however, were effectively dispelled with the November 2008 assault on Mumbai. A group of 10 terrorists launched a series of carefully planned attacks against the Taj Mahal and Oberoi hotels, the Bhikaji Cama Children's Hospital, the Chattrapati Shivaji Railway Terminus, the Leopold Cafe', and the Chabad House, a Jewish cultural center. Well over one hundred civilians, several security personnel and all but one terrorist were killed in the three-day shooting spree.

Pakistani authorities initially denied any link between the Mumbai attackers and Pakistan. Overwhelming evidence that the terrorists were members of LeT and that their operation had been planned in, launched from, and directed in real time by operatives in Pakistan, however, pointed toward the contrary. No longer able to deny the Pakistan—Mumbai connection, Pakistani officials placed Hafiz Mohammed Saeed, the head of the LeT's charitable front organization, Jamaat-ud-Dawa, under house arrest in Lahore. Before long though, Saeed was free once again after a Pakistani court released the LeTchief in June 2009, citing a paucity of evidence against him. The provincial government of the Punjab subsequently withdrew terror charges against Saeed for a similar want of evidence.

The Sorcerer's Apprentice

Analysts have often cited Pakistan's support for Islamist militancy as strategically shortsighted. Islamabad has adhered to essentially the same strategy in pursuit of the same ends for most of its history, using non-state actors in an effort to alter territorial boundaries in South Asia without triggering a full-scale conventional conflict in the region. Despite its repeated efforts, Pakistan has rarely succeeded in attaining its goals. The 1947 and 1965 Kashmir wars ended in stalemate. The Pakistan-backed insurgency in Kashmir, despite its violence, has not convinced the Indians to leave the territory. To the contrary, the Indians have become more intransigent as the carnage has increased. Meanwhile, Pakistan's provocative behavior has created serious regional tensions that could trigger a major conflict, and diverted resources away from other urgent domestic priorities such as economic development, educational reforms, and infrastructure renewal. Thus, critics argue, Pakistan's asymmetric warfare strategy has largely failed. This criticism, however, is not wholly warranted. Pakistan's asymmetric warfare strategy has in fact achieved notable successes. Its support of mujahideen forces in Afghanistan played a crucial role in the Soviets' defeat. In Kashmir, the Pakistanis have inflicted serious economic, military, and diplomatic costs on India. They have also led New Delhi to adopt draconian antiterrorism policies that have badly tarnished its international image. In neither case was Pakistan forced to engage in direct combat against a stronger adversary. Rather, the use of non-state actors enabled the Pakistanis to damage the Soviets and the Indians while avoiding direct conflict and the concomitant risk of catastrophic defeat. Whatever its shortcomings, Pakistan's strategy has achieved important goals, and should not be dismissed as an abject failure.

Despite its past successes, however, Pakistan's asymmetric warfare strategy now faces the serious problem that those militant organizations, which the Pakistanis created and nurtured to execute their policy, no longer wholly share their aims or serve their interests. The militants' goals have become increasingly maximalist. Many seek not just to liberate Kashmir or to join it to Pakistan but see eventual control of territory within India proper as the true prize in their struggle. And they will not allow the Pakistani state to prevent them from attaining it. Nasr Javed, a LeTofficial, delivering a speech at the Quba Mosque in Islamabad on February 5, 2008, declared: "India is also afraid of Jihad. India fears that if the Mujahideen liberated Kashmir through Jihad, then it will be very difficult to keep rest of the India under control. Jihad will spread from Kashmir to other parts of India. The Muslims will be ruling India again." He went on to say, "The government of Pakistan might have abandoned Jihad but we have not. Our agenda is clear. We will continue to wage Jihad and propagate it till eternity. No government can intimidate us. Nobody can stop it_be it the U.S. or Musharraf."

The jihadi organizations also oppose Pakistani efforts to cooperate with U.S. antiterrorism efforts. In the wake of the 9/11 attacks, the U.S. government realized that Islamist terrorism was not an issue isolated to the Middle East or South Asia. Rather, it was a global problem that directly impacted the United States' own security. U.S. leaders also decided that they needed Pakistan to serve as a leading partner in their new "global war on terror." Thus, Washington dramatically shifted its policy. It would no longer ignore Pakistani support for militancy in South Asia, and it would offer Pakistan substantial military and economic benefits for cooperating in its antiterror efforts. In order to reap these rewards, Pakistan agreed to serve as an ally in the U.S. antiterrorism campaign. As a result, the Pakistanis were forced to limit support for Islamist insurgents in Kashmir, occasionally even outlawing militant groups. This Pakistani cooperation with the United States alienated the militant organizations. These groups, which owed their existence to Islamabad, branded Musharraf a traitor and turned against the Pakistani government.

Meanwhile, the Taliban, whose control of Afghanistan had been strongly supported by the Pakistani government, now seeks not just to retake Afghanistan, but to seize Pakistani territory as well. Factions such as the Tehrik-e-Taliban, the main Taliban group in Pakistan, have asserted control over swaths of territory to resist the central government, enforce a strict interpretation of Sharia law, and unite with the Afghan Taliban against NATO forces in Afghanistan. Pakistan would benefit from Taliban resurgence in Afghanistan: it would mean a friendly government in Kabul, afford Pakistan badly needed strategic depth, allow it more direct access to the energy-rich states of Central Asia, and reduce Indian regional influence. Islamabad, however, does not wish to cede control of its own territory to Taliban elements. These differences between the goals of the Pakistani state and the Islamist groups it helped to create and nurture have severely undermined Pakistani security in a number of ways. First, they have led to outright violence between the militants and Pakistani forces (for example, the Pakistan army has been battling Taliban elements in South Waziristan). Such conflict is costly, both in military terms and in terms of harm to Pakistan's civilian population. Second, differences with the militants have put Pakistani leaders at risk. Musharraf survived multiple assassination attempts after siding with the United States in the war on terror. And militants associated with the Pakistani Taliban succeeded in killing former prime minister Benazir Bhutto as she sought to return to office. Third, jihadi attacks on Indian targets, such as Mumbai, do not merely threaten to undo the Indo—Pak peace process but risk plunging the subcontinent into a large-scale war. In the event of another major terrorist incident in India, Pakistan could be held responsible even if Islamabad was not involved in planning or executing the attack as it evidently was not in the Mumbai case. Even an Indian government that did not wish to respond militarily could find domestic political pressure to do so overwhelming.

Significantly, this is occurring at a time when the Pakistanis can ill afford it. Islamabad would like to deescalate tensions with New Delhi and reduce the likelihood of an Indo—Pakistani confrontation so that it can concentrate on stabilizing its internal security situation in the northwest. Instead, the danger of conflict with India forces Pakistan to divide its attention between the northwest and the East, making its task of internal stabilization significantly more difficult. Thus, the Pakistani state and the jihadis whom it no longer fully controls are, to a significant extent, working at cross purposes.

Who's Your Sorcerer Now?

Following the November 2008 attacks on Mumbai, a single question echoed from New Delhi to Washington: were the Mumbai attacks simply the work of Pakistan-based militants or were they actually orchestrated by the government of Pakistan? Given the militants' increasing autonomy, however, and Pakistan's inability to reassert control over them, this was the wrong question to ask. The relevant question is: who will now play the role of South Asian sorcerer and rein in the jihadis? The natural candidates for the sorcerer's role would be the governments of either Pakistan or India. Recent events, such as the Mumbai attacks, have shown that neither is presently up to the challenge. The government of Pakistan has publicly promised to prevent its soil from being used to launch anti-Indian terrorism, but the Mumbai attacks demonstrate that Islamabad is unable to honour this pledge. India, for its part, cannot defend itself against such attacks. Despite the fact that the Indian authorities had received credible warnings of a seaborne terrorist operation, a mere handful of terrorists were able to keep Indian security personnel at bay for nearly three days, showing that the Indian authorities were caught completely off guard. India does enjoy conventional military superiority over Pakistan. This advantage does not, however, afford the Indians many good options for dealing with the jihadis. The Indians could strike across the Line of Control against terrorist camps in Pakistan-administered Kashmir, which is the most plausible option. But even if such attacks were successful, they would yield only limited benefits because Kashmiri militant camps are transitory and lack high-value human targets or physical infrastructure.

Because strikes on militant camps are not likely to be profitable, the Indians could threaten to launch large-scale attacks deep into Pakistan proper in the event of further terrorism. Although India would eventually prevail in such a conflict, victory would be costly. Nonetheless, such a large-scale confrontation might make continued tolerance for anti-Indian militancy prohibitively expensive for Pakistan, thus finally convincing Pakistan to fully renounce the jihadi option. But even if Indian leaders decided that the possible benefits of such a policy were worth its likely costs, Pakistan's nuclear capacity makes it infeasible. Given the danger of triggering a nuclear response, it would be too risky for the Indians to launch large-scale attacks deep into Pakistan's territory. In the past, India has been willing to contemplate limited conflict with Pakistan, despite Pakistani nuclear weapons (for example, the 1999 Kargil conflict). Pakistan's nuclear capacity, however, has led the Indians to explicitly rule out the possibility of launching a full-scale conventional attack on the Pakistanis. India is unlikely to change its position in the near future. A series of rapid, more limited attacks into Pakistani territory could inflict significant costs on Pakistan without triggering a nuclear exchange. The possibility of such action might stand a better chance of convincing Pakistan to abandon its support for anti-Indian militancy than the threat of all-out conventional war. India is acquiring increasingly sophisticated conventional assets and formulating a "Cold Start" military doctrine that may afford it such a capacity. Given the jihadis' growing autonomy, however, greater Indian coercive capabilities could prove irrelevant. Pakistan may be unable to control the militants' behavior even if it wants to. Thus, Indian military threats could convince Pakistan that it must rein in the jihadis, and still fail to prevent further terrorism. The jihadi networks in Pakistan are so pervasive and their strength so significant that only a firm, unequivocal decision on the part of the country's military and intelligence services to sever all links, albeit not without costs, could bring about their eventual demise. Short of such a drastic volte-face on the part of the Pakistani security and intelligence services, the hydra-headed monster cannot be slayed. In addition, a more coercive Indian approach runs a serious risk of backfiring. Pakistan's asymmetric warfare strategy has been largely motivated by its insecurity vis-a'-vis India. Thus, by augmenting its punitive capabilities, India could render Pakistan even less secure and increase its incentives to promote militancy even further.

Neither India's nor Pakistan's domestic security nor their conventional military capabilities, therefore, are currently able to solve South Asia's sorcerer's apprentice problem. Unfortunately, their nuclear arsenals are largely useless as well. Nuclear weapons facilitated Pakistan's initial adoption of a low-intensity conflict strategy against India during the 1980s and 1990s, preventing large-scale Indian conventional retaliation while militants launched attacks in Indian Kashmir. Nuclear weapons cannot now be used to eradicate the terrorists who flourished under this strategy and today wreak havoc in both India and Pakistan. And nuclear weapons limit India's future military options in dealing with terrorism_ they prevent New Delhi from taking action that, though costly, could potentially convince Pakistan to revisit their tolerance for anti-Indian militancy.

Finally, nuclear weapons pose a danger because of Pakistan's unstable political and security environment. The army, Pakistan's most powerful institution, tightly controls the nuclear arsenal. The army has enormous incentives to ensure the weapons' security, and they do not appear to be under any immediate threat. Still, Pakistan could face situations in which its arsenal might be vulnerable. For example, if Pakistan attempted to move weapons during a crisis with India, militants could capture them as they are being transported, particularly if the jihadis had access to inside information, such as the weapons' transport schedule. Of course, even if they managed to steal a weapon, the militants would still face a number of difficult tasks, such as determining how to use it. Nonetheless, the security of Pakistan's nuclear arsenal is a genuine concern. Nuclear weapons, therefore, are not only unable to help India or Pakistan play the role of a South Asian sorcerer, they could even potentially pose dangers of their own.

ISLAMIC MILITANCY

All three militants were earlier convicted and sentenced to death for grenade attacks that killed a number of innocent people, including two judges named Jagannath Parey and Sohel Ahmed in the coastal town of Jhalkathi. Registrar of killings and tortures: Bangla Bhai and his armed group through murders and terrors created a reign of terror. Within about one year's expedition, they killed 32 tying their hands and feet, hanging. About 500 persons have become handicap. At least 3,000 were the victims of torture! Including members of the parliament hundreds of people became homeless. After being abducted from homes by Bangla Bhai-group, including religious minorities Tarun, Shufol, Shushanto of Naogaon, Atrari, Raninagar, Abu Taleb Bhutta of Shajuria village, Shahidul Islam of Baruihati village, at least 5/7 persons are still missing for the last 5 years. Police and local people think, they were all killed. No honest and effective enquiry was made for the killings and tortures by Militants. No trial was performed. The victims' family have faced much harassments and deceptions but yet they do not give up the hopes of justice. After the coming of power of Sk. Hasina Wajed, this latent hope has been revived again. In the field cases on charges of helping Militants, influential

Minister Barrister Aminul Hoque of BNP-Jamat qualition government, Rajshahi BNP-General Secretary Shish Muhammad are sentenced with 31 years of imprisonment. But the defendants could not be arrested by Police or RAB still now.

List of killeds: Identities of the 32 killed by Bangla Bhai and his group through tortures are found. They are, on 1 April 2004, Wasim alias Osman Babu, on 11 April (after tortures, on 11 April, died on 17 April), Militants hanged Golam Robbani Mukul of Kanopara, on 20 April Durgapur Awami League Leader and UP member Ajhar Ali, on 22 April Mosharraf Hossain of Belgharia, Raninagar, , Saifur of Pirgacha, Natore, on 23 July Diponkar of Kashiabari, Atrai (in the same way), on 27 April Diponkar Roy and UP Dafadar of Kashiabari, in the month of April Azahar Ali of Durgapur Awami League and UP member was tortured, he became ill and died last year, on 1 May retired army soldier Sk Farid of Bhonpara, Atrai, unknown 3 persons, on the 13 May Rabeya of Neempara committed suicide after rape on 14 May), on 15 May the deadbody of Abdul Kayyum Badsha was hanged in the tree. He was the much known Awami League and Shorbohara leader of Shafikpur, Raninnagar. On 24 June the Wami League and Shorbohara leader Khejur Ali of Shimba Village, Raninagar was killed, cut into pieces, Afzal of Borogacha of Raninnaga, on 30 June, Union Awami League Publiciy Secretary Yasin Ali of Baghmara Maria Union was hanged in the tree and killed through much torture. On the 25 June, unkown 3 persons of Bashudebpur were killed, on 14 November in the Raninagar Bheti Camp, Chatraleague leader Ziaul Hoque Zia, on 27th NovemberBNP (Mahbub) leader Ali Akbar of in Bishnupur of Taherpur, Baghmara, on 22 January 2005, Awami League Sreepur leader Mahabub was killed and attempt was made to kill Awami league popular leader UP Chairman Moqbul Hossain Mridha. Besides, the victim of the torture of Bangla Bhai, the fugitive widow old Rahima died few days back. After about five years, Abdul Bari of Baghmara came back home.

Those who helped and assisted Bangla Bhai and his group: The then SP Rajshahi Masud Mia, much discussed on the Bangla Bhai activities and now fired from the job on the same allegations,

Ex BNP MP of Puthia-Durgapur and General Secretary of Rajshahi BNP Nadim Mostofa, Ex BNP-Jamat qualition government's Housing and Public works State Minister and present LDP leader Alamgir Kabir, Ex land Deputy Minister Ruhul Quddus Talukdar Dulu, The Ex Mayor of Rajshahi City Corporation Mijanur Rahman Minu, Ex Post and Telecommunication Minister Barrister Aminul Hoq. They are all alleged to give Militants gover'nment helps. In the background of Militants' activities, it is complained that Jamat-Shibir have played a major role. From the 14 political parties including CPB and Awami League, this complain has been made. Besides against the Ex Industry Minister and Chief of Jamat (Ameer) Matur Rahman Nizami and the Secretary General of BNP Ex Social-welfare Minister Ali Ahsan Mujahid, the same complain has been made from them. But the common people believe, the real Godfathers of the Militant activities are the ,independence-opponents' murder clique. In the grass roots, all Militants had started their political career with Jamat-Shibir.

The existence of Bangla Bhai denied, then agreed and the order of his arrest: Because of the terrorist activities in the name of so-called ,Islamic Revolution', and the atrocities led by Bangla Bhai in Northbengal, Bangladesh Government, inside and outside the country faced tremendous criticism. But BNP-Jamat government Ministers and influential leaders told, ,there is no existence of Bangla Bhai and Militants in Bangladesh. ,They are creations of media.' So the government tried to avoid the responsibility. But on 23 May 2004, the then Prime Minister Begum Khaleda Zia ordered to arrest Bangla Bhai, and for the first time the important persons of the government who told about ,no existence of Militants or Bangla Bhai' became ludicrous!

On 22 January 2005 Bangla Bhai cadres came to Baghmara to kill the popular Awami League leader and UP Chairman Moqbul Hossain Mridha but they faced peoles' resistance. They threw bombs on mob and killed Awami League leader Mahabur Rahman. On this day, by the mass-beatings of furious people, 3 of Banglabhai cadres were killed. After this incidence, on 24 January 2005, the controversial SP of Rajshahi Masud Mia first confessed that ,there is a Bangla Bhai'! At the same time, Prime Minister again ordered to arrest him. After this order of the Prime Minister, in different places of the country, many Militant-cadres were arrested. From their confessional statements, the names of Bangla Bhai, his spiritual Guru Shayokh Abdur Rahman and his leader, Professor of Rajshahi University, Dr. Muhammad Asadullah Ghalib came out. At the instruction of the highest command of BNP-Jamat government, on 22 February, 2005 at early morning (23 February), Dr. Ghalib and three of his partners, Abdus Samad Salafi, Abdul Latif and Azizullah were arrested. Actually the matter of Banglabhai and Abdur Rahman was kept down. The operation to arrest Banglabhai has been faded away.

On 11 March 2005, the then Rajshahi SP masud Mia was suspended. Later on government fired him on the charges of helping the Militants. On 11 September 2005, from the Police Headquarter Awards were announced for the captures of Bangla Bhai and Shayokh Abdur Rahman. In the same year, 28 September, State Minister of Home declared the amount of this award, 1 Crore for both, 50 lakkhs for each. After much drama, on 1 March 2006, from Shaplabagh Shurja Dighol Bari in Sylhet, Shayokh Rahman surrendered to Police. In the same year on 6 March, Bangla Bhai was arrested in a house in village Rampura of Muktagacha, Mymensingh. Why Militants' activites were started: For about a decade, the terrorists of so-called Shorbohara in greater Rajshahi have changed the lives of the people to hell!

The government failed to suppress them. Because of the political bankruptcy police has never made an effective operation against the Shorobihara. The Shorbohara terrorists on 7 February 2004 in the evening, in Kamarpara Bazar, Noldanga Upozilla of Natore shot, slaughtered and killed Gama, the Jubodal leader, nephew of Land Deputy Minister. On this ground BNP supporter terrorists raided 31 houses and 15 shops belonged to Awami League leaders-supporters-workers in Kazipara, Noldanga. They plundered all, demolished and set fire. Fire was set through gunpowder. Two other Nephews of Ex Minister Dulu and Jubodal leader Dollar and Dalim led this devastating destructive event by about 200 armed cadres. In that year in February, Shorbohara killed Land Deputy Minister's Nephew and Jubodal leader Gama, his partner Jubodal leader Pakhi of Sadhonpur Puthia and Durgapur BNP leader and Ward Commissiioner Anowar. Pakhi and Anowar were very close the BNP MP Nadim Mostofa. After the nephew of Ex Deputy Land Minister was killed by Shorbohara, to suppress them, Militants were let loose in the battle field, it is heard. At the beginning, they called them as, ,Dulu Bahini, ,Gama Bahini', Al-Quaida Bahini', ,Muslim Rakhsha Parishad', ,Mujahedin Bangladesh', ,Harkat ul-Jihad', and other names.

Later on they were combined and made operations under the name, ,Jagroto Muslim Jonota Bangladesh' or JMB. Within few days after their operations against Shorbohara began, people could understand, the actual aim was not to uproot Shorbohara. Soon they were fed up with the miscreants of this new anti-constitution and anti-state activists.

Who is this Bangla Bhai? : Bangla Nhai is name of a ,panic-maker' in Northbengal.

He first appeared to uproot the Shorbohara. But his tortures, oppressions were much more! He is the Chief of Jagroto Muslim Bangladesh and operational Chief of Jamaatul Mujahidin Bangladesh (JMB), Bangla Bhai alias Siddiqul Islam (45) s/o Najir Hossain. He is from Gabtali Upozilla, District Bogra, in village Kornipara, Mohishbathan Union.

From the Sartaj Fazil Madrasha of the same Upozilla, he passed Dakhil Examination in 1989, Alim Examination in 1991. He passed B.A. (Hons) in Bengali from the Bogra Azizul Hoq College in 1995 and 1997, got the Masters Degree here. In Lathiganj School and College (Gabtali), he worked as lecturer of Bengali for 3 years. In this time he also directed Retina, Coaching Centre run by Chatrashibir in Bogra Town.

Another source says, as his result was not satisfactory, he started working with the Chatrashibir Coaching centre in Dhaka. His brother Rafikul Islam has done Chatal business in Gerírhat, Gabtoli. Another brother Jahurul Islam ist he teacher of Moksedia Alim Madrasha in Mohishbathan Union. He married the daughter of Chilmanerpara Madrasha Teacher Ibrahim Hossain, Rokeya Begum of Shaghata Village and Upozilla of Gaibandha District.

One of his brothers-in-law Omar Faruk is also a teacher of this Madrasha. As student, Banglabhai was active with Chtrashibir politics.

International Militant-connection and Bangla Bhai: He joined the Islamic extreme terrorist group in Dhaka and related with one communal leader and the dreamer of so-called Islamic Revolution, Shayokh Abdur Rahman of Jamalpur. He became a friend of Dr. Professor Muhammad Asadullah-Al-Ghalib. He directed the Motivation and Training Camps in order to create Muslim and Jihadi organisations. The poor youths of villages were recruited. In villages, in the Mosques and Madrashas, organisational and armed trainings were given. Dr. M. Asadullah al-Ghalib, ,Bangla Bhai', Shayokh Abdur Rahman, Jamaatul Mujahidin Bangladesh, Jagroto Muslim Jonota Bangladesh and Ahle Haduth Movement Bangladesh are all knoted in the same thread. The theory of Dr. Galib is to capture the state power through Jihad. But before that ,the society must be made uneasy with terrors and violence. People must be poisoned about the present social and state structures.' Taking lessons on this, including Rajshahi, Dinajpur, Bogra, Natore, Chapai Nowabganj, Shatkhira, Sylhet, Jamalpur, Comilla, Jaipurhat in about 60 Districts of Bangladesh, their activities were intensified. They have a big workers group of good organised 50,000 members. With ,Bagar' or Bangla Bhai-Ghalib and Rahman have relations with Pakistan, Lybiya, Afganistan, Kashmir, Rohinga Refugees-terrorists and with many other fundamentalists and armed organisations of many countries. These three persons arranged millions of foreign money and with this big finance, are trying to impose religious administration upon the people in the name of so-called ,Islamic Revolution' through directing terrors, bombings, murders-tortures in different places of the country.

It is complained that long 25 years they have organised secretly and only before 8/10 years, they started open terrorism. With the help of the above mentioned 3 persons, with a view to preach and extend Islam in Bangladesh, from the northern Province of India, Abdul Matin Salafi collected fund from Middle East and started to send cash money here through the borders of Chapai Nowabganj and Lalgola India and other borders. It is known as ,Salafi

Movement' in Saudi Arabia but in Bangladesh it is as ,Ahle Hadith Juboshangha or Jagroto Muslim Jonota (JMB). The same organisation is in India, ,Jayse Hind' and ,Jayse Muhammad' Militants in Pakistan. There are informations, they have also connections with Al-Quaida net work. In Bangladesh Army, there are about 3,000 Ghalib-supporters. But Dr. Ghalib and his followers claim that they have no relation with Militancy.

First operation in Nothbengal : Bangla Bhai led an armed fight agaist Police in Puthia On 1 August 2003. It happened in Maheshpur village in Khetlal Upozialla, Joypurhat. Babgla Bhai and his followers looted police arms. As Mujahid of Bangladesh of Jamaatul Mujahidin, Bangla Bhai took part in that fight against Police. It was his first operation inside Bangladesh. Here with Jihad-documents, 19 armed cadres of Bangla Bhai were arrested. After few days, while visiting his arrested partners, Bangla Bhai was also arrested.

MADRASSA STUDENTS OR ISLAMIC MILITANT

Madrassas in Pakistan are generally financed by voluntary charity provided by the bazaar businessmen and others who believe that they are earning great merit by contributing to them. Some of them are also given financial assistance by foreign governments—the Saudi government is said to help the Ahl-i-Hadith seminaries and the Iranian government the Shia ones—but there is no proof of this assistance. And even if it does exist, it goes only to a few *madrassas* whereas the vast majority of them are run on charity (*zakat* = alms, *khairat* = charity, *atiat* = gifts etc). The Zia ul Haq government (1977-1988) tried to gain influence on the *madrassas* by distributing the alms (*Zakat*) funds to them in the 1980s. The only scholarly study of this is by Jamal Malik who points out that most of the *madrassas* who received these funds were Deobandi. However, as the *madrassas* had to be registered, this increased the government's influence over them (Malik 1996: 150-153).

The government of Pakistan gives financial assistance to the *madrassas* even now for modernizing textbooks, including secular subjects in the curricula and introducing computers. In 2001-02 a total of 1,654,000 was given to all *madrassas* which accepted this help. As the number of students is 1,065,277 this comes to Rs. 1.55

per student per year. An additional aid of Rs. 30.45 million is promised for providing computers and changing the syllabi in 2003-04 and this will come to Rs. 28.60 per student per year.

However, as all *madrassas* do not accept financial help from the government the money is not distributed evenly as the above calculations might suggest. According to the Jamia Salfia of Faisalabad, the annual expenditure on the seminary, which has about 700 students, is 40,00,000 rupees. Another *madrassa,* this time a Barelvi one, gave roughly the same figure for the same number of students. This comes to Rs 5,714 per year (or Rs 476 per month) which is an incredibly small amount of money for education, books, board and lodging. In India, where condition are similar to these in Pakistan, the *madrassa* Mazahiral Uloom in Saharanpur (UP), has 1300 students and 115 employees and its income between 2000 to 2001 was Rs. 9,720, 649 or Rs. 948 per student per year (Mehdi 2005: 93).

The expenditure from the government in 2001-2002 was Rs. 1,654,000 for all the *madrassas* in the country and about 32.60 per cent *madrassas* do not received any financial support at all, the total spending on these institutions is very little (IPS 2002: 33). However, as mentioned above, there are plans to change this in a radical manner. In my survey of December 2002 and January 2003, *madrassa* students and teachers were asked about their income. Many did not reply these questions but those who did suggest that they mostly (76.62%) belong to poor sections of society. The teachers of the *madrassas* also mostly (61.11%) belong to the same socio-economic class as their students. The *madrassas* provide sustenance for all these poor people.

In short the *madrassas* are performing the role of the welfare state in the country. This being so, their influence on rural people and the poorer sections of the urban proletariat will continue to increase as poverty increases.

Poverty and the Roots of Religious Violence

While it can only be speculated that there is a connection between poverty and religious violence, the proposition does have empirical backing. Qasim Zaman tells us, for instance, that in

Jhang—the birth place of the militant Sunni organization called the Sipah-i-Sahaba—the proportion of Shias in the affluent urban middle class is higher than other areas of Pakistan. Moreover, the feudal gentry too has many Shia families.

Thus the Sipah-i-Sahaba appeals to the interests of the ordinary people who are oppressed by the rich and the influential. Indeed, Maulana Haqq Nawaz, the fiery preacher who raised much animosity against the Shias, was 'himself a man of humble origin' and 'had a reputation for being much concerned with the welfare of the poor and the helpless, and he was known to regularly spend time at government courts helping out poor illiterate litigant's (Zaman 2002: 125).

Another leader of the Sipah-i-Sahaba, Maulana Isar al-Qasimi (1964-1991), also preached in Jhang. He too denounced the Shia magnates of the area and the peasants, terrorized by the feudal magnates, responded to him as if he were a messiah. Even shopkeepers rejoiced in the aggressive Sunni identity he helped create. When the Shia feudal lords attacked and burnt some defiant Sunni shops this identity was further radicalized (Zaman 2002: 127).

In the same manner the Muslim radicals in the Philippines too attack social and economic privilege. Indeed, Islamist movements from Turkey to Indonesia talk of the poor and the oppressed and sometimes do take up their cause. This has won them votes in Turkey where they have been suppressed by the secular military. It was also a major factor for mobilization in Iran against the Shah who was seen as being rich, wasteful, corrupt and decadent. So, though difficult to demonstrate, Islamic militancy—whether by radicalized *madrassa* students or members of Islamist or Jihadi groups in Pakistan—has an element of class conflict. It is, at least in some part, a reaction of the have-notes against the haves. This is a dangerous trend for the country because *madrassa* students are taught to be intolerant of religious minorities and are hawkish about Kashmir. As they are also from poor backgrounds they express their sense of being cheated by society in the idiom of religion. This gives them the self-righteousness to fight against the oppressive and unjust system in the name of Islam.

The Worldview of Madrassa Students

The *madrassa* students are the most intolerant of all the other student groups in Pakistan. They are also the most supportive of an aggressive foreign policy. In my survey of 2002-2003 mentioned earlier the *madrassa* students were the only group of students—out of Urdu and English-medium school ones—who supported both overt and covert conflict with India over Kashmir in large numbers. They were also against giving equal rights (equal to Muslims) to non-Muslims and women (equal to men) as citizens. These figures and the survey itself are given in Rahman.

ISLAMIC MILITANCY AS PRETEXT

During the recent Awami League rule (1996-2001), India began a propaganda war which claims Islamic terrorists are becoming active in Bangladesh. A section of Dhaka-based dailies frequently made reports about the existence of the militancy in Bangladesh. They repeatedly alleged that the Muslim terrorists were being trained deep in the jungle of Chittagong Hill Tracts, or Sundarbans or different madrashas of the country. Security forces instantly rushed to those spots mentioned in the dailies, but found the reports fake and baseless. To provoke the America-led western power India deliberately launched media campaign that Bangladesh has become a safe base of al-Quada and Taliban terrorists. To promote the idea of the existence of the Islamic militant groups in Bangladesh, the government even officially published booklets on the eve of the US President Bill Clinton's visit to Bangladesh. American government, however, still officially claims that there is no real Islamic militancy in Bangladesh, rather Bangladesh is a moderate Muslim democratic country.

During its rule, AL government arrested a number of madrasha teachers and students and Imams of the mosques branding them either as terrorists or their godfathers and claimed that some of them were trained in Afghanistan or Kashmir. But the court failed to prove the allegation and they were released. But neither India nor AL stopped their fake propagation and their followers or hired columnists stopped their campaign. India and its allies in Bangladesh were cock sure about the existence of such extremist groups in the country, as they fueled them. It is unfortunate that our ministry of Home Affairs failed earlier about India's hand in floating a number of India-sponsored outwardly Islamic terrorist outfits that clandestinely served in the interest of India in justifying the allegation of India and its Bangladeshi allies.

India's constant aggressive designs to create disturbances in her neighbouring countries ventilates her expansionist as well as jealous attitude against her peace loving and innocent neighbours is known to all. But India is particularly intolerant towards her neighbouring Muslim countries, Bangladesh and Pakistan, as they were curved out of British India. India, after 58 years of the partition of the subcontinent, unfortunately failed to forget the spirit of two-nation theory. She applies this theory in dealing with the Muslims inside her own territory and beyond.

The recent bomb attacks on some NGO installations and cultural soirees and the subsequent arrest of some terrorists under the guise of so-called Islamic militants and their gangleaders unveiled India's involvement. A number of Bangladeshi dailies on February 25, 2005, quoting the interrogation of the arrested informed, that the recently banned so-called Muslim outfits-JMTB (Jagrata Muslim Janata Bangladesh) and Jamaatul Mujahiden-were the brainchildren of Indian intelligence agency-RAW. The outward and instant aim of floating these outfits was to justify Indian allegation that Bangladesh is a haven of the Islamic terrors and provoke the government to take stern action against the madrashas, their teachers and students. Such step will make the government unpopular among the people that will deter the possibility of returning to power of the alliance government and pave the way to install a puppet government in Dhaka. The long-term design is to invite American-led anti-terror invasion or get American permission to invade Bangladesh so that either the invaders or their puppets in Dhaka gradually can close down the madrashas and crush the Islamic scholars, intellectuals, and even the pro-nationalist forces and ultimately make Bangladesh a vassal state of India.

Now the question arises why India is inimical to madarasha education in Bangladesh. Historically, India believes in the unification of the pre-1947 map of the British India, which means destruction of independent Bangladesh. Indian policy makers believe that madrashas and madrasha education are main sources of inspiration of pro-nationalist forces. So long these institutions exist in Bangladesh, it will not be possible to control and keep Bangladesh under her occupation if she invades and captures it eve in remote future. Indians are aware that the maulanas, mulllahs, imams, pirs, darvishs, in brief the Muslim religious leaders, organised and led all the anti-British movements and struggles in the subcontinent when the Hindus extended their unconditional support to British occupation and exploitation.

So the real resistance in Bangladesh will come from the madashas, whenever India bids to capture it. On the other hand, this education keeps the candle of Muslim identity alive in Bangladesh, which is the main bar of the reunification of the British India. For this reason madrasha as well as madrasha education has become the prime target of India. After the emergence of Bangladesh in 1971, India tried its best to ban madrasha and Islamic education in Bangladesh alleging that all the teachers and students of madrashas were collaborators and they should be tried and given exemplary punishment.

But the then government paid no heed to pressure of Indian government, though madrahas remained closed for certain period of time. But India did not lose heart; rather worked vigorously over the years to defame the madrahas and their teachers and students branding them anti-liberation forces. Madrassas were termed as the producers of 'rajakars' and anti-liberation forces. Demand was raised from the pro-India elements to close down madrashs and madrasha education. During the immediate past AL rule, madrasha teachers and students passed hard days and many of them were the victims of harassment and persecution and thrown into jail under fake allegations. Pro-Indian print media branded the madrashas as Taliban training centres. Same of the madrashas were closed down during the AL regime (1996-2001). Moreover, all the governments were directly and indirectly influenced to change the curriculum and syllabus of the madrasha education in the name of modernisation and reformation, so that the students and teachers are gradually diverted to secularism, which is the road to the unification of dreamy 'Akhand Bharat.' Above all, the debacle of AL in the general election of 2001 scared India of and it came to this conclusion that religious parties played the vital role in installing a nationalist government in Bangladesh.

Indian intelligence are confirmed that the ruling alliance will come out victorious in the coming election scheduled to be held in 2006. Though the government adopts soft policy in dealing with India, it does not respond positively in allowing transit or port facilities to India or allow her forces to use Bangladesh territory to fight against the militants of her northeastern states. Moreover, the relatively independent foreign policy of the alliance government, its internal success stories, above all its 'look east' policy scared Indians strategists that Bangladesh would get out of Indian fold if the alliance is allowed to form government again. For all these reason, India took hard line against the alliance government. Other than disturbing the government in hundreds of ways, Indian agencies clandestinely recruited agents from those who are outwardly seen and known as religious and have relations with madrashas. This is how India now uses the card of the presence of the Islamic militancy in Bangladesh in order to crush religious education and brand Bangladesh a terror-infested country and isolate it from the international community and install a puppet government to turn it into a secular vassal state and annex it to India in course of time when Muslim identity will be replaced by secular spirit.

Quoting intelligence agencies a number of Bangladeshi dailies said, both the recently banned outfits were floated, financed and guided by RAW to carryout disruptive and subversive activities. 'The Inqilab, "The Manbjamin," The Amar Desh,' 'The Naya Diganta,' other dailies of Dhaka on February 25, 2005, unearthed how RAW floated a number of socalled Islamic militant outfits, JMJB (Jagrata Muslim Janata Bangladesh), Jamaatul Mujahideens, etc., to implement Indian design and controlled and guided their activities from across the border. Police recovered some vouchers from the house of Mantazar Rahman, which show that some unnamed persons used to come from and go to India through the

Hilly Border. The arrested cadres confessed that an assembly of learning the holy Quran used to hold at Jaypurhat residence of Jamaatul Mujahideen Commander Mantazar Rahman and others on every Sunday and Tuesday. In those gatherings vegetables were served instead of beef during dinner or launch, but in Bangladesh, beef is the main item of such occasion. The intelligence agencies believe that the avoidance of beef indicates that some Hindus used to attend in those outwardly Islamic gatherings to brief the leaders and cadres of the outfits.

Other than briefing on subversive activities, other major task of these outfits, were to award erroneous 'fatwa' (Islamic Judicial decree). The main task of these RAW-financed organisations is to derail and crush the real pro-nationalist Islamic movement in Bangladesh. Indian RAW pours huge amount of money to expand these outfits and keeps them active. No worker of Jamaatul Mujahideen knows who was the real leader of the outfit and from which source money comes.

It is learnt that a group of Rajshahi-based lawyers belonging to Awami League (AL) and a section of anti-government dailies assisted these groups in earning prominence and spreading activities of Shahadat-e-AI Hikma, another outfit. Its Amir, Syed Kaowsar Houssain was a half-educated Maulana. He was admitted into Rajshahi College in 1999, but could no sit for HSC examination due to financial crisis. Kaowsar does not have the financial or educational ability to run such a militant organisation. So the question arises, how he could gain financial ability to run the outfit. One pro-AL lawyer, Rashidul Islam of Rajshahi Bar assisted and financed Kaowsar in drafting the constitution and leaflets, posters and other publications of his outfit. Rashidul Islam also provided him legal assistance when he was arrested along with his party worker. Sanjib Roy, the President of Hindu-Buddhist-Christian Okkiya Parishad, accompanied Kaowsar on a tour to India. Kaowsar was introduced in India with an Indian citizen Ashim Kumar who later took him to a hotel and arranged his appointment with such a person who claimed himself that he was Mafia godfather Daud Ibrahim. It is suspected that he was high-ranking RAW official.

On the other hand, Jamaatul Mujahideen headed by Dr. Ghalib Rajshahi University (RU) was floated in 1998 during Awami League rule. Most the leaders and workers of this organisation are the followers of Ahale Hadith. Abdur Rahman, who once acted as the Amir of Jammatul Mujahideen, is the husband of the sister of Mirja Azam MP of Jamalpur-3 constituency belonging to AL. Using his relationship with an AL MP Abdur Rahman procured the dealership of fertiliser and earned a lot of money during AL rule. On the other hand, Dr. Ghalib of RU who now heads the outfit maintains warm relation with some influential political leaders of different parties.

On the other hand, concealing his real profession and identity secret during AL period, Dr. Ghalib using a business passport went to India and stayed there for 11 days. When this forgery came to light, the then Register of RU Prof. Mohammad Younus served showcause notice on him and took disciplinary measures against him. But the initiative deterred and foiled due to the interference of the then Home Minister Mohmmad Nasim and the Mayor of Dhaka City Corporation Mohammad Hanif. Both belong to AL. During interrogation, the arrested persons informed that an Indian prominent religious leader used to come to Bangladesh and inspired them to work for Islamic revolution. A number of Bangladeshis got huge amount of money, arms, explosives and Other materials through this Indian religious leader. As a result, the activities of these groups suddenly expanded in bordering districts like Satkhira, Chapai Nawabganj, Rajshahi, etc.

It is learnt that Indian RAW tried to brand Bangladesh as a terrorist country using these elements The coal of raisine outwardly Islamic outfits was to throw the government to an awkward position-internally and internationally. When the government would take punitive measures against the outwardly Islamic militants, the common Bangladeshis will go against it. On the other hand, if the government remain mum, it will be isolated from the international community. In that case, India will get chance to prove that the government nurses the militants. India will also try to persuade the western powers to impose punitive measures against Bangladesh, including trade embargo, economic blockade, even military invasion. Its short-term goal is to unseat the present government, while its long-term goal is to isolate Bangladesh from the international community and finally invade her.

The international community should evaluate India's historical design and evaluate its involvement in imposing terrorism in her neighbouring countries, particularly in Bangladesh. If a giant country constantly designs to undo a tiny neighbour, it can neither wipe out terrorism, nor survive. India is well aware of this evil theory and deliberately creates terrorists in different sectors to meet her ulterior goal. India is the architect of terrorism in Bangladesh. Under this situation, international community before blaming Bangladesh for all sorts of terrorist activities, should identify the real sponsor of terrorism, that let loose the terrorists not only in Bangladesh, but also in other South Asian countries and ask her to refrain from such heinous misdeeds.

AUTONOMY MOVEMENT OR ISLAMIC MILITANCY

The Kashmir problem is quite different. It existed since the time of independence and is essentially an autonomy movement. That those spearheading this movement are Muslim is incidental to the whole issue. The political, social and legal factors that have been responsible for the present situation in Jammu and Kashmir deserve separate discussion and the paper does not allow presenting it here in details. However, it must be noted here that Kashmir where nearly 80 per cent of the population was Muslim remained under Dogra rulers (Hindus) from Maharaja Gulab Singh to Maharaja Hari Singh for 106 years from 1846 and 1952, yet there never arose a communal conflict.

It was these Kashmiris who rejected the two nation theory of Jinnah in 1947 and took up arms to resist Pakistani sponsored armed infiltrators, sang national anthem on every platform of Kashmir and supported the State's accession to the Union of India signed by Maharaja Hari Singh on October 26, 1947. They lived in peace and harmony for 40 years, supported the secular fabric of the state and opposed any and every communal move of a microscopic section of Jamat-e-Islami in the Valley. The foremost

Kashmiri Muslim's leader, Sheikh Mohammed Abdullah, had to change the name of his 'Muslim Conference' to 'National Conference' because of public pressure as the Kashmiris, both Hindus and Muslims had grown together under the spirit of the Kashmiriyat.

It must be noted here that the nature of Islam in Kashmir is very different from some other parts of India. The *rishi* tradition has predominantly shaped religious and public life in Kashmir for centuries and is the basis of their self-identity as Kashmiris. Some people held Islam responsible for the uprising of militancy in the valley which shows intellectual felony. Though we can not completely deny the existence of fundamentalist strain in the present Kashmiri movement, but the fundamental question here is, whether it is religion which instigate them to fight or the situation so develops that they feel inclined to take resort to religion as instrument to easily mobilize the people? As pointed out by Engineer, though Islam was always there in the Kashmir and it could have inspired them anytime during all these years, but why extremists appeared on the scene so late, in fact only at the end of 80s.

The mistake lies with the Indian government who never kept the promise of granting autonomy and special powers to Kashmiris under Article 370. Not only that special powers promised to Kashmiris remained in the paper, but there was attempt by the Indian government to curtail the existing freedom and autonomy. Mandate of the people were hardly respected and democratically elected governments invariably were overthrown. The only fair election held was in 1977 during the Janata Government in the Centre. The movement for regional autonomy remained non-violent for four decades after independence. But when the democratic space to voice their demands shrank, people had no option but to take to arms to demand their rights which were long overdue. This provided opportunity to Pakistan to play with the heightened emotion of the people and it started providing support in the form of weapons and money to the Kashmiris to fight against the Indian government. Thus the nature of the entire movement changed form one of an indigenous movement to demand autonomy, to political aimed at destabilizing Indian government. In the light of above discussion the case of Kashmir thus can not be regarded as Islamic militancy.

Is there Possibility of Islamic Militancy in India?

The rise of Hindu communalism has gathered wide acceptance in today's environment which would have been unacceptable only a few years back. The fact that a right wing political party, BJP is ruling at the centre and in many of the states has given fillip to the Hindutva forces to impose their agenda on the national mainstream. There is an increasing tendency on the part of Hindu right-wing groups to present Muslims as the 'other' in order to unite Hindus against the Muslim so as to consolidate their hold over the power structure of the state. The rise of Hindutva forces has led many commentators to say that it will give rise to Islamic militancy in India (Narula; Kamal Chenoy; Sunil Khilnani; 2003)4. In order to deal with the issue it must be noted here that Muslim constitute largest minority in India that is 11.6 (around 120 million) per cent of total population according to 1991 census of India. Thus India is the home to the second largest Muslim population after Indonesia. This makes the issue of Islamic militancy more critical in India.

The rise of Hindutva forces in India has already resulted in some devastating consequences. In February and March 2002, over 2000 people were killed in state-supported violence against Muslims in the western state of Gujarat, led by the Hindu nationalist BJP that also heads a coalition government at the center. The attacks were carried out with impunity by members of the BJP, the Rashtriya Swayamsevak Sangh ("RSS," National Volunteer Corps), the Vishwa Hindu Parishad ("VHP," World Hindu Council), and the Bajrang Dal (the militant youth wing of the VHP) (Narula 2003).5 Collectively, these groups are known as the *sangh parivar*, or family of Hindu nationalist organizations. Police and state officials were directly implicated in many of the attacks.

Nationwide violence against India's Muslim community in 1992 and 1993 and against India's Christian community since 1998, including in the state of Gujarat, has also stemmed from the violent activities and hate propaganda of these groups. The Indian government continues to exploit rhetoric surrounding the global war on terror to silence political dissent while the sangh parivar invokes the threat of Islamic militancy in the aftermath of September 11 to justify the persecution of Muslims. Operating under the guise of patriotism, the proponents of Hindu nationalism are achieving mainstream credibility. The promotion of Hindu nationalism as a legitimate political and cultural force has consequences beyond its impact on the lives of India's religious minorities.

Attacks on Muslims in India have their corresponding effect on Hindus in Bangladesh and Pakistan. If the activities of these groups remain unchecked, violence may percolate to other parts of the South Asian region. When compounded with the growing political influence of the Islamic right and the military in Pakistan and Bangladesh, Hindu militarization may destabilize the region as a whole. The process of modernization and democratization which has been undergoing in India have also helped in the creation of minority consciousness and enabled minorities to organize them politically. They are not only determined to preserve their cultural identity, which has been threatened because of the rise of Hindutva concepts of national identity and secular state, but they also seek to grab the share in the development and prosperity resulting from ongoing process of modernization and liberalisation of the country. It must be noted here that the process of modernization has resulted in the increasing number of educated and underemployed youth within all religious communities. Further, the influx of uneducated or undereducated migrants from rural into metropolitan areas in search of jobs and better opportunities creates groups of rootless people having no ties with neighbourhood and not held together by kinship bonds. Such alienated and atomized individuals are readily available to be moblised by militant organsiations that play on their emotions (Malik and Vajpeyi 1989). Even in the face of these developments militancy within Indian Muslim community has not found widespread expression. This is not to deny that there are radical Muslim groups in India, but they have failed so far to earn wide public acceptance. The radical Muslim groups situated in the peripheral regions like Assam in the north east and Malabar region in Kerala can not be said to inspire to fight for religion. Rather their anger needs to be understood in the context of marginalization and economic deprivation which always engulf peripheral region. Their anger against the state is manifested by targeting specific groups.

Thus their struggle is to achieve political gain rather than to earn religious merit. Islamic militancy is not possible in India because of India's adoption of liberal-democratic framework after independence. India's success as a democracy lies in its successful handling of minority problems. Indian constitution like other democratic country incorporates a number of provisions which aim at safeguarding the interests of minorities and allow them to maintain their own identity through cultural and educational rights and provided special safeguards to protect their interests. However, the fruits of these special measures could not help much, especially to the Muslim minority, to achieve economic prosperity. But they could feel a sense of security. But this sense of security has been gradually, especially in the 90s, shattered owing to rise of Hindutva forces. This poses a serious question for Indian democracy; whether this will give rise to Islamic militancy? There is no any concrete answer to this question and much will depend upon the nature of Indian state, whether it will be able to maintain its democratic and secular credentials or will it allow it to be maneuvered by the right wing forces. However, since independence the political balance of power has undergone a significant change and the politico-legal system does not allow any operative system for the rise of militant Islam in India. Indian Muslims have had never in a position to give a militant response for their grievances as in such situation they are the principal sufferers. Because of the above reason and the growing power of the Indian Muslim middle class, militancy can not take root among the community. Faced with grievances, they would rather prefer to resolve it through democratic means rather than taking to arms.

Unlike migrant Islam in Europe, Indian Islam is historical Islam and there exists a very close proximity between Indian

Muslim and Indian Hindu across cultural lines, which also makes Islamic militancy a distant possibility in India. As put by Assayag, 'the continuous process of integrative and antagonistic acculturation has allowed each tradition to preserve its peculiarities and maintain a demarcating line between Hindus and Muslims'.

'This is obvious because Hinduism and Islam, as they were practiced until recently, continue to show a great deal of flexibility and a spirit of accommodation in their mutual relations.

In fact, they display an understanding that is infinitely richer than the limited sectarian approach adopted by dogmatic, fundamentalist and neotraditionalist circles on both sides' (Assayag 2004).

ISLAMIC MILITANT MOVEMENTS BETWEEN TRADITION AND MODERNITY

The Arab world is in turmoil. In most parts of the transcontinental land that extends from Casablanca to Baghdad, internal conflict has become the norm and uneasy stability is the exception. The growing cult of Islamic militancy in the Arab world owes much more to socio-political than to religious factors. The major causes of Islam being articulated as answer to the prevailing ills of the Arab polities are basically two:

1) The failure of the Arab political elites to evolve responsive political systems to take the place of traditional ones which no longer exist; and
2) The humiliating defeat of the Arabs in the Arab-Israeli Six-Day War of June 1967 causing reverberations not only in the Middle East but the wider Muslim world.

Islamic Theory

In traditional Islamic political theory the state rested on three pillars: the *Ummah* (the community of Muslim believers), the Caliphate, and the *Shariah* (Islamic Law). Except perhaps in the early decades of Islam, this theory, however, did not always conform to what happened in real life.

The *Ummah* embodied an ideal which could not be realised in full even in the early period of Islam. As long as Islam was confined to the Arabian Peninsula, the *Ummah* was a homogeneous community held together by the bonds of Islam. But once Islam spread into the non-Arab territories to the north, the dichotomy between the Arab and non-Arab Muslims arose.

The Arabs found it difficult to accept the non-Arabs as full members of the *Ummah* and gave them the unflattering title of *mawla* (client). The Persians accepted Islam but refused to be reconciled to Arab supremacy and led the revolt against the first Arab-Islamic dynasty headed by the Umayyads. The Abbasids, who succeeded the Umayyads, were accommodative to non-Arab Muslims.

From the tenth century onward, regional pressures reinforced by ethnic self-assertion splintered the Islamic empire and it was progressively displaced by feuding kingdoms across the massive arc stretching from the plains of central Asia to the Atlantic coast of Africa.

In the 16th century, the Ottomans did succeed in bringing large chunks of the Arab world under the umbrella of the Turkish empire but remained at loggerheads with the Shiite rulers of Iran, called the Safavids. Towards the end of the 19th century, the Arabs were stirred by sentiments of modern nationalism and took full advantage of the opportunities offered by the First World War to break loose from the Ottoman hegemony. The 20th century has witnessed Iran and Turkey emerge as independent states, and a fragmented Arab world into 20 odd nation-states. The *Ummah* had thus ceased to be a fact of political life long before the advent of the present day nation-states.

The institution of Caliphate emerged out of a practical necessity in the aftermath of Prophet Muhammad's death. His closest companion Abu Bakr al-Siddiq was chosen to head the *Ummah*, and he assumed the modest title of *Khalifah* ("caliph" being its Western corruption) or deputy. But within the span of a few decades the caliphate degenerated into an absolute hereditary monarchy.

Islamic political theorists supplied the necessary religious underpinnings for the institution to suit its changing requirements.

It was generally held that the caliph must be from Quraish (the Prophet's clan); he was the defender of the faith and the political leader of the *Ummah.* All Muslims were obliged to proclaim allegiance to him.

The principle of hereditary succession also found general acceptance. In later centuries, power slipped from the hands of the caliph but the caliphate lingered on as a notional institution. Kings and sultans of the Muslim world found it expedient to seek the caliph's formal recognition in return for offerings of salutations and gifts.

The *Shi'ah*, of course, did not recognise the caliphs and looked to their own *imams* for political leadership and spiritual guidance. The late Ottomans staked their claim to caliphate, if only to beef up their bargaining power *vis-à-vis* the European states. But when the empire disintegrated after the First World War, the new Turkish leaders, aspiring to build a modern republican state, abolished the caliphate in 1924.

Since then, there has been no serious proposal from any quarter to revive this supra-national politico-religious institution. Even the Islamic Conference Organisation (ICO), which pays lip-service to Islamic solidarity, takes ground realities into consideration to exclude political unification of the Muslim world from its proclaimed agenda.

In the field of *Shariah*, too, the Arab societies have traversed a long way from the early beginnings when the divine law, derived mainly from the *Qur'an* and the *Sunnah* (sayings of the Prophet), governed all aspects of life. In classical argument, the institution of caliphate itself was justified in terms of the need for a central authority to enforce the *Shariah.* Ironically enough, it was under the late Ottoman caliphate that the application of *Shariah* was progressively circumscribed. Beginning in the mid-19th century, the Ottoman sultans launched legal reforms, supplanting the *Shariah* from the penal and commercial fields, under the grand project of "*tanzimat*", or "putting things in order." The project also stipulated creation of "*nizamiyah*" (secular) courts to adjudicate the man-made penal and commercial laws.

The 1917 Ottoman Law of Family Rights made inroads into the hitherto forbidden territory of Muslim personal law by introducing administrative regulations governing divorce and relief to deserted wives. Violation of these regulations was punishable under the secular criminal law.

Most of the Arab countries, stretching from Iraq to Morocco, effected further reforms in the Muslim personal law besides endorsing the general principle of sovereignty of legislatures to enact laws for all aspects of life.

It can thus be said that in most of the Arab countries today the *Shariah* applies only to limited segments of life involving marriage, divorce and inheritance. There are, however, two sets of exceptions to this rule. At one end of the spectrum stand Saudi Arabia and the smaller states of the Arabian Peninsula which enforce, with varying intensity, the Islamic penal codes. Iran, too, falls into this category.

At the other extreme is Turkey which, in the wake of the Kemalist revolution of the early 1920s, adopted a militant secularist stance. It proclaimed modern secular laws for all areas of life including marriage and divorce. It is seldom realised that outside the "communist" fold Turkey is the only Asian nation to opt for full-scale secularisation of social and political life in a strictly modern sense of the term. And it has stayed that way since the days of Mustapha Kemal Atatürk, notwithstanding recurrent clamour by the Islamists for a return to the good old days of the *Shariah*.

It follows from the above that the concept of *ummah* and the institution of caliphate had either become dysfunctional or changed beyond recognition long before the advent of western influence in the region. It was only in the field of *Shariah* that increasing contacts with Europe and modernisation of social and economic life contributed to its shrinking influence.

ALTERNATIVE ORDER

While Arab modernising political elites can justly claim credit for managing the transition to certain areas with reasonable efficacy, they cannot escape blame for their failure to provide a credible alternative to the traditional system of government. This does not mean that no effort was made in this direction.

On the intellectual level, a whole generation of thinkers from Abdel-Rahman al-Kawakibi to Ahmad Lutfi as-Sayyid, Ali Abdel-Raziq and Taha Hussein, joined the quest, in the late 19th and the early part of this century, for an alternative order based on reason and rule of law.

The Syrian-born Abdel-Rahman al-Kawakibi argued that despotism had been the bane of Muslim polities through the ages; that the just state, in which men could find fulfilment, was one in which the individual was free and freely served the community; and that the government should be controlled by the people and act as a watchdog to ensure that freedom. Ahmad Lutfi as-Sayyid, for his part, made the case that good government is one that springs from the will of the people. All other forms end up in tyranny.

The case for an out and out secular order was, however, made by Sheikh Ali Abdel-Raziq in his book *al-Islam wa Usul al-Hukm* (*Islam and the Basis of Political Authority*, 1925). A product of al-Azhar and Oxford, Abdel-Raziq used his theological scholarship and analytical skill to advance the thesis that the entire theory of caliphate (the kingpin of Islamic political thought) had no basis in the *Qur'an* and the *Sunnah* and that the practice of the caliphate was often at variance with its theory. Abdel-Raziq's book aroused a storm of protest. But the works of Dr Taha Hussein (also an alumnus of al-Azhar) were greeted with much less hostility. For Taha Hussein approached his subject from a pragmatic rather than theological angle. In his *Future of Culture in Egypt*, he argued that the dichotomy between religious dogma and everyday secular practice is an inescapable part of life.

Early Arabs, he reasoned, had no inhibitions about borrowing extensively from Greek and Persian civilisations and they gained a great deal in the bargain. Hence, contemporary Arabs need not be averse to borrowing from the Western civilisation. On a practical footing, the quest for alternative basis of polity found expression in eclectic approach. It favoured liberal borrowings from Western constitutional forms and adapting them to local needs and circumstances. In quick succession, Iran, Iraq, Syria, Lebanon and Egypt adopted constitutions patterned after the British, French or Belgian models. This stupendous experiment in constitutionalism, however, did not carry much credibility as it was generally devoid of democratic content.

In the 1950s, most of these edifices collapsed like houses of cards. A succession of *coups d'etat* and civil disorders made the whole region reverberate with the sound of crashing thrones. Egypt and Iraq turned into republics and the soaring spirit of republicanism rattled the remaining monarchies in the region.

Then came the era of charismatic leaders espousing heady ideologies of pan-Arabism, socialism and redressal of the unequal relationship with the West. Even the Shah of Iran donned the mantle of a modernising monarch heralding his "white revolution". In most cases, where some form of constitutional structures existed, the single party system of political mobilisation was introduced. But this was mostly used as a facade behind which dictatorial rule thrived. The press and other media were firmly controlled.

The system allowed no possibility of free debate on public priorities or policies. Even the Shah of Iran felt tempted to emulate the undemocratic devices designed by the radical republics in the region which he otherwise abhorred. As for the paternalistic kingdoms and emirates of the Arabian Peninsula, the rate of their social and economic transformation in the wake of the oil boom of the 1970s has been mind-boggling. Literacy advanced in rapid strides and the benefits of housing, health and general economic welfare were extended to all sections of these sparsely populated oil-exporting countries. But there was no corresponding change in the political arena. Political power still vests in kings and sheikhs amidst growing popular clamour for accountability and rule of law.

Divisions and Disjunctions

If the absence of credible political systems responsive to popular expectations has driven the people to protest under the banner of Islam, the failure of the ruling elites to hold their own against an expansionist Israel or to contain super-power pressures on the region gave a militant edge to the call of *Jihad* against the internal and external foes of Islam.

The Islamic militants, commonly called "fundamentalists" because of their strident call for a return to the fundamental tenets of Islam, view the defeat of Arab armies at the hands of the Zionist state in a series of wars, beginning in 1947, and the loss of entire Palestine to Israel in the process, as a catastrophe for the Arab and Islamic peoples.

The fundamentalists no doubt blame the Zionist and their Western backers, in particular the United States, for this calamity; but they blame their own rulers even more.

They ascribe the Arab-Islamic defeat to the alienation of the ruling classes from Islam, their worship of the false idols of nationalism (local as well as pan-Arab) and their addiction to foreign ideologies such as socialism, communism or capitalism. The same malaise, they argue, accounts for the apathy and inaction of the present rulers in face of the ongoing tragedy in Bosnia and Herzegovina.

Exacerbating the grievous injury to the Arab sense of dignity and honour caused by defeat is the relentless pressures on and manipulations of the region by the industrialised West which not only accounts for close to two-thirds of the world's proven oil reserves but also serves as a lucrative market, thanks to the oil boom of the 1970s, for their consumer products and weapons. The Islamists see in this a replay of the medieval crusades.

It is, however, necessary to point out that the fundamentalists in the Arab world are not a monolithic entity nor is their upsurge irreversible.

The fundamentalist camp, although clamouring for Islamic solidarity, suffers from inner divisions and disjunctions. Saudi Arabia, for example, has long been the home of what might be called *controlled fundamentalism*. The Saudi royalty took shelter behind Islam to deny its own people a constitution. And to gain respectability for their archaic domestic set-up, the Saudi rulers created the *Rabitat al-Alam al-Islami* (World Islamic League) to mobilise goodwill of Muslim *'ulama'* from all over the world through an elaborate system of patronage.

With a substantial spurt in oil royalties in the 1970s, Saudi Arabia sponsored the Islamic Conference Organisation as a handy platform to demonstrate its Islamic credentials. It is hardly surprising that the United States found Saudi Arabia's championship of Islam as a convenient weapon to beat the Arab radicals with, and look benignly on it.

In the wake of the Suez War, which spelled disaster for Britain as a custodian of Western interests in the Middle East, US president Dwight Eisenhower seriously toyed with the idea of promoting king Saud as the "pope" of Islam. But the project failed to take off.

For some time now, Saudi Arabia is having second thoughts about the efficacy of its own brand of Islam as an instrument of its foreign policy. It all started with the Iranian clergy mounting a rebellion against the Shah and eventually seizing political power. In 1979, the Pahlavi monarchy of Iran was replaced by an Islamic republic with Ayatollah Khomeini as its "Supreme Guide". The cause of Saudi Arabia's discomfiture lay in the fact that whereas Riyadh had always invoked Islam to uphold political *status quo,* Iran's new rulers presented Islam in a revolutionary attire seeking to topple despotic kings, ushering in an egalitarian social and economic order, and fighting foreign dominance in the region.

The Saudis were indeed scared when, in 1979, a bunch of home-grown fundamentalists occupied the Holy Mosque of Mecca in an undisguised attempt to overthrow the monarchy, ironically, in the name of Islam.

In Iran, too, in the past 16 years since Ayatollah Khomeini returned to Iran from his long exile, public zeal for the Islamic revolution has steadily diminished. Khomeini strongly believed in the unquestioned power and efficacy of Islam to establish and sustain a just social and political order. He encouraged export of the Iranian revolution to other parts of the Islamic world and envisaged eventual triumph of Islam the world over. He came to be identified with what may be called *messianic fundamentalism.*

Khomeini, however, glossed over one basic fact about the Islamic revolution: it was made possible by the active support and sacrifices of a good section of the educated youth and the merchant class who would loathe to see Iran converted into an obscurantist theocracy. As it happened, the clergy squeezed their non-clerical partners out of the newly created governing institutions and eventually suppressed them.

The eight-year-long Iran-Iraq war, which was patently senseless for both sides, scotched all hopes of a just and humane order taking shape in Iran. In the end, Khomeini was compelled by his closest advisers to swallow his pride and call for a cease-fire. The post-Khomeini Iran is surely, though haltingly, moving towards a rational and pragmatic approach to the moulding of Iran's domestic and foreign policies. Dr Qassem Ihsanzadeh, an outspoken member of the Iranian parliament recently observed: "We must decide whether we want a parliamentary system or an Islamic government-the two are incompatible." Predictably, he was shouted down by the Islamists but not before he made it quite clear that there were many more who shared his views but would not utter them publicly.

President Ali Hashimi Rafsanjani, for his part, knows that he cannot bring the fruits of revolution to the restive people of Iran without the inputs of science and technology and modern managerial skills. He is, therefore, keen to loosen the stranglehold of clergy on the system so that Iranian technocrats who fled the country in the wake of the revolution can return and a new generation of technocrats could be trained at home. Rafsanjani admittedly sees no contradiction between modernity and Islam and he speaks of the need for close co-operation between Iran, India and China so that they can have a say in post-cold war world politics. All this is a far cry from the heady days of February 1979 when Ayatollah Khomeini had unfurled the flag of Islamic revolution.

Hence the real breeding grounds of militant Islam and Islamic fundamentalism today are not in Iran or Saudi Arabia or the mini-states of the Gulf. On the contrary, these states are either apprehensive of Islamic militancy or, as in the case of Iran, having second thoughts about its efficacy as an instrument of public policy. Islamic militancy is, however, rampant in the more populous Arab countries of Egypt, Algeria and the Sudan.

All three have certain features in common: population explosion, soaring unemployment and varying degrees of repression of political dissent. And this has given rise to Islamic protest movements which can be generally designated as *retributive fundamentalism*.

The political stalemate in Egypt during the 1940s, resulting from the triangular conflict between the British, the king and the mass-based *Wafd* Party, and public disenchantment with the politicians in the wake of Egyptian defeat in the first Arab-Israeli War of 1947-48, swelled the ranks of *al-Ikhwan al-Muslimun* (Muslim Brothers), founded by Hassan al-Banna in 1929. The *Ikhwan* preached that the redemption of Egypt (and of the Islamic world) lay neither in reform nor in reinterpretation of the Islamic doctrine but in its full-scale resurrection.

They declared that the real issue was not Islam's inadequacy to meet the challenges of modern times but that Islam was never given a chance to prove its efficacy, and that the *Qur'an* and the *Sunnah* provide essentials of a just political order and a universal brotherhood of men. Above all, the *Ikhwan* claimed that the fault lay not in Islam but in its internal and external enemies: the West strangled it politically and economically from the outside and the westernised Muslims undermined it from within.

On the eve of the revolution of July 1952, which toppled the monarchy and put General Muhammad Naguib and Colonel Jamal Abdel-Nasser into power, the *Ikhwan* claimed a million followers in Egypt alone.

Two years later the *Ikhwan* faced a showdown with the military regime and lost. For a while, Nasser's Egypt offered a future of hope to its teeming millions. Pursuit of the ideals of socialism, unification of the Arab world into a single polity, and an independent role in world affairs enthused the whole Arab world. But the defeat of Egypt in the June 1967 war turned that dream into a nightmare. Nasser's image as saviour of the Arabs was shattered and he died soon after. That was the time when the Islamists regrouped and mounted a frontal assault taking advantage of Egypt's mounting economic problems, the occupation of Sinai by Israel and the vacillations and waywardness of Anwar al-Sadat who succeeded Nasser.

Al-Sadat's compromise agreement with Israel over Sinai was seen by the Islamists as a betrayal of Egypt and Islam and as a justification to take up arms against the regime.

The turmoil gave birth to several militant groups, collectively know as *al-Jama'at al-Islamiyyah* (Islamic Groups). Currently the intensity of their violence and the virulence of their propaganda make the old *Ikhwan* look like a moderate outfit.

One such group, called *al-Jihad al-Islami,* plotted the assassination of president Anwar al-Sadat in October 1981. Amongst their principal targets are top members of the Coptic Christians, who make up over 15 per cent of Egypt's population, and foreign tourists. The most visible protagonist of the movement is a 55-year-old sightless Dr Omar Abdel-Rahman, now under detention in the United States for his alleged involvement in the car-bomb attack on the World Trade Centre at New York, in February 1993, that killed six people and injured many more.

In Algeria, the monopoly on power enjoyed by the National Liberation Front (FLN) and its failure to find credible solutions to the nation's economic problems, notwithstanding its substantial oil and gas reserves, have thrown up an Islamic backlash. Opponents of the FLN rallied under the banner of Islam not because Islam had ready-made answers to Algeria's political and economic woes but because the ruling group permitted no secular platform to exist outside its own regimented ranks.

In the early 1980s, the Algerian government launched an austerity programme to grapple with rising unemployment. But the crisis aggravated and in October 1988 widespread anti-government riots occurred.

The government then belatedly revised the constitution to permit a multi-party system. Restrictions on the press were relaxed. Among the various political parties that emerged, the most articulate was the Islamic Salvation Front (FIS), headed by Abbas Madani. It benefited greatly from Madani's previous record of opposing the FLN and gained further popularity through impressive relief operations organised in the wake of the 1989 earthquake.

Not surprisingly, therefore, the Islamic Salvation Front won 67 per cent of the provinces and 55 per cent of the municipalities in the regional and local elections held in June 1990.

And in the postponed parliamentary elections, eventually held in December 1991, when the FIS won 188 of the 231 seats in the first round of elections, president al-Shazli Ben-Jedid stepped down to make way for Muhammad Bou-Diaf.

The new president cancelled the elections. In March 1992, the FIS was outlawed. Bou-Diaf was assassinated on June 29th, 1992. Algeria's cautious advance towards democracy came to a grinding halt. In the Sudan General Ga'afar Muhammad al-Numeiri seized power in a bloodless *coup d'état* in 1969, and followed in the footsteps of Egypt's Nasser, adopting a set of socialist policies and mobilising mass support under the banner of the Sudanese Socialist Union, within the framework of a single-party system.

In the southern Sudan, assertively Christian and African in contrast to the more populous Arab-Islamic north, Numeiri followed a policy of accommodation by conceding autonomy and allocating resources for development.

Numeiri's 16-year-long stint in power, however, left the economy tottering under the weight of rampant corruption at home and the influx of refugees from Ethiopia, Uganda and Chad; the south suspicious and resentful of Khartoum's manipulations; and the disgruntled conservative groups in the north breathing down the regime's neck.

A few years before his fall in April 1985 Numeiri enlisted the support of the *Ikhwan* and Dr Hassan al-Turabi's National Islamic Front by promising to turn Sudan into a full-blooded Islamic state. This desperate act alienated the Christian south to the point of insurrection. Numeiri's exit has not made much difference to Sudan's political and economic woes.

It is noteworthy that a few months before his ouster, Numeiri's crusade for Islamisation of Sudan had resulted in the hanging of Muhammad Mahmoud Taha, the 76-year-old protagonist of a secular approach to politics. Taha's "crime" was that he and his associates belonging to the Republican Brothers had distributed a leaflet saying that the Islamic laws promulgated by Numeiri ran counter to Sudan's constitution and were indeed detrimental to integration of the Muslim north and the Christian south into one nation on the basis of equal rights for all citizens.

Taha thus became the first martyr to the cause of secularism in the Arab world. The intrepid secularist refused to defend himself in the court declaring that his persecution was unconstitutional and the judges were unqualified and technically incompetent. Secularism has been further discredited by the semi-fascist Ba'athist regime of Saddam Hussein. The Gulf War accelerated the trend in favour of fundamentalist Islamic movements and sharpened divisions among them.

Bibliography

Allana, G.: *Pakistan Movement: Historic Documents*, Karachi, Department of International Relations, University of Karachi, 1967.

Arif. S.M.: *Islamic Fundamentalism and Jihad*, MD Pub, Delhi, 2010.

Benjamin, Joseph : *Indo-Pak Relations : Prospect and Retrospect*, Reference Press, Delhi, 2004.

Bernard Wood: *Development Dimension of Conflict Prevention and Peace-building*, New York: UNDP,. 2003.

Daniel Pipes : *In the Path of God: Islam and Political Power*, New York: Basic Books Inc., 1983.

Das. P.K.: *Jihad : Terrorist Strategies Against the West*, Sumit Enterprises, Delhi, 2009.

Dekmejian, R. Hrair : *Islamic Revolution: Fundamentalism in the Arab World* Syracuse, New York: Syracuse University Press, 1995.

Dilip H. Mohite : *Rise of Islamic Fundamentalism and the Grand American Strategy* : Kalinga, Delhi, 2002.

Fox, Lisa L. : *Management Strategies for Disaster Preparedness*, Chicago, American Library Association, 1989.

Graham, Allison: *Nuclear Terrorism: The Ultimate Preventable Catastrophe*, New York: Times Books, 2004.

Greene, Mott : *Natural Knowledge in Preclassical Antiquity*, Baltimore, Johns Hopkins University Press, 1992.

Gupta, J.B. Das : *Islamic Fundamentalism and India* : Hope India Publications, Delhi, 2002.

Hassan, Lt Gen Gul, *Memoirs of Lt Gen Gul Hassan*, Oxford University Press, 1993.

Hiro, Dilip : *Holy Wars: The Rise of Islamic Fundamentalism* New York: Routledge, Chapman and Hall, Inc., 1989.

John O. Voll : *Islam: Continuity and Change in the Modern World*, Syracuse, New York: Syracuse University Press, 1994.

Khan, Major General Sher Ali: *The Story of Soldiering and Politics in India and Pakistan,* Wajidalis, 1978.

Kusum Lata Chadda: *Islamic Fundamentalism, Pakistan and the Muslim World* : Kanishka, Delhi, 2009.

Laquer, Walter, *The New Terrorism: Fanaticism and the Arms of Mass Destruction,* Oxford: Oxford University Press, 1999.

Multani, R K P : *Islamic Fundamentalism in South Asia* : Sumit Enterprises, Delhi, 2007.

Noorani, A.G.: *Islam and Jihad,* Leftword, Delhi, 2002.

Riedel, Bruce: *Deadly Embrace : Pakistan America and the Future of the Global Jihad,* HarperCollins, Delhi, 2011.

Rizvi, Hassan Askari: *The Military and Politics in Pakistan: 1947 - 86,* Progressive Publishers 1986.

Roxanne L. Euben, *Enemy in the Mirror : Islamic Fundamentalism and the Limits of Modern Rationalism : A Work of Comparative Political Theory* : Oxford University Press, 2001.

Shahid Javed: *Pakistan: The Continuing Search for Nationhood,* Westview Press, 1991.

Sharma, Rajeev: *Global Jihad : Current Patterns and Future Trends,* Kaveri Books, Delhi, 2006.

Thomas Arnold: *The Spread of Islam in the World, A History of Peaceful Preaching,* Goodword Books, 2001.

Thomas R. Metcalf : *A Concise History of India and Pakistan,* New York: Cambridge University Press, 2002).

William R. Thompson: *The Grievances of Military Coup-makers,* Beverly Hills: Sage Publications, 1973.

Index

M

O

P

R

S

T

❑❑❑